The Cherokee Indian Nation

The Cherokee Indian Nation

A TROUBLED HISTORY

edited by Duane H. King

 THE UNIVERSITY OF TENNESSEE PRESS : KNOXVILLE

Cloth: 1st printing, 1979; 2nd printing, 1981; 3rd printing, 1986;
         4th printing, 1989; 5th printing, 1997.

The paper in this book meets the minimum requirements of the
American National Standard for Permanence of Paper for Printed
Library Materials. The binding materials have been chosen for
strength and durability. Printed on recycled paper. ⊗   ♲

Library of Congress Cataloging in Publication Data

Main entry under title:
The Cherokee Indian nation.
      Includes bibliographical references and index.
      1. Cherokee Indians—History—Addresses, essays, lectures.
I. King, Duane H.
E99.C5C414   970'004'97   78-13222
ISBN 0-87049-227-6 (cloth: alk. paper)

Contents

Introduction
    Duane H. King   *page* ix
The Origins and Development of Cherokee Culture
    Roy S. Dickens, Jr.   3
A Perilous Rule: The Law of International Homicide
    John Phillip Reid   33
Distribution of Eighteenth-Century Cherokee Settlements
    Betty Anderson Smith   46
The Cherokee Frontiers, the French Revolution, and
    William Augustus Bowles
    William C. Sturtevant   61
Early Nineteenth-Century Cherokee Political Organization
    V. Richard Persico, Jr.   92
Cherokee Planters: The Development of Plantation Slavery
    Before Removal
    Theda Perdue   110
Chaos in the Indian Country: The Cherokee Nation,
    1828–35
    Kenneth Penn Davis   129
Postremoval Factionalism in the Cherokee Nation
    Gerard Reed   148
The Origin of the Eastern Cherokees as a Social and
    Political Entity
    Duane H. King   164
William Holland Thomas and the Cherokee Claims
    Richard W. Iobst   181

Observations on Social Change among the Eastern
  Cherokees
    John Witthoft   202
New Militants or Resurrected State? The Five County
  Northeastern Oklahoma Cherokee Organization
    Albert L. Wahrhaftig and Jane Lukens-Wahrhaftig   223
Contributors   247
Index   250

Illustrations

FIGURES

1. Valentine Museum poster   5
2. Cherokee burial   6
3. Archaeological phases of the Cherokee tradition   12
4. Pottery types   14
5. Boulders   16
6. Pottery types   18
7. Gorgets   19
8. Types of burials   21
9. Boulder mantles   23
10. Pottery types   25
11. Pottery types   27
12. William Augustus Bowles,
        portrait by Thomas Hardy   68
13. A member of Bowles' party,
        painted by William Hodges   69
14. A member of Bowles' party,
        painted by William Hodges   70

TABLES

1. Cherokee Lower Towns, 1721–81   51
2. Cherokee Middle Towns, 1721–81   54
3. Cherokee Valley Towns, 1721–81   55
4. Cherokee Overhill Towns, 1721–81   56

MAPS

1. Regional Developments of the Cherokee Tradition,
   A.D. 1000–1838   10
2. Cherokee Settlements, c. 1721–30   48
3. Cherokee Settlements, c. 1755–62   49
4. Cherokee Settlements, c. 1775–76   50
5. Cherokee Settlements in Northeast Oklahoma   227

Introduction

Duane H. King

At the time of European contact, the Cherokee Indian Nation occupied both sides of the South Appalachian summit region. Their towns were located on the headwaters of river systems flowing east, south, and west out of the mountainous area. In natural resources, the area was superior to much of the rest of the southeast. The mountains, the fertile valleys, and the streams provided immediate access to a variety of ecological niches which supported the Cherokees' diversified economy.

If local resources were of short supply, the Cherokees had only to venture farther into the expanse of wilderness which separated them from their neighbors. The entire range of hunting territory claimed by the Cherokees encompassed 40,000 square miles in portions of eight present states: the Carolinas, the Virginias, Kentucky, Tennessee, Georgia, and Alabama.[1] The actual land occupied was a much smaller area.

At the time of contact with Europeans, the Cherokees spoke three principal dialects; these corresponded roughly to the major geographical divisions of Cherokee settlements. The Lower (*Elati*) dialect was spoken in the settlements along the Keowee, the Tugaloo, and the headwaters of the Savannah River in what is now northwestern South Carolina and northeastern Georgia. The Middle (*Kituhwa*) dialect was spoken in the settlements on the Oconaluftee, Tuckaseegee, Nantahala, and Little Tennessee rivers in western North Carolina. The Western (*Otali*) dialect was spoken in all the towns of East Tennessee and in the towns along the Hiwassee and Cheowa rivers in North Carolina.[2]

The antiquity of the Cherokees in the South Appalachians is a subject which has generated a great deal of speculation. Some writers have felt that the Cherokees were recent arrivals who had migrated to the area shortly before white contact.[3] These writers observed that the Cherokees spoke a language unrelated to those of their neighbors, had an array of migration legends, and were unable, in the eighteenth century, to explain the origins of the artificial mounds on which many of their townhouses were built. The archaeological record, however, as Roy Dickens points out in this volume, reveals that many of the diagnostic traits of historic Cherokee culture have a long history of development in the Cherokee country. Some recognizable characteristics of Cherokee culture, according to Dickens, appeared more than a millennium ago in western North Carolina. Linguistic analysis, although not confirming the antiquity of the Cherokees in the mountains, does indicate that the group has been separate from their nearest linguistic relatives, the northern Iroquois, for at least 3,500 years.[4]

The written history of the Cherokees presumably begins with the DeSoto expedition in 1540. Sustained contact with Europeans, however, did not begin until the close of the seventeenth century. In 1673 two Virginia traders, Jems [James] Needham and Gabriel Arthur, made contact with Indians who may have been Cherokees. The murder of Needham by his Indian guide and the events which followed provide an early example of the legal concepts of international homicide shared by most southeastern Indians. As John P. Reid shows in his analysis in this volume, the tenets of blood revenge and of corporate responsibility were the basis for the Cherokee legal system.

In 1684, the first Cherokee treaty with the whites was concluded by representatives from the Lower Towns of "Toxawa and Keowa" with officials in Charlestown, South Carolina.[5] In 1693, a delegation from the Lower Towns was again in Charlestown, this time asking for guns to use in their wars against the Esaws, Savannahs, and Congarees.[6]

By the early 1700s, the deerskin trade had developed into a full-blown enterprise with more than fifty thousand hides being exported from Charlestown annually.[7] In exchange for deerskins, the Cherokees received firearms, ammunition, metal knives, axes, garden implements, as well as an assortment of beads, baubles, vermilion for paint, clothing, and quantities of rum. Of the trade goods, firearms proved to be the most important. Not only did they afford the Cherokees the means of acquiring more skins to procure more European manufactured goods, but they also provided the means for more efficient warfare. Traditionally, young men gained status in Cherokee society by demonstrating courage and valor in relatively nondestructive warfare. In the early eighteenth century the traditional enemies remained the same, but the introduction of firearms and, perhaps, the economic motivation of the fur trade brought changes in previous balance of power.

In the second decade of the eighteenth century, the Cherokees engaged in wars which ended with the dispersion and removal of the Tuscarora from North Carolina and the Yuchi and Shawnee from Tennessee.[8] During this period, the Cherokees spoke of war as their "beloved profession." They did, however, decline an invitation to assist the Carolina colonists in annihilating the Yamasees in 1715.[9]

Sir Francis Nicholson, the first royal governor of South Carolina, in an effort to systematize Indian relations, created the title "Emperor of the Cherokee Nation." The thirty-seven chiefs who met with Nicholson at Charlestown in 1721 not only agreed to accept the radical idea of a leader for all the Cherokees but also agreed to the first Cherokee land cession, yielding a strip between the Santee, Saluda, and Edisto rivers.[10]

In 1725, when Col. George Chicken visited the Cherokee country, the capital, or home of the emperor, was the town of Tunnissee, from which the Tennessee River and the state derive their names.[11] On April 3, 1730, Sir Alexander Cuming in Nequassee Townhouse arranged for the election of a new emperor, Moytoy of Great Tellico.

When Moytoy was killed in battle in 1741, the Tellico-Hiwassee power structure sought to retain the advantages of the emperorship.[12] Using the European concept of a hereditary monarchy, the Tellico council gained British recognition of Ammonscossittee, the teenage son of Moytoy, as the new emperor.[13] For more than a decade thereafter, the rising power base at Chota competed with the Tellico-Hiwassee coalition for political dominance.

In 1751, the colony of South Carolina placed an embargo on trade goods going to the Cherokees both because of altercations with several traders and also because of the tribe's persisting war with the Creeks. Realizing the need for alternative supply sources, Ammonscossittee made an ill-fated trip to Virginia the following year. Returning in disgrace, preceded by rumors of his having betrayed the best interest of the Cherokee Nation, the young emperor lost support even in his own council.[14]

With the increased political strife brought about by the faltering Tellico-Hiwassee coalition, South Carolina had no choice but to turn to Chota for leadership. In 1753, Old Hop, surrounded by a council of very capable leaders, became the emperor.

When the French and Indian War began, the British colonies invoked the Treaty of 1730, demanding that the Cherokees take up arms against the enemies of King George. The Cherokees, however, were reluctant to send warriors to the Virginia frontier unless the British assumed protection of the vulnerable Cherokee settlements. After both Virginia and South Carolina built forts in the Overhill country, the Cherokees sent several hundred warriors to fight on the frontier. The Cherokees distinguished themselves in service, and a number were killed in battle. However, when some returning Cherokee veterans were killed by Virginia frontiersmen, the alliance which Col. George Washington valued so highly was broken.[15]

Outraged clansmen of the dead were obligated by traditional law to seek revenge. Maintaining the concept of corporate responsibility, they carried the hatchet to nearby Carolina frontier settlements rather than to the offending settlements in Virginia.

The South Carolina government in turn demanded satisfaction. A peace delegation headed by Oconastota went to Charlestown in the fall of 1759 to offer reassurances of Cherokee loyalty. The delegation, accompanied by 1,300 militia, was marched back to the Cherokee country in chains. At Fort Prince George in the Lower settlements, Governor Lyttelton offered to exchange members of the peace delegation on an individual basis for the twenty-four warriors guilty of murders in Carolina since November 9, 1758.[16] It was an impossible situation for the Cherokees. They could not surrender men for execution who had acted in good conscience as agents of their society; on the other hand, they could not abandon innocent leaders who had sought only to reaffirm their allegiance to South Carolina. Finally, three alleged murderers were surrendered and several of the captives, including Oconastota, were released.

In the ensuing difficulties twenty-two members of the Cherokee delegation were murdered by soldiers from Fort Prince George, and an army of 1,650 men under Col. Archibald Montgomery invaded the Cherokee country. Montgomery destroyed five of the Lower Towns on June 1 and 2, 1760, but was later soundly defeated as he attempted to lead his army into the Middle settlements. The Cherokees, regarding their encounter with Montgomery's army as a moral victory, pressed their siege of Fort Loudoun. In August, that garrison surrendered.

The following spring, another punitive expedition marched toward the Cherokee country. Despite the Cherokees' desire for peace, there was none to be had. The army of 2,600 men commanded by Lt. Col. James Grant burned fifteen Middle Towns, destroyed 1,500 acres of crops, and created much human suffering.[17]

As a result of the political instability and resulting warfare, the pattern of the Cherokee settlement in the eighteenth century was altered considerably. Early in the century, Cherokee towns were very compact, homogenous entities, with social and political life revolving around the townhouses. By the last quarter of the century, a Cherokee town had become a sprawling community of farmsteads extending for as much as two miles along the bottomlands. Locations of townsites also changed during this period. The Lower Towns, which suffered heavily both from the Creek War in the early 1750s and the Montgomery and Grant expeditions in 1760 and 1761, were almost depopulated by the end of the Revolutionary War.

Although the political importance of the eighteenth century towns has frequently been the subject of scholarly inquiry, their geographical significance has been a source of confusion even to some prominent researchers. Movements of towns, multiple towns with the same name, and variations in spellings have contribed to the misinterpretations. In this volume, Betty Smith analyzes early maps and census data to locate the towns and correlate spelling inconsistencies. Tabulating the information on charts and new maps, she traces the changes in Cherokee settlements during the first three-quarters of the eighteenth century. Her work not only provides a better understanding of Cherokee geography but also yields an insight into the social and political factors affecting the mobility of the Cherokees.

In the Overhill country, substantial population movements did not begin until the American Revolution. By 1775, white settlement had reached only as far as the upper east corner of what is now the state of Tennessee. The frontier was rapidly expanding, however. In March 1775 at Sycamore Shoals, aged Cherokee leaders sold most of central Kentucky and most of north central Tennessee to the Transylvania Land Company. Since only the crown had authority to purchase land from the Indians, arrest warrants were issued for the company officials. They, however, quickly retired to the security of their wilderness.[18]

In the meantime, lines were being drawn in the American Revolution. War between whites who spoke the same language seemed incomprehensible to the Cherokees. Their loyalty, however, was with their trusted friend and benefactor John Stuart, now the British superintendent for the southern Indians. Stuart hoped that a war with Wataugans could be avoided and that Cherokee warriors could later supplement British regulars in the South.

When diplomatic efforts failed to bring the Wataugans to terms, Dragging Canoe could not be dissuaded from war. In July 1776, the Cherokees launched a three-pronged attack against the settlers along the Holston and Watauga rivers. The frontiersmen, forewarned, repulsed the invaders. The Cherokees did only enough damage to provide an excuse for the settlers to invade Cherokee towns. Armies were raised in Virginia, the Carolinas, and Georgia. By fall, the Cherokee Nation was in a state of devastation.[19]

Dragging Canoe and his followers withdrew to the Chattanooga area and continued their forays against the frontier settlements throughout the 1780s and early 1790s. Repeatedly, frontier armies were raised and sent against the Cherokees. By 1784, the Chickamaugas had a population "equal to that of the Upper settlements on the Little Tennessee."[20] As the frontier era in the Little Tennessee Valley drew to a close, gradual migrations depopulated the area. In 1788, after several peace chiefs including Old Tassel, Old Abram, and Abram's son were murdered under a flag of truce, the Cherokees moved their capital from Chota to Ustanali, near the present-day Calhoun, Georgia.[21]

The Cherokee political spectrum of this period was overshadowed by the continual struggle with the settlers. Marauding war parties terrorized the frontier. War chiefs such as Bloody Fellow, Doublehead, Bob Benge, and John Satts rose to prominence. The Cherokees, trying desperately to maintain their territorial boundaries, sought help from various Indian allies and European powers. Great Britain, though defeated in the American Revolution, was still looked upon as a potential benefactor. On one occasion before hostilities ceased on the frontier, several Cherokees traveled to London on a diplomatic mission. Accompanying the scheming William Augustus Bowles, they became subjects of controversy in the Nootka Sound crisis, the Prince Modoc intellectual debate, and the French Revolution before returning home. In an outstanding piece of historical detective work, William Sturtevant brings to light in this volume a very unusual episode of Cherokee involvement in international diplomacy during the last decade of the eighteenth century.

In 1794, the hostilities between the Cherokees and the whites finally ended. With the devastation of the Lower Towns by the Ore Expedition from the Cumberland settlements, the loss of much-needed Spanish support, as indicated by a letter taken from the body of Chief Breath at Nickajack, and the defeat of their northern allies by Anthony Wayne at the Battle of Fallen Timbers, the Cherokees had no choice but to pursue the road of peace.[22]

The first quarter of the nineteenth century was a time of great social change for the Cherokees. The degree of acculturation was such that the life-style of the Cherokees closely paralleled that of southern whites. Clear-cut social classes began to emerge. Attitudes toward slavery, which had been equated traditionally with war captives, began to conform to those of area whites. However, as Theda Perdue points out in this volume, despite the similarities, there were many contrasts. Dr. Perdue offers convincing evidence that the Cherokee treatment of black slaves was more refined than that of their white neighbors.

The increased pressures brought on by the flood of white settlers which engulfed the Cherokees also dictated changes in the Indians' political organization. Determined to retain the remaining tribal territory despite the 1802 promise of the United States government to extinguish Indian land titles as soon as convenient, the Cherokees reorganized their internal political structures. As Richard Persico demonstrates, traditional political concepts were altered to provide a unified front for dealing with the dominant society on more equal terms.

Despite the adoption of a constitutional government, a written language, a bilingual newspaper, and other tangible evidence of rapid acculturation, the Cherokees were subjected to relentless demands for their land. The state of Georgia enacted repressive legislation in an effort to expedite Cherokee removal. The period between 1828 and 1835, as Kenneth P. Davis points out, was especially chaotic. Repressive laws and abusive treatment by legal intruders caused some Georgia Cherokees to give up hope and to support removal. Others, even though they had been dispossessed by lottery winners, remained defiant.

On December 29, 1835, at New Echota some Cherokees who represented only a small minority signed away the entire remaining tribal territory east of the Mississippi.

In spite of the protests of the majority of Cherokees, the treaty was ratified by the United States Congress.

In June 1838, forced removal began, and immense human suffering on the "Trail of Tears" greatly compounded the political tragedy that had already taken place.

In the Indian Territory after removal, factionalism between

the Old Settlers, the Treaty party, and the Ross party (those who were forcibly removed) resulted in continued bitterness, hatred, and even bloodshed. The assassinations of Major Ridge, John Ridge, and Elias Boudinot by Ross supporters on June 22, 1839, was only one episode in a long and violent struggle. Gerard Reed provides an excellent synthesis of this difficult period in Cherokee history.

Despite the government's effort at total removal of Cherokees from the East, some were able to avoid it. Most of these were in North Carolina, where a new Eastern Band of Cherokees was formed. As I have pointed out in "The Origin of the Eastern Cherokees as a Social and Political Entity," included here, many popular beliefs about the origin of this group are contradicted by historical documentation. Even the facts concerning Tsali and his legendary sacrifice seem to have been distorted by time. Although some North Carolina Cherokees managed to avoid removal, their status was uncertain for decades to come. Richard Iobst traces the political struggle for Cherokee rights in North Carolina and the career of William H. Thomas, who led the fight for the Cherokees. By 1848, through constant war, Will Thomas was able to secure for the Eastern Cherokees some of the rights granted by the Treaty of New Echota.

Reconstruction was a time of isolation and relative stability for the Cherokees. In the West, just when the Cherokees had almost recovered from the devastation of the war, they received another blow. The Dawes Act, passed in 1887, divided the tribal land into individual allotments, with the vast surplus reverting to the United States government for homesteads. The Western Cherokees were relieved of more than six and one-half million acres, and subsequent frauds and swindles by speculators left many individuals landless and penniless.[23]

Although the New Echota treaty guaranteed that the new Cherokee land would never be part of any state, the inevitable was realized when statehood for Oklahoma came in 1907. In 1919 Cherokee veterans of World War I became United States citizens, and in 1924 all Cherokees received citizenship. Since that time many changes have taken place in Cherokee life. Social changes among the Eastern Cherokees of the past decades are discussed at length by John Witthoft in this volume.

Today, despite the level of acculturation, some vestiges of traditional culture can be identified. For instance, the Cherokee language is maintained today by about ten thousand people in Oklahoma and one thousand in North Carolina. Other traits of traditional culture—value systems, personality traits, and ways of interpersonal relations—are more subtle. The persistence and re-emergence in Oklahoma of the traditional concept of community organization is examined by Albert Wahrhaftig in this volume. Like political changes in the early nineteenth century, the development of the community organization appears to reflect reliance on a traditional means to deal with current problems.

The history of the Cherokee people is filled with pride, success, defeat, bitterness, and despair. The Cherokees' attachment to their land, the hostilities of the eighteenth century, the rapid progress of the early nineteenth century, the forced removal, and the condition of the Cherokees today are all parts of this history. The Cherokees have suffered many losses in the three-hundred-year history of sustained contact with the whites, but birthright that cannot be taken away is cultural heritage.

NOTES

1. James Mooney, "Myths of the Cherokee," Bureau of American Ethnology, *19th Annual Report* (Washington, D.C.: GPO, 1900), 14.

2. *Ibid.*, 16–17.

3. T.M.N. Lewis and Madeline Kneberg, *Hiwassee Island: An Archaeological Account of Four Tennessee Indian Peoples* (Knoxville: Univ. of Tennessee Press, 1946), 11–12.

4. Floyd G. Lounsbury, "Iroquois-Cherokee Linguistic Relations," in "Symposium on Cherokee and Iroquois Culture," Bureau of American Ethnology *Bulletin no. 180* (Washington, D.C.: GPO, 1961), 11.

5. "Document of 1691," South Carolina Hist. Soc. Collections, I, 126; cited in Mooney, "Myths," 31.

6. Alexander Hewatt, *An Historical Account of the Rise and Progress of the Colonies of South Carolina and Georgia*, 2 vols. (London: Donaldson, 1779), I, 216.

7. Mary Rothrock, "Carolina Traders among the Overhill Cherokees, 1690–1760," East Tennessee Hist. Soc. *Publications* 1 (1929), 3–18.

8. Mooney, "Myths," 32–33.

9. Charles C. Royce, "The Cherokee Nation of Indians," in Bureau of American Ethnology, *5th Annual Report* (Washington, D.C.: GPO, 1883), 140.

10. Hewatt, *Historical Account,* 258.

11. George Chicken, "Journal to the Cherokees, 1725," MS in the Public Record Office, London; C.O. 5, 12, folios 14–34; published in Newton D. Mereness, *Travels in the American Colonies* (New York: Macmillan, 1916), 97–172.

12. David H. Corkran, *The Cherokee Frontier: Conflict and Survival, 1740–62* (Norman: Univ. of Oklahoma Press, 1962), 16.

13. *Ibid.*

14. *Ibid.,* 39.

15. *Ibid.,* 142–62.

16. *South Carolina Gazette,* Jan. 12, 1760; cited in Corkran, *Cherokee Frontier,* 189.

17. Corkran, *Cherokee Frontier,* 254; Duane H. King, "The Powder Horn Commemorating the Grant Expedition Against the Cherokees," *Journal of Cherokee Studies* 1 (Summer 1976), 23–40.

18. Samuel Cole Williams, "Henderson and Company's Purchase Within the Limits of Tennessee," *Tennessee Historical Magazine* 5 (1919), 5–27.

19. Samuel Cole Williams, *Tennessee During the Revolutionary War* (Knoxville: Univ. of Tennessee Press, 1974), 48–60; William Lenoir, "Revolutionary War Diary," ed. J.G. Hamilton, *Journal of Southern History* 6 (May 1940), 247–59.

20. Samuel Cole Williams, ed., *Early Travels in the Tennessee Country, 1540–1800* (Johnson City: Watauga Press, 1928), 256.

21. Grace S. Woodward, *The Cherokees* (Norman: Univ. of Oklahoma Press, 1963), 109.

22. Mooney, "Myths," 78, 79.

23. Woodward, *Cherokees,* 320–22.

The Cherokee Indian Nation

The Origins and Development of Cherokee Culture

Roy S. Dickens, Jr.

Determining the prehistoric antecedents of the Cherokees is important to ethnohistorians, archaeologists, and other students of native American culture. However, any attempt to trace a historically documented group into the prehistoric period must ultimately rely upon material remains, even though perceived relationships in artifact styles may not be indicative of tribal or linguistic relationships. Still, if it is true that a culture can be viewed as an integrated system, then patterns in the material record should reflect some of the same processes that contributed to other behavioral patterns—social and ideological—of that system. Perhaps, therefore, the archaeological record can provide an avenue for exploring the ancestry of a historically defined group, such as the Cherokees, so long as we recognize that material traits comprise only part of the total cultural system and that considerable changes occurred in the native American cultures during the early historic period.

During the middle to late 1800s, archaeologists in eastern North America set out to prove that the prehistoric Mound Builders were part of a long and continuous development leading ultimately to known Indian tribes. In 1890, when reporting on mound investigations in eastern Tennessee, Cyrus Thomas proposed that the ancestors of the Cherokee Indians had been present in their historic homeland since the late thirteenth century. His assemblage of pre-Columbian Cherokee remains included temple mounds, engraved shell gorgets, and stone-box graves (Thomas 1890).[1] W.H. Holmes analyzed the pottery recovered from these same mound explorations, and on the question of the origins of Cherokee pottery he wrote:

3

These people [the Cherokees] were in possession of an immense tract of the South Appalachian region when first encountered by the whites, and there is nothing to indicate that they were not long resident in this region. . . . They are skillful potters, and what is of special interest is the fact that their ware has several points of analogy with the ancient stamped pottery of the South Appalachian province. . . . The question may thus be raised as to whether the Cherokees, rather than the Uchees or the Muskhogean tribes, are not the people represented by the ceramic remains of the Southeast.[2]

At about the same time that the Smithsonian crews were excavating sites in eastern Tennessee, the Valentine brothers of Richmond, Virginia, representing the Valentine Museum (fig. 1), explored sites in western North Carolina. This little-known work resulted in excavations of mounds in the area of the historic Cherokee Out Towns near the modern town of Cherokee, North Carolina. Like the Smithsonian researchers, the Valentines concluded that the mounds were built by a people who possessed "the same stage of civilization . . . as obtained among the Cherokees when first visited by the Europeans."[3] They based much of this interpretation on the fact that Cherokee women of the 1880s were making pottery in the same styles as were represented by sherds recovered from the mounds.

In 1915, the Museum of the American Indian, Heye Foundation, conducted excavations on sites in western North Carolina and northern Georgia. Their most important work was at the Nacoochee Mound in Georgia, on the headwaters of the Chattahoochee River. The excavators stated that, "while Bartram lends support to the mysterious origin of mounds occupied by the Cherokee, there is no doubt that the tribe built and occupied various mounds and that Nacoochee was one of them."[4] These archaeologists believed that the pottery they found (ranging from Etowah to protohistoric Lamar) represented a Cherokee ceramic tradition.[5]

M.R. Harrington, who explored sites on the upper Tennessee River for the Heye Foundation in 1919, was also impressed by the continuity from the earliest temple mound builders to the historic Cherokees (fig. 2). He did not hesitate to classify as Cherokee the culture Lewis and Kneberg later called Dallas,[6] and he was open

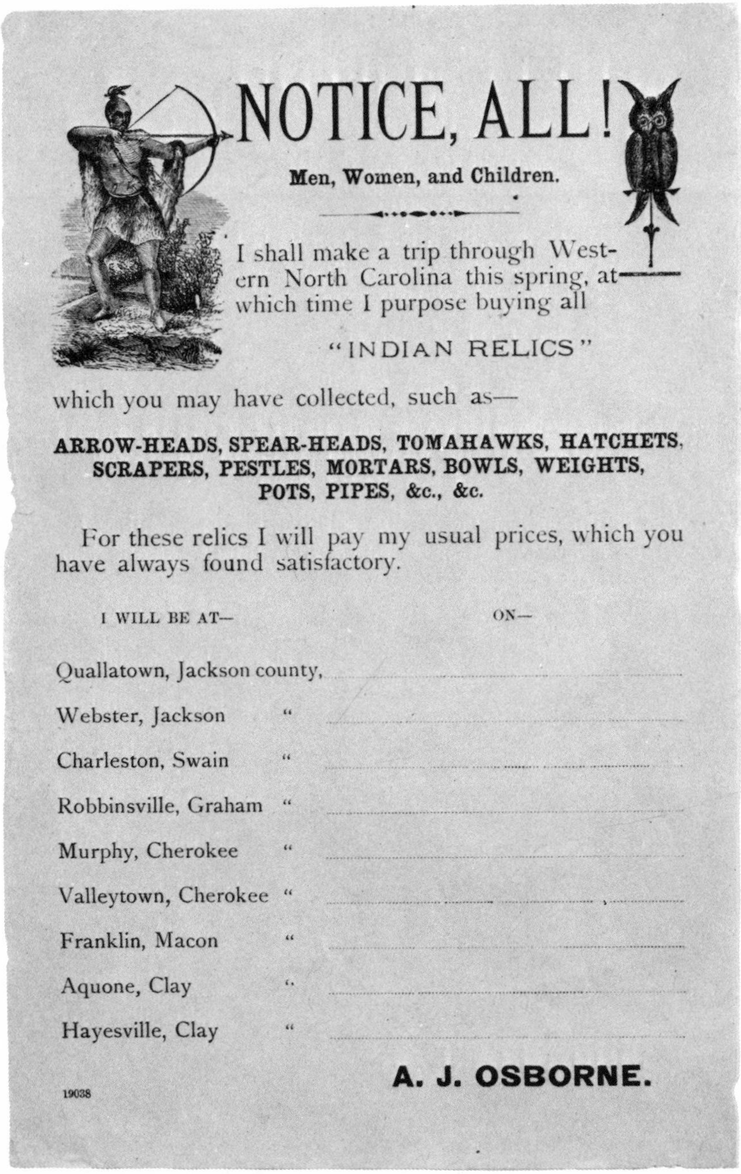

Figure 1. In the early 1880s the Valentine Museum in Richmond, Virginia, assembled a large collection of Cherokee artifacts. The poster shown above was used by A.J. Osborne of Haywood County, who was Valentine's solicitor for western North Carolina (courtesy Research Laboratories of Anthropology, University of North Carolina).

Figure 2. A member of M.R. Harrington's crew with a Cherokee burial at the Mainland Village site near Lenoir City, Tennessee, in 1919 (courtesy The Museum of the American Indian, Heye Foundation).

6

to the possibility of the same classification for the earlier Hiwassee Island culture.[7]

Between 1930 and 1950, during and immediately following the CWA-WPA excavations in the upper Tennessee Basin, interpretations of Cherokee prehistory took on a restrictive tone. William S. Webb set this tone in his Norris Basin report. After stating that "Cherokee culture cannot be exactly defined because too many traits are too widespread," he proceeded to define the Cherokees very narrowly as builders of "circular town houses on mounds erected by an earlier people."[8]

Webb based his argument on a late-eighteenth-century account —earlier rejected by Heye and his colleagues—in which William Bartram described a circular Cherokee townhouse standing on "an ancient artificial mound of earth." The Cherokees told Bartram that they had found this mound in an abandoned state when they first arrived in the area and that they had no knowledge of the original builders.[9] Webb and others were also strongly influenced by legends that brought the Cherokees to the Southern Appalachians in a migration from the Midwest during the early historic period.[10]

Since the ceremonial buildings in the Norris Basin were square or rectangular (although some did have rounded corners), and because they apparently had been constructed by the builders of the mounds on which they stood, Webb reasoned that his late-prehistoric and protohistoric cultures were Creek and Yuchi instead of Cherokee.[11] He was willing to accept the archaeological assemblages from Hiwassee Island and Dandridge farther downstream, and from Nacoochee in northern Georgia, as having Cherokee affiliations. Even though his sites agreed with these others in nineteen of twenty-four ceramic traits[12]—in fact, most of the pottery from Hiwassee Island and the Norris Basin was later classified as belonging to the same types[13]—he still based his tribal identifications on the weak evidence of Bartram's comment.

Continuing in this restrictive tenor, Lewis and Kneberg made the Cherokees Johnnies-come-lately at Hiwassee Island, Tennessee. In their report on the excellent excavations conducted at this site between 1937 and 1939, they acknowledged a late-historic Cherokee occupation, but they classified their earlier Hiwassee Island and Dallas cultures as Muskogean. Their contention was that Cherokee culture should be equated solely with complicated stamped, sand tempered pottery, which had a long history in the Georgia Piedmont region. On these grounds they were willing to grant the Cherokees some antiquity in parts of the Southeast, but they maintained, as had Webb, that in eastern Tennessee the plain and cord marked, shell tempered pottery and temple mounds were products of Creek and Yuchi immigrants.[14] They concluded that "the Cherokee never inhabited the lower Hiwassee River or Tennessee River until long after white contact."[15]

In a report on the 1933–34 excavations at the Peachtree site in southwestern North Carolina, Setzler and Jennings did not approach the Cherokee question as confidently as had Webb, Lewis, and Kneberg, but they made a couple of important observations. They noted that the four major sites thus far explored in the Cherokee area—Hiwassee Island, Etowah, Nacoochee, and Peachtree—were all known to have had Cherokee occupations in the historic period, and that there was little cultural discontinuity during late prehistory at any of them. They suggested that perhaps the Cherokees originally possessed mainly a Woodland culture and that as time went along they gradually incorporated more Mississippian traits, with the "final adoption of the general Southeastern pattern."[16]

Robert Wauchope also recognized considerable continuity in the archaeological remains from his 1938–40 survey of northern Georgia. He wrote:

> This continuity (in north Georgia ceramic traits) is so marked, one is not tempted to link any one ware with the arrival of new ethnic groups, or rather I should probably say that one does not see in ceramics here the sudden impact of a foreign dominating culture. The early Middle Mississippi traits appear at the proper place in the sequence, but they do not obliterate native pottery features. One gets no impression of dominated or dominating complexes or of retreating and returning cultures; nowhere along the line am I tempted to speculate that this is where the Cherokee arrived, or here a group of Creeks was forced into the north country and here they left again.

. . . Ceramically speaking, . . . our north Georgians seemed to rock along relatively undisturbed by the impact of clashing cultures.[17]

The next statements on Cherokee archaeology came from a series of river-basin salvage projects in northern Georgia and northwestern South Carolina in the 1950s. In his report on the Allatoona Basin project, Caldwell assigned Cherokee status only to his late-historic Galt Period, and, although he recognized many similarities between Galt ceramics and the early-historic Brewster Period ceramics, he classified Brewster as Muskogean.[18] Later, Caldwell summarized ceramic data from several historic Cherokee sites in northern Georgia. In this summary, he pointed out that the pottery from all of the sites was in the "lamar tradition," a tradition with some time-depth in the area, but he concluded — following the restrictive trend set some years earlier by Webb — that "the Cherokee appear to have been late comers into Georgia and the greater part of eastern Tennessee, displacing Muskogeans from both areas."[19]

In the meantime, Sears developed a somewhat different view of the antecedents of North Georgia Cherokee culture. After comparing and contrasting ceramics from historic Upper Creek sites with those from historic Cherokee sites, he noted that "perhaps the most important point in this attempt to understand the origins of these two cultures is that Cherokee pottery is the end product of the complicated stamped tradition, the tradition which is the hallmark of the South Appalachian province from the beginning of the Middle Woodland period." Sears then concluded that "the Cherokee ceramic assemblage is a development in this indigenous tradition, and the Cherokee culture is then indigenous. Creek culture on the other hand might well be viewed as intrusive or at least that of the upper Muskhogee-speaking Creeks."[20]

A few years later, an excellent case in point for Sears' argument for a long Cherokee tradition in northern Georgia was manifested in the findings of Kelly and Neitzel at the Chauga site in the Hartwell Basin. The first stages of the Chauga temple mound were constructed as early as about A.D. 1000. Succeeding stages were added until a documented historic Cherokee occupation, without

9

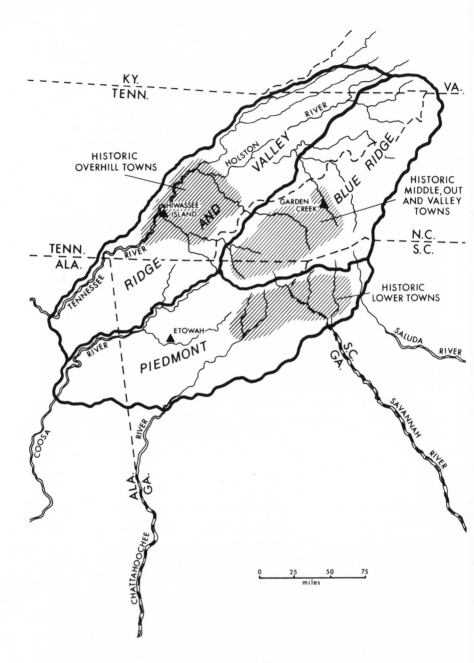

Map 1. REGIONAL DEVELOPMENTS OF THE CHEROKEE TRADITION, A.D. 1000–1838

10

a significant break in the entire sequence. In summing up their finding at Chauga and other north Georgia sites, Kelly and Neitzel wrote: "We can now regard a whole series of site situations from northeast through north Georgia . . . (as providing) a detailed continuum . . . from a perceived late Etowah-Savannah (Wilbanks) stage to an historic and modified Lamaroid complex that can be attributed on good ethnohistorical data to the Cherokee."[21]

An important statement on the Cherokee problem from the perspective of western North Carolina was made by Joffre L. Coe in 1958. Coe proposed an antiquity of more than two thousand years for Cherokee culture in the Southern Appalachians. He recognized that there were differences in the archaeological assemblages of the Tennessee River, northern Georgia, and the Blue Ridge area, but he pointed out that there were also differences between the Cherokee settlements in historic times. Why then, Coe argued, should we persist in trying to identify the prehistoric Cherokees by a single ceramic label or townhouse configuration? He suggested that the differences between such sites as Peachtree in the Valley Town area and Hiwassee Island in the Overhill area were differences of "degree rather than kind."[22]

Thus, by 1960 archaeological data was beginning to point in new directions for interpreting Cherokee prehistory. There was mounting evidence for a long and relatively unbroken continuum of prehistoric cultural development over much of the area occupied by the historic Cherokees; there was a growing recognition that Cherokee culture could not be identified at any time-level by a single archaeological assemblage; and the data suggested that the developing Cherokees participated in the generalized Mississippian pattern of the South Appalachian Province—a pattern that included the construction of platform mounds and the manufacture of a variety of ceramics including both sand tempered and shell tempered wares. Thus, archaeologists began to question the validity of Indian legends and historical accounts that brought the Cherokees into their historic homeland by recent migration.

At the time of European contact, the Cherokees exhibited many traits held in common by the terminal Mississippian cul-

11

	PIEDMONT Historic Lower Cherokee	RIDGE-AND-VALLEY Historic Overhill Cherokee	BLUE RIDGE Historic Middle Cherokee
1838 A.D.			
	Late Lamar Variants	Overhill	Late Qualla
1650 A.D.			
	Early Lamar	Late Dallas	Early Qualla
1450 A.D.			
	Late Etowah/Wilbanks	Early Dallas	Late Pisgah
1250 A.D.			
	Early Etowah	Hiwassee Island	Early Pisgah
1000 A.D.			

Figure 3. Archaeological phases of the Cherokee tradition, A.D. 1000–1838.

tures of the South Appalachian region. These traits included platform mound construction, complicated stamped ceramics, a major commitment to maize agriculture, and a settlement pattern in which groups of permanent villages were satellites of larger communities with clearly defined ceremonial precincts.[23]

These traits began to appear in the region in the closing centuries of the Middle Woodland Period, from approximately A.D. 600 to 800. Platform mounds at Garden Creek, North Carolina,[24] and Anneewakee Creek, Georgia,[25] have been dated to this period. It was at about this same time that rectilinear complicated stamping was first applied to ceramics in the South Appalachians. This style of surface finish is common on Napier and Woodstock ce-

12

ramics of northern Georgia,[26] but is only occasionally present on Hamilton ceramics of eastern Tennessee[27] and Connestee ceramics of western North Carolina.[28] Rectilinear stamped pottery may have had its origins in the Georgia Piedmont, where it is found in greatest amounts and where it seems to be oldest.

From about A.D. 1000 to 1250, three distinct subregional developments of Mississippian culture began to emerge in the portion of the South Appalachians that was occupied in historic times by the Cherokees (map 1 and fig. 3). The initial phases of these developments are the Early Etowah phase of the Piedmont province of northern Georgia, extreme eastern Alabama, and northwestern South Carolina (along the Etowah, Oostanaula, upper Coosa, upper Chattahoochee, and upper Savannah); the Hiwassee Island phase of the Ridge and Valley province in northwestern Georgia, northeastern Alabama, and southeastern Tennessee (along the lower Clinch, lower Powell, lower Little Tennessee, lower Hiwassee, and the Tennessee River proper as far south as the Guntersville Basin); and the Early Pisgah phase in the Blue Ridge province of western North Carolina, northeastern Tennessee, southwestern Virginia, and northwestern South Carolina (on the tributaries of the upper Clinch, upper Powell, Holston, Nolichucky, Watauga, French Broad, upper Little Tennessee, and upper Saluda rivers.)

Platform mounds that were either initiated or already in use during this period include Mound C at Etowah,[29] the Long Swamp and Eastwood mounds,[30] and the Chauga Mound,[31] all in the Piedmont province; the substructure mound (Unit 37) at Hiwassee Island,[32] and several mounds in the Norris Basin,[33] all in the Ridge and Valley province; and Garden Creek Mound no. 2 and Newport Mound[34] in the Blue Ridge province.

The ceramics of all three phases (fig. 4) exhibit some proportion of rectilinear complicated stamping, but this finish is more abundant in Etowah and Pisgah than in Hiwassee Island. Some Etowah and Hiwassee Island motifs are identical, and Pisgah Complicated Stamped resembles Etowah Line-Block Stamped. Check stamping forms a strong minority in Pisgah but is rarely present in Etowah and Hiwassee Island. Painted and slipped pot-

13

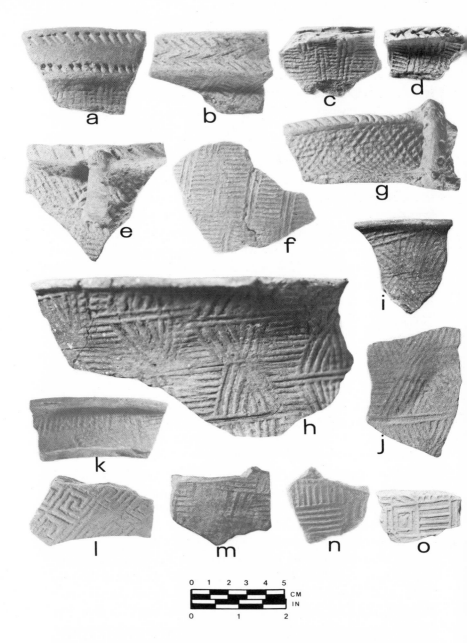

Figure 4. *A–f,* Early Pisgah Complicated Stamped; *g,* Early Pisgah Check Stamped; *h,* Hiwassee Island Complicated Stamped; *i–o,* Etowah Complicated Stamped.

14

tery, common in Hiwassee Island and present in Etowah, is lacking in Pisgah. Cord and textile marked finishes are common in Hiwassee Island but are seldom found in Etowah and Pisgah. Most of the pottery of the Hiwassee Island phase is shell tempered, while most of the pottery of the Etowah and Pisgah phases is sand tempered.

A distinctive feature of Pisgah ceramics (fig. 4) is a collared-and-punctated rim.[35] This form of rim, which has no antecedents in the Southeast, seems to have been derived from contemporary forms in the Midwest.[36] Coe has noted that these distinctive rims are significant in the interpretation of Cherokee origins because they are present on pottery in the Southern Appalachians at least as early as in the northern Iroquois area.[37]

In the period from about A.D. 1250 to 1450, Early Etowah evolves into Late Etowah/Wilbanks,[38] Hiwassee Island develops into Early Dallas,[39] and Early Pisgah becomes Late Pisgah.[40] The Late Etowah/Wilbanks and Dallas phases are strongly affected by the Southern Cult (Southeastern Ceremonial Complex), and their influence on neighboring cultures is clearly documented in the archaeological remains. Early Dallas ceramics replace Pisgah ceramics on sites in northeastern Tennessee and are found on sites deep in northern Georgia and Alabama. Lewis and Kneberg have suggested that at the Hiwassee Island site the development of Dallas culture was accompanied by an augmentation of the existing population by a new group moving up the Tennessee River.[41] Late Pisgah becomes restricted mainly to the Blue Ridge basins of western North Carolina and northwestern South Carolina.

There are significant similarities in mound architecture in the three provinces during this period. In several instances substructure mounds were raised over collapsed semisubterranean earth lodges, and stone mantles or irregular groups of stones were incorporated in mound stages. Collapsed earth lodges (fig. 5a) have been found beneath the Wilbanks[42] and Bell Field mounds,[43] in the Piedmont province; several mounds in the Norris Basin[44] of the Ridge and Valley province; and the Garden Creek Mound no. 1[45] and Peachtree Mound[46] in the Blue Ridge province. Stone features (figs. 5 and 9a) are present in mounds in the Norris Basin in

a

b

Figure 5. A, stone feature at the base of the Cox Mound, Norris Basin, Tennessee (courtesy Smithsonian Institution); *b,* stone mantle and collapsed earth lodges at the base of Mound no. 1, Garden Creek site, North Carolina (courtesy Research Laboratories of Anthropology, University of North Carolina).

16

Tennessee; at Garden Creek and Peachtree in North Carolina; at Wilbanks and Nacoochee[47] in Georgia; and at Chauga[48] in South Carolina.

Some important changes are evident in ceramics (fig. 6) during this period. In Early Dallas pottery, there is a decline in complicated stamped wares and an increase in plain, cord marked, and incised wares. However, it should be noted that complicated stamping does not disappear entirely. In Late Etowah/Wilbanks pottery, stamped motifs are boldly executed, and there is a marked increase in curvilinear designs. Also present in small amounts are plain, red filmed, and check stamped finishes. Connections between the Wilbanks series and the Savannah series of the Atlantic Coastal Plain have been pointed out by Sears[49] and Wauchope.[50] Ceramic changes from Early to Late Pisgah are subtle. Rectilinear motifs are bolder, some curvilinear stamping is now present, and check stamping (usually bolder) continues as a strong minority finish. Influences on Late Pisgah ceramics from both Dallas and Wilbanks, as well as from Pee Dee ceramics of the Carolina Piedmont, are indicated.[51]

The spread and elaboration of the Southern Cult already has been noted for this period. Cult manifestations are considerably stronger in Late Etowah/Wilbanks and Early Dallas than in Late Pisgah; however, one cult-related artifact is duplicated almost to the detail by all three cultures. This is a circular shell gorget with coiled rattlesnake motif (fig. 7) called the "Lick Creek" style.[52]

Another comparable feature in all three phases is the shaft-and-chamber burial (fig. 8). In the Blue Ridge[53] and the Piedmont provinces[54] these include both central-chamber and side-chamber varieties, with the openings of the chambers covered by logs or, occasionally, stone slabs. In Dallas sites of the Ridge and Valley province there are central chambers with log or stone slab coverings.[55] In all three areas, logs or stone slabs are sometimes used to construct formalized tombs or vaults.[56]

In the next two centuries, between about A.D. 1450 and 1650, there were several important changes in the cultures of the Southern Appalachians. Stimuli for some of these changes were indigenous, while others probably resulted from initial contacts with

17

Figure 6. A and *b*, Late Pisgah Complicated Stamped; *c*, Late Pisgah Check Stamped; *d*, Late Pisgah Complicated Stamped (incised rim); *e*, Dallas incised; *f, g,* and *h*, Wilbanks Complicated Stamped.

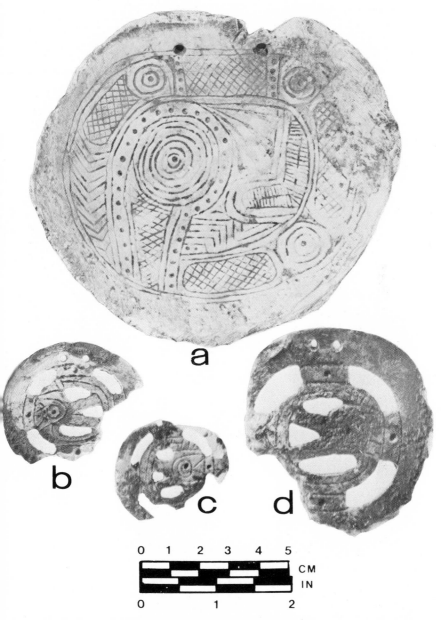

Figure 7. A, "Citico" style gorget from the Little Egypt site in Georgia (courtesy Laboratory of Archaeology, University of Georgia); *b, c,* and *d,* "Lick Creek" style gorgets from the Warren Wilson and Garden Creek sites in western North Carolina.

Europeans. In the Piedmont, Wilbanks becomes Lamar, in the Ridge and Valley province, Early Dallas becomes Late Dallas, and in the Blue Ridge, Late Pisgah becomes Early Qualla. During this period there is an apparent overall decline in the importance of the Southern Cult, and the Lamar culture of northern Georgia seems to exert the strongest and most far-reaching influence, at least in pottery styles.

Mound construction continues in all three provinces, and considerable effort is expended on enlarging already existing platforms. Although there is little archaeological evidence for earth lodges in this period (an earth-covered building found at the base of the Tugalo Mound in northeastern Georgia may date to this period), there are later historical accounts of such structures. Also, stone mantles have not been conclusively documented for mounds of this period, but they definitely were used in historic-period mounds.

Very important at this time is the development of Lamar ceramic styles in Piedmont Georgia, and the ultimate spread of these styles to the north and east. In northwestern Georgia, Lamar pottery is used along with and then replaces Dallas styles. This mixed assemblage has been documented at several sites in the Carters Reservoir on the Coosawattee River[57] and at the King site on the Coosa River west of Rome.[58] It has been termed Dallamar by Kelly[59] and Barnett phase by Hally.[60] Some researchers have resurrected the Cherokee-replacement-of-Creek hypothesis to explain this ceramic relationship,[61] but Hally has suggested, and more correctly I think, that it may "reflect only the ebb and flow of ceramic styles independently of social and political boundaries."[62] Lamar pottery (fig. 10) includes bowls and jars having bold complicated stamped, bold check stamped, plain-roughened, plain-smoothed, and burnished surfaces finishes. Jars and simple bowls have notched or finger impressed rim fillets, while steep-shouldered (cazuela) bowls have incised decorations.

Late Dallas ceramics differ little, on the whole, from those of Early Dallas contexts, but there is an increase in plain wares, and Lamar influence is indicated by the presence of incised cazuela bowls and a few vessels with bold complicated stamping.[63] The

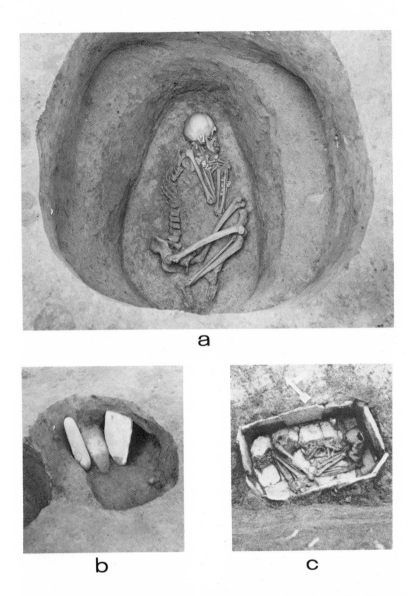

Figure 8. A, Central-chamber burial of an adult male at the Warren Wilson site, North Carolina (Late Pisgah phase); b, side-chamber burial of an infant at the Warren Wilson site (Late Pisgah phase); c, stone-vault burial of an adult at the Peachtree Mound, North Carolina (probably Early Qualla phase). (Photographs a and b provided courtesy of the Research Laboratories of Anthropology, University of North Carolina; photograph c provided courtesy of the Smithsonian Institution.)

transition from Late Pisgah to Early Qualla ceramics is clearly documented at several sites in western North Carolina.[64] Lamar traits are gradually incorporated into the Pisgah repertoire, and by the middle-to-late 1400s the transformation is complete. Qualla pottery (fig. 10) differs from North Georgia Lamar pottery in that angular complicated stamping and check stamping are more important, cord marking is a minority finish, and there are some unique rim treatments that are probable holdovers from Pisgah.

Two distinctive shell gorget styles are present in all three phases of this period. The first has a rattlesnake motif (fig. 7) which is a conventionalized descendant of the Lick Creek style of the previous period. This is termed the "Citico" style by Muller,[65] and it has been found at the Etowah, King, and Little Egypt sites in Georgia, at the Coweeta Creek and Birdtown mounds in North Carolina, and at the Hiwassee Island and Citico sites in Tennessee. Muller makes the following important comments: "At the present time, I would speculate that there is a direct relationship between the Citico and Lick Creek styles, that is that they represent the different styles of the same society or societies at different points in time. . . . As to the identification of these societies, the distribution of the Citico style gorgets is the same as that of the Cherokee group in large part."[66]

A second gorget style, the elongated "mask" type, is found on many of the same sites as the Citico style, occasionally in the same burial.[67] The face motifs found on these gorgets are executed in a very similar fashion whether they are found in Lamar, Dallas, or Qualla contexts.

Chambered burials, begun in the previous period, persist in the Lamar, Late Dallas, and Early Qualla phases. In the Blue Ridge province, Early Qualla burial practices are almost indistinguishable from those of the Late Pisgah culture; the side-chamber pit and a comparable assemblage of shell grave furniture continue to be used.[68]

In the period between 1650 and Indian removal, the archaeological record and historical documentation can be combined to produce a comprehensive view of the end products of the three re-

a

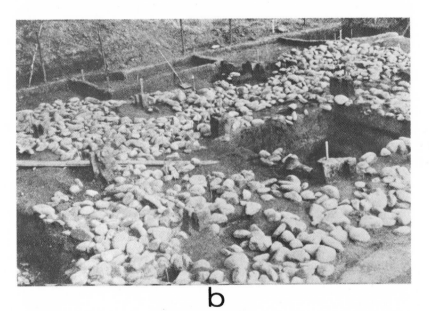

b

Figure 9. *A,* stone mantle overlying collapsed earth lodge at the base of the Peachtree Mound, North Carolina (courtesy Smithsonian Institution); *b,* stone mantle in lower stage of the Estatoe Mound, Georgia (courtesy Laboratory of Archaeology, University of Georgia).

gional developments. In the Piedmont province, Early Lamar evolves into Late Lamar, which is represented at many documented Lower Cherokee sites; in the Ridge and Valley province, Late Dallas interacts with Lamar and Qualla to become Overhill Cherokee; and in the Blue Ridge province, Early Qualla evolves into Late Qualla, which is represented at identifiable Middle, Out, and Valley Cherokee sites.

Platform mounds constructed during this period are small and composed of sequential townhouse floors separated by thin lenses of sand and clay. Examples are the Estatoe Mound (fig. 9b) in northeastern Georgia[69] and the Coweeta Creek Mound in western North Carolina.[70] Many of the large mounds begun in previous periods saw continued use in historic times, but it would appear that additions or alterations were minor. Examples include the Chauga Mound in the Lower Towns,[71] the Cowe Mound in the Middle Towns,[72] Garden Creek Mound no. 1 in the Out Town area,[73] the Peachtree Mound in the Valley Town area,[74] and the substructure mound at Hiwassee Island in the Overhill region.[75]

Two features of mound architecture for which we have seen ample evidence in the prehistoric phases are again present in the historic period. Earth-covered ceremonial buildings are clearly documented at Chota in the Overhill Towns by Timberlake[76] and at Cowe in the Middle Towns by Bartram,[77] and a massive stone mantle is found in an early historic phase of the Estatoe Mound (fig. 9b) in the Lower Towns.[78]

By 1650, ceramics in all three provinces are dominated by Lamar styles. In the Piedmont province, in historically documented Lower settlements, several localized "Lamaroid" wares (fig. 11) have been defined. These are the Boyd series on the upper Chattahoochee River,[79] the Tugalo series on the upper Savannah tributaries,[80] and the Galt series on the Etowah.[81] These series are closely related, and they all manifest considerable likenesses to the Late Qualla series of North Carolina. In general, this pottery is characterized by the use of heavy, poorly executed complicated stamps (with mostly angular motifs) on jars and bowls having abundant sand or grit temper. Check stamping is also present, as is incising on cazuela bowls. Caldwell[82] has suggested that, as the historic

Figure 10. A, b, e, and *f,* Qualla Complicated Stamped; *c,* Qualla Incised; *d,* Qualla Cord Marked; *g* and *h,* Qualla Check Stamped; *i,* Overhill Complicated Stamped; *j–l,* Early Lamar Complicated Stamped; *m–o,* Early Lamar Incised; *p,* Early Lamar Check Stamped.

period progressed, check stamping increased in importance while incising decreased.

In the Ridge and Valley province, terminal Dallas ceramics are found on some early contact sites, while most eighteenth-century sites contain a Lamar/Qualla-related ware called Overhill.[83] The Overhill series (fig. 10) differs from contemporaneous ceramics of the Piedmont and Blue Ridge provinces in the abundance of a plain surface finish and in the presence of shell temper,[84] although grit temper is found in a small percentage of sherds.[85] Nevertheless, a regular occurrence of complicated stamping serves to tie the Overhill series to historic Cherokee pottery of the other two provinces. In the Blue Ridge province, there is little change in ceramics from Early to Late Qualla, but Egloff has noted that complicated and check stamped motifs become a little cruder, incising and burnishing decrease in frequency, and cord marked and corncob impressed finishes increase in frequency.[86] Qualla style pottery persisted in the Middle and Out Towns until Indian removal, and was produced at the Qualla Reservation as late as 1880-1900.[87]

Shell gorget styles and burial pit forms described for the previous period continued to be used into the late seventeenth and early eighteenth centuries in the Overhill Towns at Hiwassee Island[88] and in the Middle Towns, where Citico gorgets have been found in chambered burials at the Coweeta Creek site.

During the historic period a number of demographic and economic changes occurred in the Cherokee area. Many of these changes can be linked through good ethnohistorical and archaeological data to European intervention, which after 1650 was intensified through warfare, disease, and the deerskin trade.[89] The result was a depopulation of the Cherokee area as a whole and a dispersion of the remaining people within the areas still occupied. Settlements, most of which had conformed to a nucleated pattern in the prehistoric setting, spread out to take advantage of larger farming and grazing plots; this movement led to the occupation of some new sites and left fewer residents at many older sites. Also, with a depleted labor force and weakened village structure, less effort was expended on mound and townhouse construction. This historic-period shift in settlement and decline in attention to

26

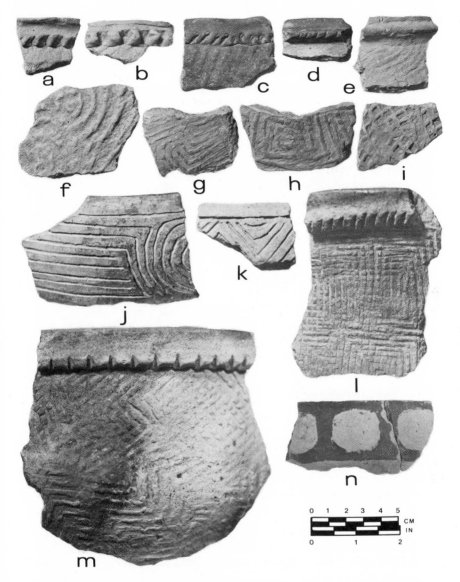

Figure 11. *A–h,* Late Lamar (Tugalo series) Complicated Stamped; *i,* Late Lamar (Boyd series) Check Stamped; *j* and *k,* Late Lamar (Tugalo series) Incised; *l* and *m,* Late Lamar (Galt series) Complicated Stamped; *n,* painted rim. Sherds *a–k* are from the eighteenth-century Cherokee Lower Town of Tugalo in Stephens County, Georgia; *l–n* are from an 1800–36 Cherokee single-family site in Bartow County, Georgia.

public structures have contributed through the years to the idea that the Cherokees arrived late in the Southeast and did not build platform mounds.

Another well-documented change occurred in the broader sociopolitical realm. The late seventeenth and early eighteenth centuries saw the development of a loose "tribal state,"[90] which was quite different from the more autonomous village-ceremonial-center groupings that characterized the late prehistoric and early historic periods. In spite of this change, however, the generalized boundaries, both geographical and social, of the Cherokee group seem to have remained about the same as they had been in pre-contact times.

In conclusion, it now seems that three subregional developments —Piedmont, Ridge and Valley, and Blue Ridge—of the South Appalachian Mississippian tradition were important in the evolution of Cherokee culture. These developments, which began around A.D. 1000, included the Etowah/Wilbanks-Lamar, Hiwassee Island-Dallas, and Pisgah-Qualla phases. Through time there was interaction between these phases, and some important traits were introduced from the outside, but a measure of regional distinctiveness was maintained and was reflected in the Lower, Overhill, and Middle divisions of the Cherokee towns in the eighteenth century.

Some important archaeological traits of the Cherokee tradition are ceremonial earth lodges, stone features in mound construction, shell gorgets with a rattlesnake motif, and chambered burials. There is also continuity in ceramic styles, although this is stronger in the Pisgah-Qualla and Etowah-Wilbanks-Lamar developments than in Dallas to Overhill. Nevertheless, bold complicated stamping represents an important trait of the Cherokee tradition. These archaeological traits need not be identified solely with the Cherokees, nor are they the only traits by which Cherokee culture can be defined. They are, however, part of a common material tradition, and they may indirectly reflect a common social and ideological tradition. This suggests, at the least, that Cherokee culture was the end product of a long, continuous, and multilinear development in the South Appalachian region.

ACKNOWLEDGMENTS

I am grateful to Leland G. Ferguson, David J. Hally, Bennie C. Keel, and William H. Sears for reading and commenting on this paper. Richards Jefferies and David Hally contributed photographs of several of the artifacts illustrated in figures 6 and 7. The Research Laboratories of Anthropology at the University of North Carolina, the Laboratory of Archaeology at the University of Georgia, the Museum of the American Indian–Heye Foundation, and the Smithsonian Institution were sources of other photographic material. Many of the ideas expressed in this paper owe their origins to Joffre L. Coe, who suggested as early as the 1950s that there had been a long Cherokee tradition in the Southern Appalachians. My association with Coe during the Cherokee Archaeological Project between 1965 and 1970 led directly to my interest in this subject.

NOTES

1. Cyrus Thomas, *The Cherokees in Pre-Columbian Times* (New York: Hodges, 1890).

2. W.H. Holmes, "Aboriginal Pottery of the Eastern United States," in Bureau of American Ethnology, *20th Annual Report* (Washington, D.C.: GPO, 1903), 143.

3. G.G., B.B., and E.P. Valentine, *Catalog of Objects,* in the Valentine Museum (Richmond, Va.: 1898), 53.

4. George G. Heye, F.W. Hodge, and G.H. Pepper, "The Nacoochee Mound in Georgia," *Contributions from the Museum of the American Indian, Heye Foundation,* vol. 2, no. 1 (New York: Museum of the American Indian, Heye Foundation, 1918), 13.

5. *Ibid.,* 56.

6. Lewis and Kneberg, *Hiwassee,* 10–12.

7. M.R. Harrington, "Cherokee and Earlier Remains on the Upper Tennessee River," *Indian Notes and Monographs* (New York: Museum of the American Indian, Heye Foundation, 1922), 272–93.

8. William S. Webb, "An Archaeological Survey of the Norris Basin in Eastern Tennessee," in Bureau of American Ethnology, *Bulletin 118* (Washington, D.C.: GPO, 1938), 378.

9. William Bartram, *Travels of William Bartram,* ed. Mark Van Doren (New York: Dover, 1940), 232–33.

10. Mooney, "Myths," 17–23.

11. Webb, "Archaeological Survey," 379–82.

12. *Ibid.*, 373.

13. Lewis and Kneberg, *Hiwassee,* 9-10, 94.

14. *Ibid.*, 92-94.

15. *Ibid.*, 17.

16. Frank M. Setzler and Jesse D. Jennings, "Peachtree Mound and Village Site, Cherokee County, North Carolina," in Bureau of American Ethnology, *Bulletin 131* (Washington, D.C.: GPO, 1941), 52-57.

17. Robert Wauchope, "The Ceramic Sequence in the Etowah Drainage, Northwest Georgia," *American Antiquity* 13, no. 3 (1948), 209.

18. Joseph R. Caldwell, "Survey and Excavations in the Allatoona Reservoir, Northern Georgia," MS, n.d., on file at the Univ. of Georgia.

19. Joseph R. Caldwell, "Cherokee Pottery from Northern Georgia," *American Antiquity* 20, no. 3 (1955), 277-80.

20. William H. Sears, "Creek and Cherokee Culture in the 18th Century," *American Antiquity* 21, no. 2 (1955), 143-49.

21. A.R. Kelly and R.S. Neitzel, *The Chauga Site in Oconee County, South Carolina,* Univ. of Georgia Laboratory of Archaeology series, no. 3 (Athens, 1961), 64.

22. Joffre L. Coe, "Cherokee Archaeology," in "Symposium on Cherokee and Iroquois Culture," ed. John Gulick, Bureau of American Ethnology, *Bulletin 180* (Washington, D.C.: GPO, 1961), 53-60.

23. Leland G. Ferguson, "South Appalachian Mississippian," Ph.D. diss., Univ. of North Carolina, 1971.

24. Bennie C. Keel, "Woodland Phases of the Appalachian Summit Area," Ph.D. diss., Washington State Univ., 1972.

25. Roy S. Dickens, Jr., "A Processual Approach to Mississippian Origins on the Georgia Piedmont," Proceedings of the Southeastern Archaeological Conference (1975), 3-42.

26. Robert Wauchope, "Archaeological Survey of Northern Georgia: With a Test of Some Cultural Hypotheses," *Memoirs of the Society for American Archaeology,* No. 21, 57-62.

27. Lewis and Kneberg, *Hiwassee,* 84-88.

28. Dickens, "The Pisgah Culture and Its Place in the Prehistory of the Southern Appalachians," Ph.D. diss., Univ. of North Carolina, 1970, 19.

29. Lewis H. Larson, Jr., "Archaeological Implications of Social Stratification at the Etowah Site, Georgia," *American Antiquity* 25, no. 3 (1971), 58-67.

30. Wauchope, "Archaeological Survey," 301-14, 347-52.

31. Kelly and Neitzel, *Chauga Site,* 57-60.

32. Lewis and Kneberg, *Hiwassee,* 28-34.

33. Webb, "Archaeological Survey," 12-25, 69-83, 145-59.

34. Dickens, "The Pisgah Culture," 195-96, 223.

35. *Ibid.*, 27-57.

36. *Ibid.*, 85-87. John T. Dorwin, *The Bowen Site: An Archaeological Study of Culture Process in the Late Prehistory of Central Indiana,* Prehistoric Research series of the Indiana Hist. Soc., vol. 4, no. 4 (Indianapolis, 1971).

37. Coe, "Cherokee Archaeology," 59.

38. Sears, "The Wilbanks Site (9CK-5), Georgia," in Bureau of American Ethnology, *Bulletin 169* (Washington, D.C.: GPO, 1958), 129-94.

39. Lewis and Kneberg, *Hiwassee,* 10.

40. Dickens, "Pisgah Culture," 198, 206.

41. Lewis and Kneberg, *Hiwassee,* 10, 37–41.

42. Sears, "Wilbanks Site," 129–85.

43. A.R. Kelly (personal communication, 1973).

44. Webb, "Archaeological Survey," 69–82, 163–66.

45. Dickens, "Pisgah Culture," 207–18.

46. Setzler and Jennings, "Peachtree Mound," 14–26.

47. Sears, "Wilbanks Site," 471; Heye, Hodge, and Pepper, "Nacoochee Mound," 14–26.

48. Kelly and Neitzel, *Chauga Site,* 11–20.

49. Sears, "Wilbanks Site," 172–76.

50. Wauchope, "Archaeological Survey," 77–79.

51. Dickens, "Pisgah Culture," 58–60.

52. Jon D. Muller, "Archaeological Analysis of Art Styles," *Tennessee Archaeologist,* 22, no. 1 (1966), 24–39.

53. Dickens, "Pisgah Culture," 226–27.

54. A.R. Kelly, "Explorations at Bell Field Mound and Village, Seasons 1965, 1966, 1967, and 1968," MS, n.d., on file at Southeastern Archaeological Center, National Park Service, Tallahassee, Fla.

55. Lewis and Kneberg, *Hiwassee,* 144.

56. *Ibid.,* 144; Heye, Hodge, and Pepper, "Nacoochee Mound," 14–27; Setzler and Jennings, "Peachtree Mound," 33–34.

57. Kelly, "Explorations," 5; David J. Hally, *Archaeological Investigations of the Potts' Tract Site (9–mu–103)m Carters Dam, Murray County, Georgia,* Univ. of Georgia Laboratory of Archaeology series, no. 6 (Athens, 1970).

58. Patrick H. Garrow and Marvin T. Smith, "The King Site (9Fl-5) Excavations, April 1971 through August 1973"; collected papers (Rome, Ga., 1973).

59. Kelly, "Explorations," 5.

60. Hally, "Archaeological Investigations," 1.

61. Carole E. Hill and Margaret V. Clayton, "The Ethnohistory of the Carters Site," paper presented at the joint meeting of the Southern Anthrop. Soc. and the Am. Ethnol. Soc., New Orleans, 1969.

62. Hally, "Archaeological Investigations," 20.

63. Lewis and Kneberg, *Hiwassee,* 99–102.

64. Dickens, "Pisgah Culture,"; Brian J. Egloff, "An Analysis of Ceramics from Historic Cherokee Towns," master's thesis, Univ. of North Carolina, 1967.

65. Muller, "Archaeological Analysis," 25–30.

66. *Ibid.,* 37.

67. Madeline Kneberg, "Engraved Shell Gorgets, and Their Associations," *Tennessee Archaeologist* 15 (1959), 26, 27.

68. Dickens, "Pisgah Culture," 131–33.

69. A.R. Kelly and Clemens de Baillou, *Excavations of the Presumptive Site of Estatoe,* Southern Indian Studies 12 (Univ. of North Carolina, 1968), 3–21.

70. Egloff, "Analysis of Ceramics," 9–10.

71. Kelly and Neitzel, *Chauga Site,* 59–60.

72. Bartram, *Travels,* 297.

73. Dickens, "Pisgah Culture," 217.

74. Setzler and Jennings, "Peachtree Mound," 18.

75. Lewis and Kneberg, *Hiwassee*, 33.

76. Henry Timberlake, *The Memoirs of Lieut. Henry Timberlake . . .* , ed. Samuel Cole Williams (Marietta, Ga.: Continental, 1948), 59.

77. Bartram, *Travels*, 232-33.

78. Kelly and de Baillou, "Excavations," 16-21.

79. Caldwell, "Cherokee Pottery," 277-80.

80. Sears, "Creek and Cherokee Culture," 143-49.

81. Caldwell, "Survey and Excavations," 54-55.

82. Caldwell, "Cherokee Pottery," 277-80.

83. Lewis and Kneberg, *Hiwassee*, 105-6.

84. Duane H. King, "The Study of Eighteenth Century Cherokee Ceramics," paper presented at Southeastern Archaeological Conference, Macon, Ga., 1971.

85. Egloff, "Analysis of Ceramics," 73-74.

86. *Ibid.*, 38-43.

87. G.G., B.B., and E.P. Valentine, *Catalog of Objects*, 51-52; Harrington, "Cherokee and Earlier Remains," 195-204.

88. Kneberg, "Engraved Shell Gorgets," 39.

89. Dickens, "Settlement Pattern Changes in the Middle Cherokee Area, A.D. 1300-1838," paper presented at Am. Soc. for Ethnohistory, Athens, Ga., 1971.

90. Fred O. Gearing, *Priests and Warriors: Social Structures for Cherokee Politics in the Eighteenth Century*, Am. Anthrop. Assoc., *Memoir 93* (Menasha, Wis., Am. Anthrop. Assoc.)

A Perilous Rule:
The Law of International Homicide

John Phillip Reid

Homicide was the exception of Cherokee law. No other event of which we know brought into action legal forces beyond the individuals involved. When a Cherokee was the manslayer and another Cherokee the victim, two Cherokee clans would confront one another to settle the matter by the customary rules of domestic law. If a member of the Long Hair clan should be killed by a Cherokee of another clan, the Long Hairs would be owed one life. If a Long Hair should kill a member of one of the other six clans, the Long Hairs would pay with a life.

Consider by way of illustration an average Cherokee, named Ditiyohi, living in the Valley Town of Nikwasi near what is today Franklin, North Carolina. He is a member of the Deer clan and is married to a woman of the Paint clan. If a homicide occurs in Nikwasi, Ditiyohi's role will be determined by the clan ties of the manslayer and the manslayer's victim. Should neither belong to the Deer clan, he will not be involved. This fact is true even if the manslayer is a member of the Paint clan. Ditiyohi may well be worried. After all, his wife, his children, and his wife's brothers are liable, along with every other Paint, but he himself has no role to play in the legal resolution of the affair.

If the victim was a member of Ditiyohi's own clan, the Deer, Ditiyohi may have a duty to participate. Should the victim have been close kin, he will have much to say. Like many other rules of law, it is a matter of degree. If the victim was his brother, or his sister's son, Ditiyohi may well be the one to decide on the direction of vengeance. If the manslayer is still in Nikwasi, his life will almost certainly be forfeited. Cherokee law does not demand an eye for an eye, and Ditiyohi will not seek satisfaction for his brother's life by killing the manslayer's brother, rather than the manslayer. Should the manslayer flee, however, Ditiyohi would select some other member of the manslayer's clan to kill. Undoubtedly, it would be the manslayer's brother or another of his close-clan kin. The knowledge that his brother will die in his place is the best guarantee that the manslayer will not flee, or if he does, that he will return, thus insuring a degree of certainty and uniformity to the law and curbing the discretion of the avenger of blood.

If the manslayer's clan is the Paint, Ditiyohi will find himself aligned against his wife, his children, and his wife's brothers. It is unlikely that he will select one of them to render the blood price, but he would be within his rights to do so.

Finally, there is the situation in which the manslayer is a Deer. Again Ditiyohi is involved, for, along with all the other Deers, he is liable. Still, his life is not in absolute jeopardy. If the manslayer is not his close-clan kin, he probably need not worry. He will be more concerned if the relationship is near, especially if the manslayer has fled. If the absent manslayer is his brother, there is little doubt that Ditiyohi will be a likely target. One rule is undisputed: neither he nor any other member of the Deer clan can either prevent the execution or seek retaliation. Vengeance is the right of the victim's clan—a privileged act which evens the score and cannot be revenged.[1] It was that doctrine—that interclan vengeance was privileged—that distinguished the Cherokees' domestic law of homicide from their international law of homicide. Intertribal killings were never privileged, for they did not set into motion the legal mechanics of vengeance. In most cases, whether intentional, a hunting accident, or what we would call self-defense, an international homicide led to war.

The adventures of the first British subjects to enter the Cherokee mountains, James Needham and Gabriel Arthur, illustrate the legal consequences of international homicides. It is a story of risk and peril—risk for the Europeans and peril for the southern Indians. Although it does not tell us all that we would like to know, still it tells us much about the dangers faced by American natives when unprotected British traders intruded into their homeland.

The first European traders to visit the Cherokee country came from Virginia. It has been suggested that Virginia traders were in the Nation as early as 1612,[2] but that date is wildly improbable. Credit for being the first Europeans to see the Tennessee Valley probably belongs to Needham and Arthur, and to Arthur for being the first to travel through Kentucky, but history does not often list them among North American explorers because they did not map unknown lands or report new discoveries. All accounts of their travels describe people and events, not scenery or locations. They went west searching for trade, and to contemporaries who recorded their adventures, whom they met was more important than what they saw.

James Needham was a freeholder who worked for Abraham Wood, the proprietor of Fort Henry (now Petersburg) on the Virginia frontier and a promoter of Indian trade. Arthur was probably Wood's indentured servant. During April 1673, the two men left Fort Henry and by July had arrived at an Indian village somewhere in eastern Tennessee.[3] After remaining there for several months, Needham started back toward Virginia accompanied by a few natives and by his guide, a member of the Occaneechi nation, known as Indian John. The fact that he left Arthur at the village implied the mission had been successful — that they had negotiated a trade — for it is unlikely Arthur would have remained had they failed. While on the path to Virginia, Indian John quarreled with Needham, shot him, stole his goods and pack-horses, and sent runners back to the village to have Arthur killed. When they learned what had happened, the men of the village tied Arthur to a stake and would have burned him had not their "king" intervened. He shot one Indian who defied him, persuaded the others to acquiesce, and Arthur's life was spared. Arthur remained at the village for about a year, during which time he accompanied his hosts on war parties against the Shawnees on the Ohio, the Spaniards in Florida, and a coastal tribe located near

35

Port Royal, South Carolina. Finally, the king took him back to Fort Henry, where having told his story, he disappeared from history.[4]

Arthur identified the Indians with whom he stayed as "Tomahitans," and most writers think they were Cherokees.[5] Because their location seems to have been on the Watauga and Nolichucky rivers,[6] and also because the Shawnees were their particular enemies, an argument could be made that the Tomahitans were either Overhill or Out Town Cherokees. There are doubts, however. One of the strongest doubts comes from the fact that the Tomahitans were trading in Florida and had about sixty Spanish flintlock muskets.[7] It is possible, but unlikely, that by that date the Upper Cherokees could have been so well armed. Since the Lower Towns lay much closer to Saint Augustine, whatever the Overhills obtained from the Spaniards we would expect the Lowers to have in greater abundance. Twenty years later, however, the Lower Cherokees would imply that they had no guns.[8]

The fact is that the Tomahitans could have been any one of a half-dozen southern nations.[9] Aside from their geographical location, the best evidence that we have—the law controlling the events that Arthur reported—cannot be used to establish a positive identity. Even though that law corresponds to everything we know of the Cherokees, it is not sufficient to prove that the Tomahitans were Cherokees; since most of the surrounding nations had comparable legal systems, the law would have fit other tribes as accurately as it did the Cherokees. Yet the similarities between Tomahitan and Cherokee law are so striking that, even if we cannot be certain that they were the same people, the events surrounding the killing of James Needham serve to illustrate the legal problems faced by the Cherokees when they first made contact with Europeans. At least seven lessons were taught.

First to be noticed is the fact that there were aliens in the Tomahitan village, complicating international relations and jeopardizing domestic tranquillity. Indian John, who guided the two Virginians to Tomahitan, was an Occaneechi: a nation of Siouan stock occupying an island in the Roanoke River near the present town of Clarksville, Virginia.[10] He was undoubtedly a visitor who came to trade, not a permanent resident, yet he could bring with him third parties for whose safety the Tomahitans were responsible under southern-Indian law. Another non-Tomahitan was the man who defied the "king" and was shot. Though apparently living in the village, he was a Waxhaw, a small Carolina tribe believed to have been closely related to the Catawba, another Siouan-speaking nation.[11]

A second lesson concerns the instability being introduced into southern-Indian life by European trade—a problem that had two aspects. One consideration is the attitude of Indian John, who, as an Occaneechi, belonged to a nation conducting a profitable business as middlemen in the trade between Virginia and the interior. The facts will never be known, but it has been suggested that, since the Occaneechi jealously guarded their monopoly, the quarrel between Needham and Indian John arose from Needham's plan to bring trade directly to the Tennessee area, bypassing the Occaneechi.[12] On the other hand, there is the surprising fact that the Tomahitans were dealing with the Spaniards. Recently a party of Tomahitans trading in Florida had been attacked.[13] As a result, Tomahitan was at war with Spain, which may explain why Needham's talk of a Virginia trade (with its promise of an alternative market where guns could be obtained) received a hearing from the Tomahitans, and why one of the raids in which Arthur took part was directed against Florida. Chances are that Spanish-affiliated Indians, not Spanish white men, had been responsible for the attack. The Tomahitans, however, held the Spaniards liable, for such was the prevailing law of the southern nations.

Indeed, there was no set of more precisely defined legal rules than that governing liability between nations, although, true enough, there were grey areas where troublesome questions found no answers. These were, however, grey areas for us, not for a southern Indian, presenting questions to trouble us, not the Tomahitan king or his southern-Indian compatriots. They knew as much as they needed to know. Presented with a factual situation involving an international homicide, not only would they have known their own duty and rights, but also they could have been sure how a Creek, a Catawba, a Chickasaw, or a Choctaw would act. Should a Tomahitan kill a Yamasee, for example, the Tomahitans could expect a Yamasee war. It was a matter of corporate liability, and all the Tomahitans were in danger, not merely the manslayer or his close-clan kin. If the Yamasees attacked, they were not limited to retaliation in kind — to one life in satisfaction of the one life lost. Since their vengeance was not privileged, they would have taken as many Tomahitan scalps as they could, coming back again and again until they tired of the war or became preoccupied elsewhere. The same rule was true if the Waxhaw who lived in Tomahitan killed a Yamasee. The Yamasee might also make war on the Tomahitans. Had the entire Waxhaw nation been adopted by the Tomahitans, both the Waxhaws and the Tomahitans would have been liable — a principle that explains the Tomahitan-Spanish conflict if, as suggested, Indians and not Spanish soldiers had attacked the Tomahitans. The mission Indians of Florida were so much under Spain's influence that, from the southern-Indian point of view, they were virtually adopted by Saint Augustine, and Spain was responsible for their actions. Had the Waxhaw been adopted as an individual and not as a member of his nation, and if he lived exclusively in Tomahitan, the Yamasees would probably make war only on the Tomahitans. If, on the other hand, he was merely a resident, the Yamasees might hold both nations liable, or might be pragmatic and declare war on the weaker, or the one they most detested. The operative principle was that intertribal homicide led to war, for vengeance was not privileged, and was seldom overlooked.[14]

Far more difficult is the case when a temporary visitor such as Indian John killed, not in the Tomahitan village itself, but out on the path. Most of our available information indicates that the victim's nation would retaliate only against the Occaneechi, not against the Tomahitans. That the rule was not absolute, however, is seen by the reaction of the Tomahitans who were present when Indian John shot Needham. They tried to stop him but were not quick enough; when they saw that Needham was dead, the Tomahitans "all fell a weepeing and cried what shall wee doe now you have killd ye English man we shall be cut of[f] by ye

English."[15] Obviously they thought the British would hold them accountable. It is too late for us to learn the legal theory they were applying. Of only one fact may we be confident: they were thinking of southern-Indian law, since they had not sufficient experience with the British to be misinterpreting English law.

It is, of course, possible that practical rather than legal considerations motivated the Tomahitan despair. They could have premised their liability on the mere facts that, because they had been present when the killing occurred, or because Needham had been visiting Tomahitan, the British would assume he had been killed by them. However, our interpretation of law may have had no meaning to a southern Indian. Categories become blurred when we seek definitions from foreign crimes, and what is clear to other nationalities may be hazy to us. The Tomahitans who wailed at Indian John expected that the British would hold them liable. That their legal premises were vague to others might not matter to them. If they could predict that the British would retaliate, then categories became blurred for them as well. While we may never be certain, it is difficult to doubt that they were predicating European behavior on southern-Indian law.

Another lesson revealed by Needham's death points up the precarious situations in which southern nations could find themselves because of acts of alien visitors or alien residents in their towns. No one punished Indian John because no one had the responsibility. If the Tomahitans were in fact Cherokees, their reasoning is easy to explain, for only a Cherokee clan-kin of the victim would have killed Indian John out of duty. Under the same rule, any Cherokee angry at Indian John could kill him with impunity. Just as there was no one to call Indian John to account, so there would have been no one to call his manslayer to account. A Cherokee could well have decided to kill Indian John, not for reasons of domestic law, but for reasons of international law. The idea would have been to cut off his head and carry it to Fort Henry or Jamestown in hope of appeasing the British. If some trader recognized it and the Cherokee story was believed, war would be avoided with Virginia, though war with the Occaneechi would be almost a certainty. Choosing between alternative wars posed a cruel dilemma

39

for individual Cherokees, usually calling for such protracted discussions among the headmen that any action became unlikely.

Another lesson from the Needham affair was the rule of passion when strangers were involved. Law went from one extreme to another. The calm, nonaggressive conduct and deliberate circumspection characterizing relations between Cherokees did not always carry over into their dealings with non-Cherokees. True, national habits and ingrained social values were not easily shed, but events fed upon events, and the collective passions of the Cherokees were more easily aroused when strangers were there to scorn. The Tomahitans who witnessed Needham's death may have been momentarily stunned by the suddenness of the act and anguished at the thought of British retaliation. But they were southern Indians: they could be moved by violence to commit violence, and the Occaneechi manslayer was enough of a student of psychology to move them. "Indian John drew out his knife stept acrosse ye corpes of Mr. Needham, ript open his body, drew out his hart, held it up in his hand and turned and looked to ye eastward, toward ye English plantations and said hee vallued not all ye English."[16] It may have been melodrama, yet it was effective. Indian John knew his men. When he urged them to rush home and kill Arthur, they were ready to do his bidding. Perhaps it is too strong to assert that they transferred their hostility from Indian John to Gabriel Arthur. If they were already at war with Virginia, they might as well kill whatever Virginian was near at hand.

The events that occurred at the Tomahitan village provide our lessons from domestic law:

Ye Tomahittans hasten home as fast as they can to tell ye newes. ye King or chife man not being att home, some of ye Tomahittans which were great lovers of ye Occheneechees went to put Arthur to a stake and laid heaps of combustible canes a bout him to burne him, but before ye fire was put too ye King came into ye towne with a gunn upon his shoulder and heareing of ye uprore, for some was with it and som a gainst it. ye King ran with great speed to ye place, and said who is that that is goeing to put fire to ye English man. a Weesock [Waxhaw] borne started up with a fire brand in his hand said that am I. Ye King forthwith cockt his gunn and shot ye wesock dead, and ran to Gabriell and with his knife cutt ye thongs that tide him and had him goe to his house and said lett me see who dares touch him.[17]

Rescues such as Arthur's, occurring frequently in the southern nations during the colonial era, were misunderstood by the British, at least from the perspective of the law involved. Their chief mistake was to call the headman a "king," giving him a European title and assuming that he occupied a kingly office with kingly powers. The king had prevented Arthur's execution; hence it followed he had authority over life and death. If the Tomahitans were, in fact, not Cherokees, we cannot say that this king was without such prerogatives. In some of the smaller southern nations individual warriors even could be restrained from torturing or killing their war prisoners, whom they owned as personal property. Such power was not the general rule, however, and considering the circumstances of Arthur's rescue, we may doubt if it was vested in the Tomahitan king. That he had to shoot the Waxhaw does not prove he was without power, for the Waxhaw, as a stranger, may have felt no compulsion to obey his commands. We should expect, however, that a headman with constitutional authority to prevent executions would not have had to take such drastic steps (which risked Waxhaw retaliation), as he could have called upon the Tomahitan warriors to restrain the Waxhaw. A Cherokee headman could not have done so, and all the facts in Arthur's case indicate that the Tomahitan king was acting in a similar vacuum and that the legal principles upon which he depended were the same as those a Cherokee headman would have followed in a similar situation.

An Overhill headman seeking to save Arthur from the pyre would not have acted differently than the Tomahitan king. His town was divided, passions ran high, and the two leadership techniques upon which he relied—persuasion and reason—were of diminished effectiveness, considering the circumstances of the moment. He could count upon his prestige to dampen some of the high spirits—many of those intent on burning Arthur would reflect on the consequences once a respected headman expressed opposition. Reluctance to disrupt village harmony could be expected to calm even heated passions. Then, too, the headman had a stroke of luck when it turned out that the hottest firebrand was a Waxhaw whom, we may assume, no clan had adopted. Had it been a Cherokee whom the headman had shot, his clan would have killed the headman in return. With the Waxhaw, or any other alien, rules were different. No Cherokee was legally concerned, and anyone who avenged his death by killing the headman would have had to answer to the headman's clan. Of course, when the headman shot the Waxhaw he risked provoking a Waxhaw war. It was the price of avoiding trouble with the British, and the cost depended on circumstances. If the Waxhaw was a renegade from his nation, the headman may have felt that the risk was small. We will never know whether the king reflected, but if he did, he probably concluded it was better to insult the Waxhaws than chance a war with Virginia.

The last bit of law to be extracted from the Needham affair relates to the headman's decision that Arthur, while living at Tomahitan, should accompany war parties. Considering the fact that one of the raids, which took the Tomahitans into British-held South Carolina, occurred only after Arthur was promised that no white people would be attacked, we can be reasonably certain that the headman gave reflection to the question of taking Arthur along. There seems little doubt that his reasons were legal. While in the company of the headman, Arthur was relatively (though not absolutely) safe. If the headman left the village and Arthur remained, anything could happen. Those who had wanted to burn him and still harbored animosity might again decide to tie him to the stake once the headman was out of town. The headman could leave instructions that Arthur not be harmed, but no one had to obey, and promises among southern Indians were easily forgotten. Thus it is reasonable, even logical, to surmise that the headman could have included Arthur in the war parties to protect him from harm.

A more subtle legal doctrine, and the one that the headman could have had in mind, was the rule that a man who went to war should be exonerated for his faults. A Cherokee manslayer, for example, who hoped to escape execution at the hands of his victim's close-clan kin would take to the warpath and, if he obtained a scalp, would offer it to them. It was a legal principle akin both to compensation and to forgiveness. The close-clan kin of the victim were not obliged to accept, but often did, especially when the homicide had not been intentional. On the other hand, should the manslayer be killed, the victim's clan was usually satisfied and did not seek vengeance against his brother or other close-clan kin.[18] Taking Arthur along may have been designed to foster similar attitudes: to persuade his enemies among the Tomahitan to think good thoughts and forget their frustrations.

After the Tomahitan king returned Arthur to Fort Henry, and he told of his rescue, the way was open to trade. There was no difficulty now identifying the nation visited. The Tomahitans disappeared, and the impressive trading caravans sent by William Byrd from Virginia to the Tennessee country went to the Cherokees.[19] After the Virginians would come the Carolinians, and all would change on the southern frontier. Before this happened, however, the international law of the nations would help to shape events.

There are lessons to be drawn from our evidence. First of all, historians and anthropologists should abandon the misconception that Europeans introduced the idea of corporate responsibility by treating a nation as a political entity for purposes of demanding satisfaction for homicide.[20] It was southern-Indian law that held the manslayer's nation collectively liable; British law tried to introduce the concept of personal guilt, but traditional ways were not easily changed.[21] The right of a private citizen to take vengeance for an international homicide meant that the question of war was left to individual Cherokees. When the right was seen as a duty, the nation was unable to control its fate.

A law indigenous to one culture may serve its society's needs until it must compete with a stronger law. An international law that entailed small risks when neighbors were Creeks, Catawbas, or Tuscaroras could spell disaster if enforced against Europeans with their superior weapons and disciplined organization.[22] When Cherokees were killed on the Virginia frontier in 1759 and their clan kin took vengeance against Carolinians whose only "guilt" (in British eyes) was that they belonged to the same nation as the Virginians, Cherokee headmen were helpless to avoid a conflict they knew could destroy their villages.[23] We cannot claim that a different law would have saved the Cherokees, but the international law they did have meant only peril and could lead only to war.

NOTES

1. John Phillip Reid, *A Law of Blood: The Primitive Law of the Cherokee Nation* (New York: New York Univ. Press, 1970), 73-112.

2. Williams, ed., *Early Travels,* 18.

3. *Ibid.,* 21-22; Paul M. Fink, "Early Explorers in the Great Smokies," East Tennessee Hist. Soc. *Publications* 5 (1933), 57; W. Neil Franklin, "Virginia and the Cherokee Indian Trade, 1673-1752," East Tenn. Hist. Soc. *Publications* 4 (1932), 4-5.

4. Clarence Walworth Alvord and Lee Bidgood, *The First Explorations of the Trans-Allegheny Region by the Virginians 1650-1674* (Cleveland: Clark, 1912), 84-85; Williams, *Early Travels,* 32-34. (Letter from Abraham Wood to ed., John Richards, Aug. 22, 1684.)

5. Charles M. Hudson, *The Catawba Nation* (Athens: Univ. of Georgia Press, 1970), 33 n.4; Harriette Simpson Arnow, *Seedtime on the Cumberland* (New York: Macmillan, 1960), 114 n.17; Donald Davidson, *The Tennessee: The Old River; Frontier to Secession,* Rivers of America Series, vol. 1 (New York: Rinehart, 1946), 65; Wilma Dykeman, *The French Broad,* Rivers of America Series (New York: Rinehart, 1955), 29; Williams, ed., *Early Travels,* 22; Mary U. Rothrock, "Carolina Traders among the Overhill Cherokees, 1690-1760," East Tenn. Hist. Soc. *Publications* 1 (1929), 4-5; Alvord and Bidgood, *First Explorations,* 81-92.

6. It has also been contended that Needham and Arthur reached the Little Tennessee River. A.J. Morrison, "The Virginia Indian Trade to 1673," *William & Mary Quarterly* 1, 2d ser. (1921), 235.

7. Rothrock, "Carolina Traders," 4-5; Alvord and Bidgood, *First Explorations,* 83.

8. John Phillip Reid, *A Better Kind of Hatchet: Law, Trade, and Diplomacy in the Cherokee Nation During the Early Years of European Contact* (Philadelphia: Pennsylvania State Univ. Press, 1975), 28-29.

9. Another guess, for example, is that they were Yuchi; Thomas M.N. Lewis and Madeline Kneberg, *Tribes That Slumber: Indians of the Tennessee Region* (Knoxville: Univ. of Tennessee Press, 1958), 140-42.

10. Frederick Webb Hodge, "Handbook of the American Indians North of Mexico," 59 Cong., 1 sess. 1910, *House Doc. 926* II, 103.

11. Hudson, *Catawba Nation,* 1-2, 7, 15, 26-27.

12. Rothrock, "Carolina Traders," 5; Alvord and Bidgood, *First Explora-*

tions, 33; John R. Swanton, "The Indians of the Southeastern United States," in Bureau of American Ethnology, *Bulletin 137* (Washington, D.C.: GPO, 1946), 164.

13. Alvord and Bidgood, *First Explorations,* 83.
14. Reid, *Law of Blood,* 153-61.
15. Williams, ed., *Early Travels,* 32-33.
16. *Ibid.,* 33.
17. *Ibid.*
18. Reid, *Law of Blood,* 98-100.
19. W. Stitt Robinson, "Virginia and the Cherokee-Indian Policy from Spotswood to Dinwiddie," in *The Old Dominion: Essays for Thomas Perkins Abernathy,* ed. Darrett B. Rutmand (1964), 26; Franklin, "Virginia," 4-19; Williams, ed., *Early Travels,* 30 n.26, 94; "Letters of William Byrd, First," *Virginia Magazine of History and Biography* 28, (1920), 23 n.6.
20. Gearing, *Priests and Warriors,* 85.
21. Reid, *Law of Blood,* 80-82.
22. *Ibid.,* 181-84.
23. *Ibid.,* 66.

Distribution of Eighteenth-Century Cherokee Settlements

Betty Anderson Smith

During the eighteenth century, Cherokee towns were visited by many outsiders who left descriptions of what they considered to be of interest and significance. A number tried their skills at cartography, with varying degrees of reliability. Although political significance of the more important eighteenth-century towns has been the focus of ethnohistorians, very little attention has been given the precise locations and spatial distribution of these towns. This paper is the summary analysis of twenty-two eighteenth-century maps and documents giving names and descriptions of Cherokee towns. A comprehensive table correlating the names of towns found in the various maps and documents was prepared. Because this original compilation covers twenty-one pages, only a portion of it is presented here in tables 1 through 4. The discussion of Cherokee towns which follows is, however, based upon the original table and data.

In addition to the table correlating town names, several maps were prepared to show the spatial distribution of Cherokee towns in the eighteenth century. Three of these maps, showing Cherokee settlements during selected periods in the eighteenth century, are presented here with some explanatory notes on changes in number or location of towns through time.

Before proceeding with the discussion of eighteenth-century Cherokee settlements, however, it is necessary to outline a few of the problems encountered in dealing with the early maps and documents. Variations in the spelling of town names make correlation among the sources difficult. Occasionally, a town is listed twice in one source. Bartram, for example, lists Big Island and

Nialque as two separate towns, but Harper indicates, probably correctly, that the two names represent the same place.[1] Some towns may be listed in the wrong group.[2] For example, Beamer in 1756 listed six Middle Towns as Lower Towns. This was an obvious error and easily corrected, but other similar errors more difficult to identify may exist. A fourth problem is the occasional difficulty in determining the authenticity of a particular map. Some maps are merely copies of earlier ones and may not, therefore, reflect changes in the number and/or location of settlements that may have taken place after the original was made. Errors can also occur during the reproduction of a map. Swanton, in his "Early History of the Creek Indians and Their Neighbors," reproduced a portion of the Mitchell map.[3] His reproduction, however, omits at least one Cherokee town and the symbols indicating the different kinds of towns that were shown on the original map, thus distorting the data.[4] In the discussion which follows, the reader is asked to refer frequently to maps 2 through 4 and tables 1 through 4 in order to visualize better the changes described.

Maps 2 through 4 represent an effort to plot the distribution of as many Cherokee towns as possible during three selected periods in the eighteenth century. The twenty-two sources used yielded a list of over one hundred and sixty town names. The location of some of these towns could not be determined. In most cases, however, those towns which could not be placed are those which appear only once in the sources and so may represent semipermanent hamlets that someone happened to list as towns. This seems indicated by a report in the *South Carolina Gazette* of June 28–July 5, 1760, that "the Cherokees allow no settlements to be called towns, except where they have a house [townhouse] for their own public consultations."[5] Those names that appear consistently in the sources, therefore, may be towns with townhouses; semipermanent hamlets were probably smaller villages occupied for a while, then abandoned as natural resources were depleted.

Map 2, spanning the period from 1721 to 1730, is based primarily upon the 1721 census of Cherokee population, the Barnwell map of 1722, and the Hunter map of 1730 (these and all the other sources used are listed in the Appendix). Fifty-nine town

47

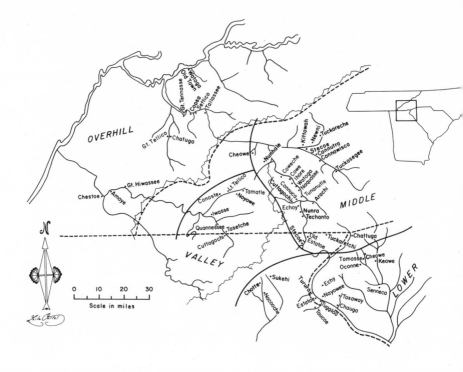

Map 2. CHEROKEE SETTLEMENTS, *c.* 1721–30

names are shown on map 2. Note that most of the settlements
were in the Lower and Middle territories. This may only reflect,
however, the British mapmakers' greater familiarity with these regions than with the others at this time.

Map 3 represents the period from 1755 to 1762. Several of the
Lower Towns shown on the previous map were abandoned during
this period. One reason for this was that Cherokee and Creek Indians were engaged in open hostilities during the 1750s. In 1750,
the Creeks destroyed Echy and Estatoe. In 1752, Keowee, Echy,
Tugalo, Oconne, and Tomassee were destroyed, with "some of
their harrowed people joining Toxaway and Estatoe, others moving to the Middle Settlements or the Overhills."[6] The Cherokees

48

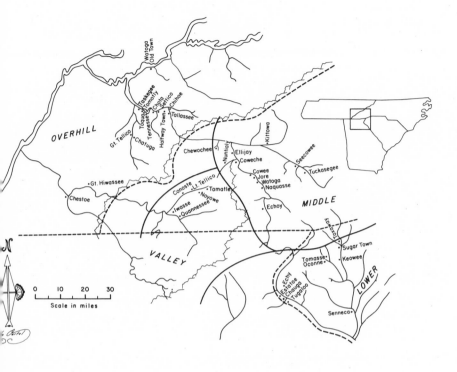

Map 3. CHEROKEE SETTLEMENTS, *c.* 1755–62

were at war with the British in the early 1760s. In 1760, all the Lower Towns were reportedly burned by Colonel Montgomery, and fifteen Middle Towns were destroyed by Colonel Grant in 1761.[7]

Even though several of the towns mentioned above were rebuilt, map 3 shows a decrease in the number of Lower and Middle Towns and an increase in the number of Overhill settlements. Forty-four names are included on this map, reflecting a reduction in the overall number of settlements; this trend continued, as will be seen on map 4.

Map 4, representing the years 1775 and 1776, depicts only thirty-one towns. Most were destroyed by the Americans during

49

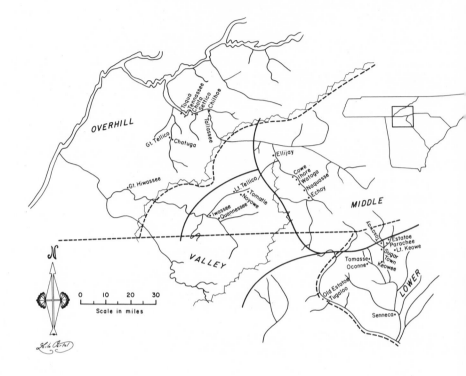

Map 4. CHEROKEE SETTLEMENTS, *c.* 1775-76

the American Revolution. The Cherokees were, by this time, moving farther down the Tennessee River to the vicinity of present-day Chattanooga, Tennessee, and northern Georgia. These later settlements are not included in this study.

Of the Lower Towns (see table 1), Keowe, Toxaway, Estatoe, Tomassee, and Tugalo appear most frequently between 1721 and 1781. Bartram, speaking of Keowe in 1775, wrote that "there are several Indian mounts or tumuli, and terraces, monuments of the ancients, at the old site of Keowe, near the Fort Prince George, but no Indian Habitations at present; and here are several dwellings inhabited by white people concerned in the Indian trade."[8]

Table 1. CHEROKEE LOWER TOWNS, 1721–81

Town Names	Census–1721	Herbert–1725	Hunter–1730	Hunter–1751	Mitchell–1755	Stuart-Purcell–1775	Romans–1776	Brown-Purcell–1781
Keowe	x		x	x	x	x	x	x
Toxaway	x		x	x	x	x	x	x
Estatoe	x	x	x	x	x	x	x	x
Tomassee	x		x	x		x	x	x
Tugaloo	x	x	x	x	x	x	x	x
Echie	x		x	x	x		x	
Oconne	x		x	x	x	x		x
Nougouche		x	x		x			
Lt. Chota		x	x		x			
Old Estatoy	x		x					
Cheewokee	x		x	x				
Seneca	x		x				x	x
Turrurah	x	x					x	
Tecoee			x	x			x	
Chauga	x	x	x	x	x			
Sukahe		x	x					
Noyouwee		x	x					
Tasse		x						
Catasue		x						
Sugar Town						x		x
Qulatch						x		x
Old Estatoe							x	
Parachee							x	
Lt. Keowe						x		x
Ustaly						x		

However, Bartram does include a town called Keowe in his list of Cherokee towns "inhabited at this time."[9] Keowe is listed as one of the towns destroyed by Williamson's force in 1776. From this it may be inferred either that Keowe's location had been moved from the area of Fort Prince George or that the Keowe listed by

51

Bartram and destroyed in 1776 was Little Keowe. Both Keowe and Little Keowe appear on the Brown-Purcell map (1781). Whether this map included not only inhabited towns but also known locations of former towns is not clear, but the latter seems more likely.

The town name Estatoe presents an even more complicated problem. The 1721 census lists an Old Estatoy and Estatoy. The Herbert (1725) and Mitchell (1755) maps show Estatoe on the Tugalo River. The Kitchin map (1760) has Estatoe in approximately the same place and Old Estatoe farther north. The Mante map (1756) shows Old Estatoe on the Tugalo River, Estatorie Old Field on the Keowe River south of Keowe, Estatoe on the Keowe River northeast of Toxaway, and Old Estatoe on the Keowe River north of the Estatoe just mentioned. The Woolley map (1776) places Old Estatoe on the Tugalo River and Estatoe on the upper Keowe River. The Romans map (1776) shows Old Estatoe on the Tugalo River and Estatoe on the Keowe River. About the only thing that can be deduced from this is that there were at least two, and perhaps as many as four, separate Estatoes among the Lower Towns.

On some lists Toxaway and Sugar Town are indicated as being identical, but this is not the case. Toxaway appears on the lists from 1721 to 1781. Sugar Town, on the other hand, does not show up on any map or list until 1756. Toxaway appears on the Hunter (1730) and Kitchin (1760) maps on a branch of the Tugalo River. On the Mitchell map (1755) and all subsequent ones, it is on the Keowe River above Keowe. The Hunter map was based both upon the Herbert map (1725), which does not show Toxaway at all, and upon Hunter's own observation; consequently it must depict a different town from that shown on the Mitchell map.[10] The Kitchin map was, however, based upon the Mitchell map and should, therefore, locate Toxaway where Mitchell does.[11] Sugar Town, also known as Connasetchi, was near Toxaway on the Keowe River.

Chauga presents a different kind of problem. It appears consistently between 1721 and 1755. It is not listed after 1755 until the Woolley map of 1776, on which the name appears in approximately the same location as previously. Why is there a twenty-year gap here? Does Woolley merely indicate an old town name, or had a new town been built and given the old name? The archaeological work done at Chauga sheds little light on the problem. Kelly and Neitzel conclude that it was probably destroyed in 1761 when several other Lower Towns were destroyed.[12] They apparently were not aware of the existence of the Woolley map since they do not refer to it.

Seneca was described by Bartram as a new town built after 1760.[13] However, the name appears on the 1721 census and Hunter map (1730), as well as on the Kitchin map (1760), Drayton list (1775), and the Woolley (1776), Romans (1760), and Brown-Purcell (1781) maps. Bartram indicates that Seneca was north of the confluence of the Tugalo and Keowe rivers and about sixteen miles below Fort Prince George.[14] The Kitchin, Woolley, and Romans maps show it in the same general vicinity. Map 2 presented here, using the Hunter map, locates Seneca farther north than it appears on maps 3 and 4. However, after looking again at the Hunter map, it appears that an argument can be made for placing Seneca in 1730 in the *same* place as it appears after 1760. Since this conflicts with Bartram's statement, there seems to be no ready solution to this dilemma other than to state that there may have been two successive Senecas, since there is a gap of thirty years during which the name does not appear anywhere.

Of the Middle Towns (see table 2), Echoe, Naquasse, Cowe, Ellijay, Sticoe, and Kittowah appear most frequently between 1721 and 1781. The Cherokees sometimes referred to themselves as *ani-Kituhwagi* ("people of Kituhwa"), a fact which prompted Mooney to conclude that Kittowah was "apparently the original nucleus of the tribe."[15] Watoga and Jore do not appear before 1730 but are listed consistently from then to 1781.

Several towns with similar names are found in the Middle settlements. These are Tuckaretchi, Tuckorechee, Tuckilegee, Tuckaseegee, and Taskeegee. Tuckaretchi and Tuckorechee appear as two separate towns on the Kitchin map (1760); however, the latter appears nowhere else. Tuckaretchi and Tuckilegee could be the same if the *r-l* is merely a dialectal difference. How-

Table 2. CHEROKEE MIDDLE TOWNS, 1721–81

Town Names	Census-1721	Herbert-1725	Hunter-1730	Hunter-1751	Mitchell-1755	Stuart-Purcell-1775	Romans-1776	Brown-Purcell-1781
Echoe	x	x	x	x		x	x	x
Naquassee	x	x	x	x	x	x	x	x
Cowe		x	x	x	x	x		x
Ellijay	x	x		x	x	x	x	x
Tuckaretchi		x	x	x		x		x
Sticoe	x	x	x	x	x	x	x	x
Kittowah	x	x	x	x	x	x		x
Nunay		x	x		x		x	
Coweche		x	x	x	x	x		x
Tuckaseegee	x		x		x			
Stickoes	x		x				x	
Econorocti		x		x			x	
Tumatly		x						
Cheowhee	x	x	x		x		x	
Erachy	x	x	x					
Tuckoe	x	x						
Chattoogie	x		x					
Cunasege		x						
Taskeegee	x							
Watoga			x	x	x	x	x	x
Jore			x	x	x	x		x
Tarsarla			x					
Tuckoreche			x					
Cuttagochi			x					
Cunnaer			x					
Tunanutte			x					
Cunnawishee			x					
Newni			x					
Iorsee				x				
Ounenuste				x				
Oustanarle				x				
Tawsee						x		x
Burning Town						x		x
Kenoche					x			
Tuckilegee							x	
Quannessee							x	
Ussanah						x		x
Tessantih						x		x
Neowee							x	
Techanto			x					
Connutra			x					

Table 3. CHEROKEE VALLEY TOWNS, 1721–81

Town Names	Census–1721	Herbert–1725	Hunter–1730	Hunter–1751	Mitchell–1755	Stuart-Purcell–1775	Romans–1776	Brown-Purcell–1781
Lt. Hiwassee	x	x	x	x	x		x	
Lt. Tellico	x			x	x	x	x	x
Tomotly	x	x	x	x	x	x	x	x
Cunnookak	x							
Turrurah						x		x
Quannessee	x	x	x		x		x	
Taskaye		x					x	
Castoe		x					x	
Cuttacatchi		x	x		x			
Tasatche	x	x	x		x			
Suquache		x						
Lt. Tunnissee	x							
Econorocti							x	
Nuntially				x				
Cotocanahut								x
Noyowee				x	x	x		x
Cheeowie				x		x		x
Conoste			x	x	x			x
Natally						x		x
Esthenore						x		x
Nacutche							x	
Nehowie								x
Tasetche			x					

ever, presumably the "-chi", "-gee" endings indicate different sounds and hence different words. Tuckalegee and Tuckaseegee might be the same name with an *s-l* difference. Taskeegee seems to be totally different.

Of the Valley Towns (see table 3), Little Hiwassee, Little Tellico, Tomotly, and Noyowee appear most frequently between 1721 and 1781. Little more can be said of the Valley Towns except that a division seems to show up on table 3: the first several

Table 4. CHEROKEE OVERHILL TOWNS, 1721–81

Town Names	Census–1721	Herbert–1725	Hunter–1730	Hunter–1751	Mitchell–1755	Stuart-Purcell–1775	Romans–1776	Brown-Purcell–1781
Chilhoe	x					x	x	
Settico	x	x	x		x	x		x
Chota*		x		x	x	x	x	x
Tennassee	x	x	x	x	x	x		
Tomotly		x				x		x
Gr. Tellico	x		x	x	x	x	x	x
Chatuga				x	x	x	x	x
Tallassee	x	x	x	x	x	x	x	x
Gr. Hiwassee	x	x	x		x		x	x
Watoga Old Town	x	x			x			
Amoye		x					x	
Chestoe Old Town		x			x		x	
Tarrawatee	x							
Toqua				x	x		x	x
Taskeegee	x	x						
Soo Sen			x					
Clokastowin				x				
Tellico				x				
Big Island							x	

*Charna, on the Herbert map, is here equated with Chota.

towns listed appear almost invariably throughout the period, but the towns on the last half of the list appear only after 1730.

Of the Overhill Towns (see table 4), Chilhoe, Settico, Chota, Tennassee, Great Tellico, Tallassee, and Great Hiwassee appear most frequently between 1721 and 1781. Great Tellico and Chatuga are usually listed together because the two towns existed side by side. They were considered by the Cherokees to be two separate towns because each had a townhouse. Colonel George Chicken, a British agent who visited several Cherokee towns in 1725, described Great Terriquo [Tellico] thusly: "This Town is very Compact and thick settled which they are obliged to, otherwise they would be Cut off by the Enemy who are continually within a Mile of the Town lurking about the Skirts thereof and very often Cut of their People and make their Escape. Here are two town Houses by reason they are the people of Two towns settled together which are both Enforted."[16]

Toqua does not appear on the lists until 1751, but it does show up consistently after that date. Watoga Old Town appears on the 1721 census and the Herbert (1725), Popple (1733), Bowen (1747), and Mitchell (1755) maps. It does not appear after 1755. Since all of these maps were based upon the Barnwell map (1722), the existence of Watoga Old Town after the 1720s may be open to question.

Towns were a very important part of Cherokee culture. Smaller villages and hamlets were located within easy reach of the towns, for it was there that the people congregated for their most important ceremonies and council meetings. Many of these towns were destroyed several times, only to be rebuilt. The total number of towns seems to have decreased, but some names appear consistently throughout the period from 1721 to 1781. It seems likely that most of the towns that appear so consistently were those with townhouses and hence the most important settlements. This lends credence to the hypothesis that some of the more than one hundred and sixty names recorded were, indeed, hamlets and not towns in the sense described by the *South Carolina Gazette*.[17]

ACKNOWLEDGMENTS

I should like to thank Mr. Marshall Williams for generously loaning me materials pertaining to the Lower Towns in his possession and Professor Louis DeVorsey, Department of Geography, University of Georgia, for his thoughtful comments and suggestions.[18]

APPENDIX

Description of the Sources Used in the Compilation of the List of Eighteenth-Century Cherokee Towns

1721 Census of Cherokee population. Society for the Propagation of the Gospel in Foreign Parts, ser. B, vol. 4, pt. 2, item 173. Microfilm copy in De Renne Collection, Univ. of Georgia Library.

1725 Herbert map. Herbert-Hunter, "A New Map of his Majesty's Flourishing Province of South Carolina showing ye Settlements of y' English, French and Indian Nation." De Renne Collection, Univ. of Georgia Library. Listed by William P. Cumming, *Early Maps*, 213, as Herbert-Hunter, 1744. Derived from Barnwell, *c.* 1722.

1730 Hunter map. Based on Herbert's map and Hunter's observations. Cumming, *Early Maps*, 196.

1733 Popple map. "A Map of the British Empire in America with the French and Spanish Settlements adjacent thereto," in John R. Swanton, "Early History of the Creek Indians and Their Neighbors," in Bureau of American Ethnology, *Bulletin 73* (Washington, D.C.: GPO, 1922), Plate IV.

1747 Bowen map. "A New and Accurate Map of the Province of North and South Carolina, Georgia." A copy of the Carolina portion of Popple, 1733, with a separate title. De Renne Collection, Univ. of Georgia Library.

1751 Scheme for regulating trade. William L. McDowell, Jr., *Colonial Records of South Carolina: Documents Relating to Indian Affairs May 21, 1750–Aug. 7, 1754* (Columbia: South Carolina Dept. of Archives, 1958), ser. 1.

1755 Mitchell map. "A Map of the British and French Dominions in North America . . . ." De Renne Collection, Univ. of Georgia Library. Based on Barnwell, *c.* 1722. Also in Cumming, *Early Maps*, 224.

1756 Beamer trader's report. McDowell, *Records of South Carolina* (Columbia: Univ. of South Carolina Press, 1970), ser. 2, 3–28.

1757 Bogges list. McDowell, *Records of South Carolina*, ser. 2, 3–28.

1760 Kitchin map. "A New Map of the Cherokee Nation with the Names of the Towns and Rivers . . . ." De Renne Collection, Univ. of Georgia Library. Based on Mitchell, "Map of the British and French Dominions." Also in Cumming, *Early Maps*, 231.

1760 Colonel Montgomery's expedition. *South Carolina Gazette*, June 28–July 5, 1760. Courtesy of Mr. Marshall Williams.

1761 Journal of Christopher French, 1761. Microfilm courtesy of Mr. Marshall Williams.

1762 Timberlake map. "A Draught of the Cherokee Country, on the West Side of the Twenty Four Mountains, commonly called Over the Hills . . . ," *Lieut. Henry Timberlake's Memoirs 1756–1765*, ed. S.C. Williams (Johnson City, Tenn.: Watauga Press, 1927), 14–15. Listed in Cumming as Timberlake, 1765.

1764 Stuart list. "List of Cherokee Towns," unpublished manuscript. Courtesy of Professor Louis DeVorsey.

1773 Stuart-Purcell map. "A Map of the Southern Indian District of North America." De Renne Collection, Univ. of Georgia Library. Indian towns shown on this map are similar to those shown on the Stuart map, *c.* 1761. Also in Cumming, *Early Maps,* 251.

1775 Bartram List. *Travels of Bartram,* 271–92.

1775 Drayton list. John Drayton, *Memoirs of the American Revolution* (Charleston: A.E. Miller, 1821), 99–103.

1776 Woolley map. "Cherokee Country Prior to 1776." De Renne Collection, Univ. of Georgia Library.

1776 Romans map. "A General Map of the Southern British Colonies in America . . . 1776." De Renne Collection, Univ. of Georgia Library.

1781 Brown-Purcell, "A New Map of the Southern District of North America . . . compiled in 1781 . . . ." De Renne Collection, Univ. of Georgia Library.

NOTES

1. William Bartram, *The Travels of William Bartram, Naturalist's Edition,* ed. Francis Harper (New Haven: Yale Univ. Press, 1958), 574–75.

2. The British divided the Cherokee towns into four groups: Lower, Middle, Valley, and Overhill.

3. John R. Swanton, "Early History of the Creek Indians and Their Neighbors," in Bureau of American Ethnology, *Bulletin 73* (Washington, D.C.: GPO, 1922).

4. Symbols on the Mitchell map of 1755 distinguished towns, enforted villages, and deserted villages.

5. *Gazette,* courtesy of Mr. Marshall Williams.

6. David H. Corkran, *The Cherokee Frontier: Conflict and Survival, 1740–62* (Norman: Univ. of Oklahoma Press, 1962), 23, 35–36.

7. Chapman J. Milling, *Red Carolinians* (Chapel Hill: Univ. of North Carolina Press, 1940), 302–6.

8. Bartram, *Travels,* 210.

9. *Ibid.,* 235.

10. William P. Cumming, *The Southeast in Early Maps* (Chapel Hill: Univ. of North Carolina Press, 1962), 196.

11. *Ibid.,* 231.

12. A.R. Kelly and R.S. Neitzel, *The Chauga Site in Oconee County, South Carolina*, Univ. of Georgia Laboratory of Archaeology series, no. 3 (Athens, 1961), 5.

13. Bartram, *Travels*, 209.

14. *Ibid.*

15. Mooney, "Myths," 15.

16. Newton D. Mereness, *Travels in the American Colonies* (New York: Macmillan, 1916), 111–12.

17. *Gazette*, June 28–July 5, 1760, courtesy of Mr. Marshall Williams.

18. John Stuart, "List of Cherokee Towns" (1764), unpublished MS courtesy of Professor Louis DeVorsey.

The Cherokee Frontiers, the French Revolution, and William Augustus Bowles

William C. Sturtevant

In the archives of the Quai d'Orsay, Paris, is a curious document, unsigned, and only later dated simply "1792." Headed "Notes given to M. de Montmorin in 1791," it begins as follows:

> In April, 1791 I had the honor to write from London a letter to M. de Montmorin, by which I announced to him that I had discovered that the six Cheerokoës who had then been in London for a year, and whom the English government was passing off as Indian chiefs from the neighborhood of the bay of Nootka Sound, were not Indians at all, but on the contrary that three of these gentlemen were English and the other three Spaniards, and that they all spoke French and English, that these men were intended to take part, as chiefs, in the projected operations against Santo Domingo and that they would soon leave. . . . During the month of June following I wrote from London to M. de Montmorin that the six Cheerokoës had left and that the conspiracy against Santo Domingo no doubt would not be delayed in execution, and that I would not delay in returning to Paris to give him the most circumstantial details on the affairs of that colony.[1]

The rest of the document concerns other details of the supposed British complicity in a conspiracy against Santo Domingo, without again mentioning this strange group.

I have not tried to identify the French agent in London. He may have felt it necessary to summarize for the Paris authorities the messages he had sent the previous year because his correspondent had fallen from favor: Armand-Marc, comte de Montmorin-Saint-Hérem, minister of foreign affairs from 1787 and minister of the interior from January 1791, was expelled from the Club des Jacobins as an aristocrat in June 1791, arrested on August 21, 1792, condemned by the Revolutionary Tribunal, and executed on September 2.

There are several puzzles in this brief document. Who were the masqueraders? Why the confused connection between Cherokees and Nootka Sound, on Vancouver Island at the opposite corner of the continent? What was the conspiracy against Santo Domingo? Why would anyone suppose that Cherokee chiefs would be useful in Haiti? The answers to these questions illustrate the role, or the potential role, of the Cherokees in international colonial power politics.

In the years between the American and the French revolutions, Santo Domingo—Haiti—was an extremely productive colony, very valuable to France and of interest to England, especially after the loss of the Thirteen Colonies. It was a stratified society, ruled by European bureaucrats, with some 24,000 whites of two classes, the *grands blancs* (the planters) and *petits blancs* (the middle and lower class), about 20,000 *gens de couleur* (mulattoes and free blacks), and 408,000 black slaves. When the Estates-General convened in Paris in May 1789, *grand blanc* delegates joined the National Assembly. But the antislavery *Amis des Noirs* forced the reduction of their representation because mulattoes were excluded, while the Declaration of the Rights of Man and Citizen, adopted on August 26, 1789, implied rights for *gens de couleur*. The National Assembly, however, failed to seat the Haitian mulatto delegates, causing one of them, Vincent Ogé, to leave Paris for London, where the abolitionists provided him with money and letters of credit to purchase arms and ammunition in the United States. He went to Charleston, and then to Haiti, landing near Cap François on October 21, 1790.

From September 1789, when news of the fall of the Bastille had arrived in Haiti, until June 1790, the *grands* and *petits blancs* had stood together against the royal bureaucracy. In April and May a general assembly of the colony developed a constitution giving power to the *petits blancs*; in June the *grands blancs* in the north joined the bureaucrats, and royal authority was restored.

Soon after arriving, Ogé raised a force of about seven hundred mulattoes. His revolt failed; he was captured and hanged on March 9, 1791; some two hundred of his followers were soon executed. Two French regiments arrived in that month, sent to support the bureaucracy — but they mutinied and went over to the *petit blanc* National Guard. Ogé's death led the French National Assembly to pass the Decree of May 1791, giving full citizenship to propertied mulattoes. In Haiti the whites were outraged at this — a letter in the London *Times* on August 31, 1791, reported that they talked of killing mulattoes, seceding from France, and calling in the English. A letter in the *State Gazette of South Carolina,* August 8, 1791, reported that, when troops landed to enforce the Decree of May, the whites at Cap François sent to England and Jamaica requesting British protection.

On August 22, 1791, the slaves revolted. The Colonial Assembly then appealed for assistance from the British in Jamaica, the Spaniards, and the Americans. Arms, ammunition, and black soldiers were sent from Jamaica to assist the *grands blancs.* The Assembly even offered the colony to the British, who refused because acceptance would have meant war with France. But British interference in the complex, many-sided conflict remained a strong possibility. In December 1792, a British West Indian expert suggested to the prime minister, William Pitt the Younger, that "the deplorable situation of the French West Indies seems loudly to crave the protection of Great Britain." When war did break out between England and France in September 1793, the British landed in Haiti a force of nine hundred men from Jamaica. After initial successes they were thrown back when Toussaint L'Ouverture changed sides on learning of the French Republic's abolition of slavery.

Thus it is clear that the French had cause in 1791 and 1792 for concern about British interest in Haiti, and for suspecting that British interests in North America might well be involved also.[2]

The idea that the Cherokees in London were from the neighborhood of Nootka Sound can only be an effect of the Nootka Sound crisis, which had come to an end about six months before our French informer's first letter. This conflict between Spain and England had its origins in the discovery of Nootka Sound and its rich resources in sea-otter furs and commercially oriented Indians. The first European sighting of Nootka Sound was by a Spanish expedition in 1774, which traded with the Indians but did not go ashore. The next visitor was Captain James Cook, who did land there in 1778. From his experiences developed the sea-otter trade by British and a few American ships. Finally, in May 1789, a Spanish force was sent from Mexico to occupy Nootka Sound and protect Spanish claims against anticipated Russian encroachment from the north. The energetic Spanish commander Esteban José Martínez arrested four British ships at Nootka between May and July and imprisoned their crews for what was, from the Spanish point of view, illegal intrusion into Spanish territory.

News of this affair first reached London in January 1790. The early accounts were fragmentary, garbled, and immediately exaggerated. William Pitt seized the opportunity to build a confrontation with Spain, where the weak and inexperienced Carlos IV had just acceded to the throne. Because the French Revolution, in its early stages, was seen to jeopardize traditional French-Spanish cooperation, Pitt construed the clash at Nootka as an insult to the English flag and pressed not only for compensation but also for Spanish recognition of a new principle: prior discovery alone did not yield sovereignty, but colonization and effective control were necessary also. The confrontation had a clear economic basis in the fur trade and in freedom to trade with Spanish settlements in America. Spain and Great Britain both mobilized their navies as the crisis developed. Propagandists in London mentioned the 1783 Spanish repossession of Florida (by the Treaty of Paris) among English grievances, and secret orders were sent to the governor-general of Canada, Lord Dorchester, regarding plans against Spanish Louisiana and Florida.

In early May 1790 Spain applied to Louis XVI for support under the terms of the Bourbon Family Compact. This precipitated a famous debate in the revolutionary National Assembly which ended in August 1790 with the voting down of the Family Compact.

Word of the Nootka crisis first reached the United States in late June; it was the first foreign policy crisis faced by the new American government. American desire for freedom of navigation on the Mississippi was involved, as were the activities of Spain in building alliances with the southern Indians against the expanding American frontier. Seeing a risk to his support from Spain, the Creek leader Alexander McGillivray was led to conclude the Treaty of New York, signed on August 7, 1790, by which the Creek Nation ceded land to the United States and moved away from its commitments to the Spanish in Florida and New Orleans. The British were kept informed of American policies and activities through Alexander Hamilton's secret negotiations in New York with an agent reporting to Lord Dorchester.

The loss of firm French support — a result of the Revolution — weakened Spanish resistance. Finally Spain backed down and the crisis was ended, short of war, by the signing of the Nootka Convention on October 28, 1790. Spain gave up her claims to exclusive dominion over Nootka Sound and the rest of the Northwest Coast and conceded British rights to trade there and wherever else Spanish settlements had not existed before April 1789. The wording was ambiguous, but the British interpreted it as applying to the whole coast north of San Francisco, thus opening the way for eventual Anglo-American settlement of the Oregon country. As Warren Cook, the author of a fine recent history of these matters, has remarked, "The Nootka crisis signals the beginning of the end of the Spanish Empire in America."[3]

Who were the six Cherokee chiefs, or the Englishmen and Spaniards masquerading as Cherokees, in London in 1790 and 1791? The number, description, and dates fit only a group led by William Augustus Bowles, whose presence in London was widely reported in the contemporary press. Bowles himself was indeed no Indian, but a Tory American, an early "Indian hobbyist" who was perhaps the most colorful adventurer and imposter of the southern frontier. His companions were, however, Indians, and it is clear from several contemporary references that three of them were Cherokee and two Creek. Bowles himself wrote out their names at the head of a letter to the king, in the order given below.[4]

65

His spelling was rough, but not unusually so for the period, and some of the names can be positively identified, others tentatively.

1. Unatoy. Elsewhere this is spelled "Uniotowy".[5] This is the most obscure of the names. By elimination it is probably Cherokee. Duane King notes the vague resemblance to the Cherokee word *inata* ("snake") and points out that a man well known in the early nineteenth century (but probably not one of Bowles' men) bore the name *inatana?i* ("Going-snake").[6] Bowles' handwriting is clear; if it were not, or if we could suppose he were copying the name as written by someone else, then there is a possible resemblance to the name of Moytoy, the "emperor" of Tellico in 1730. Mooney says the same name appears as "Moyatoy" in an unidentified 1792 document and that in his own day an Eastern Cherokee boy bore the unanalyzable name *matayi*.[7]

2. Kuahtekiske. This seems clearly to be Cherokee, ending in *-tikiski* ("eater"), as in the Western Cherokee surname k^hwan *tikiski* ("Peacheater").[8]

3. Seponejah. This is probably Creek. The final part resembles *-ha·čô·* ("crazy, furious in war"), a common Creek ending for adult men's names (an hypothesis strengthened by the spellings -hojah, -ijah in Creek Council 1789), and the first part contains "p," representing a sound common in Creek but absent in Cherokee. Either this individual or the next must have been "Tom Lewis, a half Breed boy," whom Alexander McGillivray interviewed on his return, remarking that Bowles had "Seduced [him] away" from the Lower Creek country.[9]

4. Tuskeniah. This is plainly the Creek man's name *taski hinihâ·*, often abbreviated to *taskinihâ·*. The name appears in Swanton's lists,[10] and was borne by a Creek emissary to Tecumseh in 1811; this was the eldest son of *tastanâki łákko* ("Big Warrior"), of Tukabahchee, then the speaker for the Upper Creeks.[11]

5. Wosseo. This clearly represents *wohsi*, a borrowing of the English "Moses" that is still a current Cherokee name.[12] That he was Moses Price is certain: in 1792 "Moses Price, a sensible half-breed, who can read and write, and who was in England with Bowles" was at the Cherokee town at Lookout Mountain;[13] a Welsh crackpot in London spoke with "Mr. Price, one of the com-

panions of Mr. Bowles, who was born among the Creeks . . .
[who] declared that his father . . . was a Welshman . . . [who]
had lived the greatest part of his life and died in the Creek Country."[14] Moses Price was living in 1788-89 at the Cherokee Crow
Town.[15] He was the son of Captain Thomas Price, who served as
an interpreter of Cherokee in the 1770s.[16] In 1799 Moses was living at Coyotee Old Town at the mouth of the Little Tennessee
River. In an encounter with two Moravian missionaries at Tellico
Blockhouse, he refused to serve as their interpreter, claiming
"that for that purpose, another interpreter would be needed, as
he understood nothing of such matters and could talk with the Indians only of every day matters."[17]

We know what three of the delegation looked like: "they are all
. . . handsome men, not exceeding in age twenty-five or twenty-
six years,"[18] and three portraits have survived, executed by well-
known artists at the high point of English portraiture. Bowles was
painted by Thomas Hardy; a mezzotint reproduction often published bears the caption "William Augustus Bowles, Chief of the
Embassy from the Creeke & Cherokee Nations. Published as the
Act directs, March 26 1791 by T. Hardy";[19] the original in oils
(fig. 12) survives at Upton House, Warwickshire. At the Royal
College of Surgeons of England, in London, there are two unsigned paintings for which the only documentation is in manuscript catalogs compiled by the first conservator of the collection.
He wrote in 1816 and 1820 that they were painted by William
Hodges for John Hunter (who died in 1793), and that the subjects
were Cherokees whose names were not remembered who were
supposed to have fought on the British side in the American Revolution and were in London about 1790-91 where they were often
seen at Sir Joseph Banks' parties.[20] One of them (fig. 13) looks as
though he may have been part white. A duplicate of this painting
in the Yale Art Gallery was received as a portrait by Benjamin
West of the Mohawk leader Joseph Brant, but it does not resemble other portraits of Brant and the documentation is not good.
The other man portrayed, younger, appears to be entirely Indian
(fig. 14). Unfortunately, neither can be positively identified, even
as to tribe. While we know that Moses Price was half white and

67

Figure 12. William Augustus Bowles, painted in London in 1791 by Thomas Hardy. His complexion is Caucasoid, his eyes blue or grey. His turban is of white cloth below and red cloth (striped in yellow, black, and white) above, with a large set gem or bit of glass, a white aigrette, and pheasant (?) and red-dyed ostrich (?) feather plumes. Around his neck is a belt of white and purple wampum and a silver gorget. He has a ruffled white shirt, a silver arm-band, and on his right hip a red pouch on a narrow red strap that runs over his left shoulder (courtesy The National Trust, London).

Figure 13. A member of Bowles' party, painted by William Hodges (oil, 75 x 62 cm). The ear lobes are cut, stretched, and wrapped with two silver plates. The cutout ear ornaments and the gorget are silver. He wears a white ruffled shirt with black neckcloth, and a dark-blue robe edged with blue and a red stripe. His complexion is Indian, although his features seem to indicate some White ancestry (courtesy Royal College of Surgeons of England).

Figure 14. A member of Bowles' party, painted by William Hodges (oil, 75 x 62 cm). The downy white feather is touched with red towards the base. His ear ornaments, gorget, and arm-band are silver. He wears a white ruffled shirt with a black neckcloth, and a dark blue robe edged with red and a yellow stripe. Both his complexion and his features are very Indian (courtesy Royal College of Surgeons of England).

probably older than Tom Lewis, we do not know that none of the other three were part white. The clothing and ornaments are not tribally distinctive. In any event, the French informer was mistaken in claiming that none of the six was Indian. Another painting brought back to the Cherokee country has disappeared. Showing Bowles flanked by two "Cherokee chiefs," it was labeled "General Bowles, commander-in-chief of the Creek and Cherokee nations," and was seen in February 1792 at Lookout Mountain in the house of the Cherokee Richard Justice, along with "a number of dining cards, (copper plate) addressed to Bowles while in England, styling him 'commander-in-chief of the Creek nation.'"[21]

The delegation, an invention of Bowles, cannot be understood apart from his biography and his personality.[22] He was born in 1763 in Frederick, on the Maryland frontier, the son of Thomas Bowles, an immigrant from London, and his wife Eleanor. At the outbreak of the Revolution the family were Tories, and William went to Philadelphia in the fall of 1777 to enlist as a common soldier in one of Gen. William Howe's infantry regiments. He soon shifted to the new regiment of Maryland Loyalists, which included nine ensigns (the lowest rank of officer) of whom Bowles was one, at age fourteen. Soon the regiment was shipped to Jamaica and thence to Pensacola, where it arrived at the end of December 1778. By April 1779 Bowles' name was dropped from the rolls without a court-martial because, according to Bowles, he had insulted a superior officer. He said that he then joined a party of Lower Creeks who had come to Pensacola for presents. "I took the Indian dress, soon habituated myself to their manners, and became at length, from custom, and from choice attached to the Nation."[23] The "Creek chief" who took him in may have been Tom Perryman, from the lower Chattahoochee River, with whom he was later closely associated. Nevertheless, he soon returned to Pensacola, where he lived for a time with a baker; but finding it difficult to support himself, he went back to the Lower Creeks. He seems to have stayed for less than a year. Wright has invented a Cherokee wife and son for Bowles at this time, in order to account for the name of The Bowl or Colonel Bowles, a leader of

71

the Western Cherokees killed by Texans in 1839.[24] Mooney, however, says The Bowl's English name was a translation of his Cherokee name, *tiwahli*, and it is very likely that he is the same person as The Bowl who was born about 1756, became a town chief in 1792, and led Chickamauga Cherokees in a fight at Muscle Shoals in 1794—if so, he could not have been fathered by William Augustus Bowles.[25]

In 1780 Bowles returned to Pensacola, accompanying Creek warriors coming to aid the British defense against Spanish attack. He claimed that this time he "served as an Indian";[26] it was then that Alexander McGillivray first met him.[27] He seems to have participated in the failed British attack on Spanish Mobile. Perhaps as a result of this service, he was given back his ensign's commission as Pensacola was about to fall to the Spaniards in May 1781. Bowles and the other troops were paroled by the Spanish, going first to Havana, then to New York, where they arrived in July. In September 1783, before the British evacuated New York, Bowles claimed, he obtained a leave of absence and "returned to the country of the creeks."[28] He elided, however, for it is clear from other sources that in 1783 he went with other Loyalist refugees to the Bahamas, where he was put on half-pay.

His activities for the next four or five years are obscure. He may have visited his father in Frederick; much later reports put him in St. Mary's, Savannah, and Augusta, Georgia, painting portraits and perhaps spying for the Creeks.[29] Also during this period he probably began his association with John Miller, a Loyalist merchant in Nassau, and with John Murray, earl of Dunmore, the governor of the Bahamas. Both men were commercial and political rivals of the Bahamian firm of Panton, Leslie and Company, to which the Spanish had granted a monopoly for trade with the Creeks through Pensacola and their store in St. Marks—a firm in which McGillivray also had an interest. It is tempting to speculate that it was during these years that Bowles allied himself with Tom Perryman's daughter Mary, by whom he had a son, Little Billy,[30] and perhaps a daughter—for a daughter of Perryman's was at one time the "concubine of Colonel [Thomas] Brown in Providence," in the Bahamas.[31]

In any event, the first sure report of Bowles' return to the Creek country seems to place it in April 1788,[32] in June, and again in August. McGillivray reported his arrival as a "Stranger," a "Strange man," a former Loyalist officer who brought a supply of arms and ammunition which McGillivray accepted, as his supplies through Panton, Leslie and Company were then inadequate.[33] McGillivray's initial evaluation of him as "a Gentleman" did not last long. By August Bowles was back in Nassau to get more supplies that he had promised the Creeks and to recruit a party of thirty men for an attack on Panton, Leslie's store at St. Marks. When they landed on the Indian River in November 1788, the Indians were disappointed that he brought so little, and twenty-six of his men soon deserted to the Spanish. Bowles returned briefly to Nassau, but in December he was again on the Florida coast[34] and in January 1789 he was at Perryman's village on the Chattahoochee, claiming to await the arrival of a shipment from Nassau that evidently never came. McGillivray lost patience with him, writing to Leslie on February 8, 1789, that "it seems to me that his backers have chosen an instrument not at all appropriate for such undertakings. He could pass, eating and drinking like the other sons of his mother, but he does not seem to be suited to great things."[35]

We know from McGillivray that in May 1789 there was a meeting of the Lower Creeks that included many Cherokee chiefs, presumably mainly Chickamauga Cherokees.[36] But we have only Bowles' word that he was present, and only from copies he provided do we have the two documents, addressed to George III and supposedly signed then, that validated his expedition to London. The first of these is headed "The Memorial of the Kings and Cheifs [sic] of the Cherrokee Nation given at the great Convention of the Creek Nation on the Banks of the Chattahooche River near the Cowetah Town this 6th day of May 1789." It complains that Americans are encroaching onto Cherokee territory and reports that at a meeting at Chilhowie called by the "Virginians" in June 1788 they had killed five old Cherokee chiefs—after first sending medals, two of which are sent to the king via Bowles. Alluding to the previous Cherokee alliance with Great Britain, they ask that British soldiers be landed in Carolina and Georgia and promise Cherokee assistance for such an invasion. They also complain that the price of trade goods has risen and ask that someone be sent to reduce prices and ensure fair measures. This rings true, as does the prose style.[37] One sentence, however, sounds rather like Bowles' handiwork: "The Warrior whom we beg to deliver this to your hand is one of your Warriors who has been among us and knows what we speak is truth, as he has seen our situation himself." At the end are transcribed thirteen names, most of them recognizable and some belonging to Cherokee leaders of the period: "Kaanittuh or Little Turkey" (*khv·n anita* ["Little Turkey"]); "Usqualkuttah or Hanging Maw" (*uskwo·l kata·* ["his stomach hangs out; Hanging Maw"]); "Chenkunnasnah or Dragging Canoe" (*tsiyu ka·nsi·ni* ["canoe—he is dragging it; Dragging Canoe"]);[38] "Richard Justice" (reported by Craig 1792 as the Cherokee conjuror at Lookout Mountain[39]); "Ishettechi"; "Unenegatee" (perhaps *unine·katihi* ["White men killer"]); "Aguttahee" (perhaps *aka·taʔi* ["he is hanging"]); "Nehenoataah" (perhaps Nenetooyah Bloody Fellow, who by 1791 had changed his name to "Iskagua" ["Clear Sky"]);[40] "Skaantee" (*askayatihi* ["man-killer"]); "Catakish" (*kataki·ski* ["the picker"]); "Tekakolohan"; "Cheesquatelone" (*tsiskwa talonikeʔi* ["bird, yellow"]); "Chuleon" (*tsuliʔe·ni* ["deaf in both ears"]).[41]

The other petition to the king is headed "The Address of the Cheifs [*sic*] of the Creek Nation" and concludes "Done in Council this 7th day of May at the Cussatees in the Lower Creeks." This document complains that Americans are taking Creek land and property and killing Creek hunters, and requests arms and ammunition needed for defense against anticipated Georgian aggression. Surprisingly, the firm of Panton, Leslie and Company is not mentioned. An appeal is made to the previous Creek alliance and friendship with the British, and a medal is sent to be exchanged for a new one. Bowles' sentence is included: "Father we have sent two Warriors with our beloved Warrior who is one of yours, he came back to us after your people left our Land and he has lived with us ever since, he has seen our distress and knows what we say to be the truth." The ten names appended are worse-spelled than the Cherokee ones (perhaps Moses Price helped with the latter), and the four personal names that head the list are not easily recognizable: "Kalishiniah" (-*hinihâ·* is a standard Creek final name element), "Cowappah," "Cohogijah," and "Fullalhojah." Each of these is identified as "Tustunuka" (i.e., *tastanâki* ["warrior"]) of a Creek town, respectively "Cowetah" (*kawíta*), "Claae cotsca" (*łi·ká·čka* ["Broken Arrow"]), "Cussatee" (*kasíhta,* or perhaps *kowassá·ti* ["Koasati"]), and "Usache" (*o·sočí*). Six final titles are labeled "Signed on behalf of the Nation"; these are merely the town names "Cussetatee" (*kasíhta* or *kowassá·ti*[?]), "Cowetah" (*kawíta*), "Oaknnulga" (*okmolkí*), "Usache" (*o·sočí*), "Ufallaugh" (*yofá·la* ["Eufaula"]), and "Ichetee" (*hičíti*), with the ending "Micko" (*mí·kko* ["chief"]) added to each.[42]

With these two petitions as credentials — genuine or forged or a combination of the two — Bowles set off for London, having "address enough to prevail on two three half Breeds of the cherokees & a Couple of Young fellows from the Creeks to accompany him," as his enemy William Panton later wrote.[43] They went first to Nassau, arriving on July 28, 1789.[44] According to Panton, Bowles was there thrown into jail for debt, but was released by the governor, Lord Dunmore.[45] While in Nassau Bowles wrote to the Conde de Floridablanca, the Spanish minister of state, asking Spanish protection for the Creeks and Cherokees, urging a Choctaw-Chickasaw-Creek-Cherokee alliance, and requesting that the Creek trade monopoly given to Panton, Leslie and Company be lifted and Florida ports opened to hitherto nonexistent Creek ships. The answer was to be sent to him in London via the Spanish ambassador.[46]

Wright says that Bowles and his party went to Florida to await there a ship promised by Nassau merchant Miller. When that did not arrive, they got a small vessel and sailed south, heading for Jamaica. However, in the Keys they found a wreck; as they began salvaging it, its captain arrived. A deal was made by which he would carry them to Halifax, Nova Scotia, in exchange for the salvage. They were overtaken by a ship finally sent by Miller to take them to Canada, and transferred to that.[47]

75

Panton's version is different:

> [Bowles and his party] escaped over to the Florida Point [the Miami region], where it is said the Indians had resolved to kill him, and would have done it for the deception he had practiced on them, if accident had not preserved him by throwing a Spanish vessel ashore near where he and his Indians were encamped. The crew of the vessel & passengers having left the wreck Bowles and his people took possession of Her wherin they found a Considerable booty, and among other things some suits of very Rich Gold laced Clothes with which he equiped his party and having hired a fishing Boat that happened to be there catching Turtle he proceeded to Nova Scotia where he introduced his Indians & himself to Govr. Parr as Men of the first rank & Consequence of the Creek & Cherokee Nations. And So artfully did he Conduct himself, that the Governor listened to his Storry and believed it. From Nova Scotia he was Sent on to Lord Dorchester, the Governor Genl. of Canada, [in Quebec].[48]

Some weight is lent to this second version by an exchange between Bowles and Lord Dorchester; the latter remonstrates with him for having drawn a bill, while in Halifax, on Sir John Johnson of the Indian Department; Bowles explains that he did so on Governor Parr's advice in order to pay off the captain, who put them ashore at Halifax when his ship ran out of wood and water. At any event, the party arrived in Quebec at the beginning of July 1790.

Bowles now had the double problem of explaining his presence to the skeptical Governor-General and persuading him to foot the bill for the remainder of the trip to London. Bowles wrote to Lord Dorchester that when he arrived in the Bahamas in July 1789, he "received intelligence of preparation making [by the Americans], intending to attack the British Posts at Niagara"; therefore he decided to go via Canada in order to get instructions from Lord Dorchester. Since he also alluded to "the present prospect & appearance of an approaching war with Spain," he had obviously heard of the Nootka Sound crisis — news which he could not have known when he left Nassau. Lord Dorchester replied that if, in fact, there had been an attack on Niagara, Bowles would have arrived too late, or if not too late, his presence would have been of no help; in any case he had conveyed the news outside proper channels, which would have gotten it to Lord Dorchester "with fidelity and dispatch." To this Bowles responded that if an attack had occurred, he would have sent a message to the Creeks and Cherokees to attack the American frontiers. Lord Dorchester advised Bowles that he should have gone directly to England, which would have been quicker and cheaper than going to Halifax. By now he was cautiously replying in the third person, rather than by formal letters, evidently because Bowles had asked for a written explanation of the Governor-General's oral refusal to send him to England. He offered to forward to the king any message Bowles might have, and to see that any reply reached Bowles. Besides, "in London it would be thought very extraordinary, that Six Young men should be sent to carry a letter, that they should wander about so long, and so far out of the way." Bowles responded that his commission from the Creeks and Cherokees required him to present their messages to the king directly, before returning home. He went on to explain that it would cost the government about the same — £60 — to send his party home as to England and that additional expenses for their stay in Canada amounted to £40. (This sum no doubt included rent of the private lodgings Bowles had taken in Quebec, rejecting the government quarters offered by Lord Dorchester, to the latter's annoyance.) Lord Dorchester sent a brief reply authorizing the £100, but carefully not specifying that he was underwriting their trip to London. At the same time, he forwarded a bundle of his correspondence with Bowles to W.W. Grenville, secretary of state for the Home Department; it arrived in London on September 3, nearly two months before Bowles appeared there. The covering letter explained that he did not want to alienate the party any further, "as in case of a war with Spain they might be of considerable use, as their confederacy is very numerous, in both the Floridas." He also mentioned McGillivray, "the leading man among the Creeks," who was suspected of involvement with Panton, Leslie and Company, against whose monopoly Bowles had complained.[49] Clearly, the Nootka crisis affected his decision, as did recent word of the impending Treaty of New York to be signed by

77

McGillivray. It is certainly the latter threat, and the publicity McGillivray received as a result of it, that caused Bowles to emphasize in the next few months his Cherokee connections, rather than the more valid Creek relationships to which he limited himself in his subsequent career.

Bowles and his party took passage on the merchantman *Lord Dorchester,* which arrived at Spithead on October 28, 1790. Bowles immediately got in touch with the press. An early report describes the arrival of "six Cherokee chiefs of the first rank . . . dressed in the habits of their country, with their faces painted in an extraordinary manner. . . . One of them, who was born in England, named Bowles, speaks English tolerably well, and is extremely communicative. He went over to America with his parents, who were in the army, when a boy, and by some means strayed to an Indian camp, where he was most hospitably received, and afterwards raised to the highest honours of their nation."[50]

Bowles' plans began auspiciously: the same brief news item reports that the commander of a seventy-four-gun ship sent his barge to take the party to Portsmouth and that the Cherokees are in the country to make an alliance to support their attempt at the conquest of Mexico, "near which place they have 20,000 men in arms; and can raise 30,000 more in a short time," thus opening "a source of trade and wealth to this nation, that will more than compensate for the loss of America, and the expence of attaining that grand object." The next weekly issue of the same newspaper explains that "the Indian Chiefs lately arrived in town are six in number. They have been indiscriminately styled Cherokees, but three of them only are of that nation, and three of them Creek Indians." Immediately following in the same issue are three news items reporting the cancellation of preparations for war with Spain, for the Nootka Convention was signed in Madrid on the day Bowles arrived at Spithead.[51] Thus the wind was taken out of Bowles' sails, and the next week the *Sheffield Register* reports, in an item datelined London, November 12, that "the Cherokee Chiefs are not to be presented at Court. After seeing everything of notoriety in London and other parts of the kingdom, they will again return to America in the Spring."[52] By November 13 "the

Cherokee Chiefs" had twice conferred with Grenville, the secretary of state, but to little avail.[53]

Bowles and, presumably, his five companions, stayed at Osborne's Hotel at Adelphi in the Strand. During the following months they saw and were seen by a great part of London society. They were received by the Prince of Wales, the Duke of Gloucester, and Lord Townshend. Bowles attended Dr. George Pearson's Chymical Lectures and met some refugee Loyalists, including Captain Benjamin Baynton, who took notes for his brief biography of Bowles published in early 1791.[54] As we know, they had their portraits painted, and went to dinner more than once at the house of Sir Joseph Banks, president of the Royal Society and an old hand at such affairs since, years before, he had entertained and displayed Omai, the young Tahitian man who had returned with Captain Cook from his first voyage.

Bowles became involved in a current intellectual controversy over whether, and where, there were Welsh-speaking Indians in America.[55] William Owen-Pughe, an enthusiast for the theory that Prince Madoc had left Welsh-speaking descendants in America, interviewed Bowles and Moses Price and reported the results in the *Gentleman's Magazine*. Bowles told Owen that these were the "Padoucas," or "White Indians," a numerous and warlike nation well known to the Creeks, and that he had "travelled their Southern boundary, from one end to the other." Owen was especially impressed by the resemblance, as he heard it, between "Padoucas" and "Madawgwys" as he supposed the people of Madoc ["Madawg"] must call themselves. Bowles went on to say that he knew among the Creeks a Welshman who had escaped from the Spaniards in Mexico and walked across the continent, stopping among the Padoucas on his way. He had told Bowles that their language was Welsh and that they kept as religious objects books, wrapped in skins, that described their origins. Moses Price, playing along, told Owen that his father, a Welshman, had talked with the Padoucas in Welsh.[56] However, after Bowles had left England, the *Gentleman's Magazine* published a retort dated London, May 8, and signed merely "L." which demonstrates that at least one man in London knew Bowles better than Owen did:

It is not my intention to controvert what your correspondent, p. 329, advances respecting "the settlement of the Madawgwys" in America; but only to request to know what degree of credibility is due to the evidence advanced by Mr. Bowles, who, if I mistake not, came down to Pensacola, in West Florida, in 1777 or 1778, in the very humble station of an Indian packhorse-man, or trader, and always so much affected the manners and dress of his colleagues, that he never could be induced even to speak English, although it was supposed at the time that he was an Irishman, of very low birth and manners. There are merchants now in this city, who can, I believe, speak more particularly concerning him. I do not recollect that he was considered as a Chief, or a person of any intelligence, but, as I have mentioned above, occupying a menial station. — These hints are simply with a view to your correspondent's information, that he may not offer to the publick any other evidence than such as can be stamped with respectability and certainty.

An Indian Chief of the Creek nation frequently came down, and his name was the *Mad Dog* Indian. — Perhaps some ingenious commentator may discover an affinity between it and *Madawg*; for, barbarous as they may be supposed, and fond as the Chiefs are of titles, no one would imagine that any man would take up one that carries an idea so vile; and particularly the Chief I speak of, whose good-nature was remarkable.[57]

The final dig, while appropriate, reflects a poor translation: Mad Dog's Creek name was *ífaha· čô·* ("dog-crazy, furious in battle"). However, as the young Tom Lewis reported to McGillivray after he returned home, "in England where Bowles was not known, they were all treated with extraordinary Kindness; but when they arrived at the Bahamas where he has been known before, he Bowles was treated as a Vagabond, except by [the governor] Lord Dunmore, John Miller & one or two others his Lordships friends."[58]

Bowles' final attempt to get a hearing seems to have been a long letter written from Osborne's Hotel to the king on January 3, 1791, and sent through Lord Grenville, minister of state, with a follow-up letter to the latter alone sent ten days later. The letter to George III — who no doubt never saw it — is a masterpiece, skillfully combining some grains of truth with a great deal of imagination (or optimism) that Bowles hoped would appeal to English preconceptions and prejudices. He begins with allusions to the "old alliance" of the Creeks and Cherokees with the British and their desire to renew it "more, perhaps, from predelection [*sic*] & affection, than from the dictates of a sound & interested policy." The more powerful Creek Nation has, he says, united with the Cherokees under a single Council of some seventy-two chiefs— hereditary titles limited to noble families, "though there is no law against confering that honour on strangers, as they did on myself." This Council solemnly convenes for days and nights at a time, with "examples of acute deliberation, & considerable shew of oratory." The "United Nation of Creeks & Cherrokees" has formed an "offensive and defensive" alliance with the Choctaw and Chickasaw nations. The former can field "near Twenty thousand warriors" and nearly as many more can be raised among the Choctaws and Chickasaws. The old Indian military tactics have been abandoned; the hatchet has been given up in favor of the musket and "a long spear with which they form a phalanx, as forcible and effectual as the bayonet: They submit to regular engagement, & will stand in the field, like European troops of the best discipline." These troops are commanded by chiefs headed by a Council-appointed "Generalissimo" who serves also as president of the Council for a one-year term that is renewable— "this office I had the honour of holding, at the time I left the Nation." The United Nation has given up hunting for agriculture: "the woods [are] deserted, & towns built; & [they have decided] that the plantation & farmyard were the best resources for the supply of a family. . . . The Creeks & Cherrokees are now become a people, that live in a fixed society; have their town, & their country life; are mechanics & farmers; . . . they have stemmed the course of waste & decay; their population encreases; individuals have property, & the blessings of civil society multiply every day." Private property and wealth increase, and taxes on agricultural produce support the "public services." There is already an economic surplus, of which some is exported and more could be. Among possible exports are indigo, tobacco, drugs, dye woods, saltpeter, furs, hides, tallow, wax, ship timber, tar, turpentine, hemp, and flax. Seagoing vessels have been acquired from Europeans and built by the Indians.

Bowles then complains, justifiably, that the British have

handed over Creek and Cherokee country in the peace treaty with the United States and Spain "without any reserve, or mention of them, or their rights, at the conclusion of a war, in which they had involved themselves, as allies of your Majesty, and at the instance of your Majesty's Governors, & Commanders." Thus they have been abandoned to the mercy of their enemies, although previously they have been treated as independent allies rather than British subjects, and much of their territory was never claimed by the British. "But there is a way of defining the boundaries of sovereignty, by lines on paper, that supercedes all local distinctions, and every actual circumstance of nations, and of tribes; so that people are parcelled out by latitude, and longitude, and not by a due consideration of their situation, and pretensions."

Although the Spanish did not claim sovereignty over the Creeks, their attempts at commerce were "restrained & annoyed by their *guarda Costas* at sea." Creek relations with Georgia were, however, hostile. American enmity was aroused, the pro-British sentiments of the United Nation were demonstrated, by their admitting and protecting over one thousand families of Loyalist refugees, from whom the Indians expected to learn "their skill, their arts, & their manners."

The present delegation is sent to assure the king of their continued loyalty, and to ask for renewal of the old alliance. Bowles is commissioned to present to George III "a silver medal suspended to a belt of peace, according to the manner of the Indian nations," which the Creeks received from the British governor of East Florida at a treaty in 1764. If the king wishes to continue the alliance, they ask him to so signify by presenting a new medal and belt; if the delegation must return empty-handed, the Council of the United Nation "will then be at liberty to take measures for its own security and welfare." Also, Bowles has been asked to present two medals which the Americans put on the bodies of the Cherokee chiefs they killed in 1788, stripping them of the British medals they were then wearing.

Specifically, the Creek and Cherokee Nation asks permission to carry their trade to free ports in the British West Indies, an exception to the law limiting such access to the subjects of European states. Such trade, Bowles remarks, would result in the Creeks buying £200 to £300 worth of British manufactures each year; presently they must get such goods through Panton, Leslie and Company, whose monopoly allows them price markups of 200 to 300 percent, thereby holding down British exports to one-twentieth of the amount the Creeks actually could absorb. Bowles admits that the Creek and Cherokee Nation is "not yet sufficiently ripe" to develop its own merchant marine to carry this trade, but they are forced to do so by the terms of the Treaty of 1783, which made Florida a Spanish colony, and by the terms of the Nootka Convention, which precluded British trade within ten leagues of the limits of Spanish settlements.

Bowles adds some information concerning his own career and position, concluding, "Your Majesty sees one of your subjects, becoming the adviser, & the leader of an independent & populous Nation, presenting to your Majesty their devotion & services as allies, both in peace & war; and under circumstances highly advantageous to the commerce, and Interest of Great Britain."[59]

Bowles' letter to Lord Grenville, dated January 13, is more pointed and flamboyant. He reports that he has asked Spain to allow him two ports on the Florida coast. If this is refused, as soon as he returns he will attack the Spanish forts in Florida and in two months will drive Spain from the Floridas and Lower Louisiana, capturing them for "the Creek and Cherrokee Nation." He will then "march a strong force across the Mississippi towards Mexico." Having already "marched seven hundred miles in that country, for the purpose partly of exercising troops, that [he] had been training in a New Method," he found that he could have "proceeded to the centre of Mexico and . . . been received as a deliverer." Next time, therefore, he expects to reach Mexico City "and in conjunction with the Natives declare it independent of the Spaniards," or at least force Spain to cede the Floridas to the Creeks and Cherokees. "It was the opinion of Lord Clive, that by the Troops of the Country, only, India was to be conquered and retained. Experience has shewn he was right; and it may be worth consideration, if the Maxim is not as good in America as in Indostan." Bowles would expect at least 6,000 men to be provided by the Cumberland settlers, who have already asked him to lead them against the Spanish settlements. He elaborates on the story he has given Lord Dorchester, this time claiming that in April 1788 the Americans secretly proposed that he should lead his Indians in an attack "upon the Northern tribes, and the British Posts." His refusal, out of loyalty to the king, led to attempts on his life in August and September 1788. Now he suggests that an alliance between Great Britain and "the Nation of Creeks and Cherrokees" could gain the support of the Indians on the Canadian border — support which would be useful in any quarrel with the United States or Spain (a prefigurement, in another form, of Tecumseh's later scheme). Such a political and military alliance would require supplying Bowles with British arms and ammunition. Lacking British support, the Creeks, taking the northern Indians with them, might choose an alliance with the Americans and attack the British posts, jeopardizing Canada.

However, realizing perhaps the improbability of this grandiose plan, Bowles claims that the principal object of his embassy is to secure a "wholly Commercial" treaty involving the admission of ships of the Creek and Cherokee Nation to the British free ports, or at least to Nassau. If this can be assured, even privately without a treaty, he is willing to forgo the public exchange of medals with the king.[60]

Here was a compromise which could be agreed to, in order to get rid of the delegation, for it must have been obvious that no ships of the United Nation were likely to show up in Nassau. Lord Grenville reports this solution in a letter to Lord Dorchester dated March 7, 1791: "Such of their requests as related to views of hostility against the United States have met with no kind of encouragement, but they will in some degree be gratified in their wish of intercourse with the British Dominions by an admission to the free ports in His Majesty's West Indian Islands, supposing that they should find themselves in a situation to avail themselves of this indulgence."[61]

Bowles' time was running out. On March 15, he and his delegation dined with the Spanish ambassador[62] and on March 25 he again addressed a letter to the Conde de Floridablanca, repeating his previous request from Nassau for Spanish protection and freedom of trade.[63] On March 29 the "Cherokee Chiefs" had a farewell breakfast with the first clerk in Lord Grenville's office.[64] A couple of days later they boarded the *Mercury* and sailed for Nassau, where they arrived in early June.[65]

The French agent in London was a bit behind the times, for he first wrote to Paris concerning the matter in April, after Bowles had left and the danger—if, indeed, there were any—had long passed. By June he realized that they had gone, but he feared they were headed for Santo Domingo rather than Florida.

In the Bahamas, John Miller and Lord Dunmore once more outfitted Bowles. In August or early September he and his party arrived by schooner at the mouth of the Ochlockonee River in Apalachee Bay, near St. Marks, where Panton, Leslie and Company had a store. It was rumored, according to Lord Dorchester's secret agent in New York, that he had brought £50,000 worth of presents for the Indians,[66] and, according to Spanish sources, ammunition and arms including several three-pound bronze cannon. (Of this store, in fact, fourteen weapons, two rammers, and two muskets were later captured.)[67] A small Spanish force, with a pilot from Panton, Leslie and Company's store, was sent to capture him. Bowles' luck, however, held: the Spanish officer in charge reported that Bowles' wife, Molly Perryman, who had "lived as if married" during his absence with a factor at the store, upon learning of his arrival rejoined him and warned of the Spanish search in time for him to escape.[68]

Bowles returned to Perryman's town of Osochi on the Flint River.[69] Although McGillivray put a price on his head, his agitation did not diminish: Lord Dorchester's agent, George Beckwith, reported from Philadelphia on December 2, 1791, that Bowles had told the Creeks and Cherokees that the British had authorized him to reestablish the boundary with Georgia that existed before the 1790 Treaty of New York, "and, that he has solicited their having recourse to Arms to effect this, promising them an English reinforcement in the Spring, to which the Indians replied, that prior to their commencing hostilities they would await

85

the arrival of these succours."[70] Moses Price, back among his people in February 1792, was still enthusiastic (at least when talking to an American official): "He speaks of Bowles as a very great man; that he can actually procure for the Southern tribes, from England, men and arms to defend them against the United States; and that he can obtain a free port in East Florida to extend trade to them directly from England. He says, while he was in England, he was informed that England, by treaty of peace, did not cede the lands claimed by the Creeks and Cherokees, to the United States, and, consequently, the United States could have nothing to do with the government of them, or their trade."[71]

However, Bowles had already made a serious mistake. Having captured Panton, Leslie and Company's store at St. Marks in January, with a party of some one hundred Creeks, he rashly accepted an invitation to board a Spanish ship (actually sent to capture him) to pay a visit to the new governor in New Orleans.[72] Finding himself a prisoner there, rather than a diplomatic envoy, nevertheless he continues his spirited letter-writing. In one, to the Spanish governor, he presents still a third version of the offer he refused in 1788. This time he says that the Americans in Kentucky and Cumberland asked the Creek council for protection and proposed a joint attack on the Spanish settlements in Louisiana and Florida, "with an offer to support me with 10,000 Men." When Bowles rejected this, he says, in order to silence him "in the Month of March 1789 several attempts was made to cut me off."[73]

From New Orleans, Bowles was sent to Spain. Still objecting to his prisoner's status, he was shipped to Manila in 1795. After fifteen months the authorities there tired of him and put him aboard a ship bound back to Spain. Off the African coast Bowles was caught in a plot to take over the ship and was transferred to an escorting French frigate. At Gorée, near Dakar, the convoy was attacked by a British frigate. In the confusion Bowles dived out a porthole and was picked up by a nearby American merchantman, which put him ashore in Sierra Leone. He caught a British ship bound for Tobago, but when it was disabled by a storm Bowles transferred to a passing British warship headed for

London. Arriving there in August 1798, he costumed himself once again as a Creek, bestowed on himself the title "Director-General of the Muscogee Nation," and began his customary politicking.[74] It was apparently at this time that he adopted a Creek name, "Eastajoca." That cannot readily be interpreted as one of the usual Creek adult names. I am tempted to suggest an etymology: can it be that, searching his memory, Bowles recalled that Creeks had sometimes called him *ísti čó·ka* ("writings person")? That would certainly have been an appropriate nickname for the letter-writing, petition-collecting, precedent-citing foreigner.

In March 1799 Bowles obtained passage to Barbados on a warship. From Barbados he went to Jamaica, and thence to Nassau. As it arrived in Apalachee Bay, his ship ran aground and sank in a storm. Bowles, unharmed, went up the Apalachicola River in a canoe and returned to the Creek country in August 1799, some seven years since he had left it. About two months later he issued a proclamation expelling — with only eight days notice — all United States and Spanish agents from "the territories of Muskogee," concluding "God save the state of Muskogee" and signing as "Director General of Muskogee."[75] The next year Bowles captured the Spanish fort at St. Marks but soon lost it. In 1803 the Creeks, encouraged by the American agent Benjamin Hawkins, finally turned Bowles over to the Spanish in Mobile. He was sent to Havana, where he died a prisoner in El Morro on December 23, 1805.[76] The closest he had gotten to Haiti was on his way from Jamaica to Nassau in 1799.

NOTES

1. État des Notes données a M^r De Montmarin en 1791 Au mois d'Avril 1791 J'eus l'honneur d'écrir de Londres une lettre a M^r De Montmorin, par laquelle Je lui annoncui que J'avois decouvert que les six Cheerokoes qui alors étoient depuis un an a Londres, et que le gouvernement Anglais s'étoit et faisoit passer pour des Chefs de sauvages, voisins de la baye de Nootka sond, n'étoient point des sauvages, mais au contraire que trois de ces messieurs étoient anglais et les trois autres Espagnols, et qu'ils parloient tous français et Anglais, que ces Gens étoient destines a agir comme Chefs, dans les Opérations projetées contre st Domingue et qu'ils

devoient bientot partir. . . . Dans le Courant du mois de Juin suivant
J'écrivis de Londres a M^r De Montmorin que les six cheerokoés étoient
parti et que la Conspiration de st Domingue ne tarderoit sans doute pas a
être éxécutée, et que Je ne tarderois pas a me rendre a Paris pour lui
donner les détails les plus circonstanciés sur les affaires de cette Colonie.[1]

Archives des Affaires étrangères, Correspondence politique, Angleterre, 585
(1792) Supplement, f. 219^r.

2. The preceding section is based on C.L.R. James, *The Black Jacobins:
Toussaint Louverture and the San Domingo Revolution* (London: Secker and
Warburg, 1938), *passim;* Thomas O. Ott, *The Haitian Revolution, 1789–1804*
(Knoxville: Univ. of Tennessee Press, 1973).

3. The preceding section is based on Warren L. Cook, *Flood Tide of Empire:
Spain and the Pacific Northwest, 1543–1819* (New Haven and London: Yale
Univ. Press, 1973), 63–269.

4. William Augustus Bowles, "The Representation of Wm. Augustus Bowles
. . . To His Britannic Majesty," MS dated Osborns Hotel, London, 3 Jan. 1791,
in Public Record Office, London, F.O. L/9, S/J.9756, folios 5-17 (crown
copyright).

5. Anonymous. *General Bowles.* Pp. 118-54 in *Public Characters of 1801–
1802,* 2d ed. (London: J. Adlard, 1804), 137.

6. Duane H. King (personal communication, 1974).

7. James Mooney, "Myths," 526.

8. King (personal communication, 1974).

9. McGillivray to William Panton, dated Little Tallassie, 28 Oct. 1791, MS
copy in Archivo General de Indias, Seville, Papeles de Cuba, legajo 2362; printed
in John Walton Caughey, *McGillivray of the Creeks* (Norman: Univ. of Oklahoma Press, 1938), 298-300.

10. John R. Swanton, "Social Organization and Social Usages of the Indians
of the Creek Confederacy," in Bureau of American Ethnology, *42d Annual Report* (Washington, D.C.: GPO, 1928), 105-6.

11. R.S. Cotterill, *The Southern Indians: The Story of the Civilized Tribes
before Removal* (Norman: Univ. of Oklahoma Press, 1954), 166; John R. Swanton, "Social Organization," 328.

12. King (personal communication, 1974); Mooney, "Myths," 545.

13. David Craig, "The Report of David Craig to William Blount, Superintendent of Indian Affairs for the Southern District, made at Knoxville, March 15th
1792," in *U.S. Congress, American State Papers,* Class II, *Indian Affairs,* vol. 1.
(Washington, D.C.: Gales and Seaton, 1832), 264-65.

14. William Owen, "Discovery of the Madawgwys," *Gentleman's Magazine*
61 (1791), 329, 396-97. Owen here confused *Creek* with *Cherokee.*

15. J.G.M. Ramsey, *The Annals of Tennessee to the End of the Eighteenth
Century* . . . (Philadelphia: Lippincott, Grambo & Co., 1853), 514.

16. Williams, ed., *Early Travels,* 248, 465; Ramsey, *Annals,* 120, 172.

17. Williams, ed., *Early Travels,* 465; (Duane H. King pointed out the last
two sources.)

18. *Sheffield Register,* Nov. 12, 1790.

19. Cotterill, "Southern Indians," facing p. 230; J. Leitch Wright, Jr.,

William Augustus Bowles: Director General of the Creek Nation (Athens: Univ. of Georgia Press, 1967), frontispiece.

20. William LeFanu, *A catalogue of the Portraits and Other Paintings, Drawings, and Sculpture in the Royal College of Surgeons of England* (Edinburgh and London: E. & S. Livingstone Ltd., 1960), 82.

21. Craig, "Report."

22. Undocumented assertions in this section are based on the 1967 biography of Bowles by Wright, who has located a remarkable number of very widely scattered documents on Bowles' entire career and has usually been scrupulous in identifying the source of each part of his text. Unfortunately, however, what seems to an anthropologist a mistaken conception of Creek polity at the period and the narrowness of his focus on the historical literature have led Wright to accept uncritically too many of Bowles' own statements about his activities and his own importance among the Indians. Each source must be scrutinized, and all information that derives from Bowles' own word must be doubted unless corroboration can be found elsewhere. My own study of primary sources concerning the short period of Bowles' life examined here has shown many contradictions, exaggerations, and errors in Bowles' statements, confirming the necessity for reexamination of his career. Of course, given his precarious position and his ambitions, such self-serving distortions, when detected, are themselves evidence on the nature of this remarkable man and on the fluid frontier affairs in which he was engaged.

23. Bowles, Representation, f. 17[r].

24. Wright, *Bowles*, 13.

25. Mooney, "Myths," 100, 516; John R. Swanton, "The Bowl," p. 163 in "Handbook of American Indians North of Mexico," ed. Frederick Webb Hodge, Bureau of American Ethnology, *Bulletin 30* pt. 1 (Washington, D.C.: GPO, 1907), 163; Dorman H. Winfrey, "Chief Bowles of the Texas Cherokee," *Chronicles of Oklahoma* 32 (1954), 29–41.

26. Bowles, Representation, f. 17[r].

27. McGillivray to John Leslie, dated Little Tallassie, 20 Nov. 1788, manuscript Spanish translation in Library of Congress, East Florida Papers, 114J9; printed in English translation in Caughey, *McGillivray*, 205-8.

28. Bowles, Representation, f. 17[r].

29. Wright, *Bowles*, 23; Caughey, *McGillivray*, 203 n.158.

30. Wright, *Bowles*, 13.

31. Arturo O'Neill to Estevan Miró, 22 Dec. 1788, MS copy in Archivo General de Indias, Seville, Papeles de Cuba, legajo 38; printed in translation by Caughey, *McGillivray*, 211-12; for Brown, see Caughey, *McGillivray*, 203 n.156.

32. Caughey, *McGillivray*, 186 n.130.

33. *Ibid.*, 186, 192, 194-95.

34. *Ibid.*, 214.

35. *Ibid.*, 223.

36. McGillivray to Vicente y Folch Juan, dated Little Tallassie, 14 May 1789; MS in Archivo General de Indias, Seville, Papeles de Cuba, legajo 52; printed in Caughey, *McGillivray*, 230-32.

37. On the murders of Chilhowie, perpetrated by Tennesseans from the "State of Franklin," see Mooney, "Myths," 65; Cotterill, *Southern Indians*, 79.

38. These and the following interpretations of the Cherokee names are supplied by Duane King (personal communication, 1974).

39. Craig, "Report," I, 264-65.

40. Mooney, "Myths," 69-70, 522.

41. Cherokee Chiefs, "The Memorial of the Kings and Cheifs [sic] of the Cherokee Nation . . . [to George III]," MS copy in Public Record Office, London, C.O. 42/68, X/J. 9756, ff. 296-98 (crown copyright).

42. Creek Council, "The Address of the Cheifs [sic] of the Creek Nation [to George III]," MS copy in Public Record Office, London, C.O. 42/68, X/J.9756, ff. 292-94 (crown copyright).

43. William Panton to Estevan Miró, dated Pensacola, 8 Oct. 1791, MS in Archivo General de Indias, Seville, Papeles de Cuba, legajo 203; printed in Caughey, McGillivray, 295-97.

44. Bowles to Lord Dorchester, dated Quebec, July 7, 1790, manuscript copy, encl. no. 1, with Guy Carleton, First Lord Dorchester, to W.W. Grenville, dated Montreal, July 26, 1790, manuscript in Public Record Office, London, C.O. 42/68, X/J.9756, ff. 282-84.

45. Panton to Miró, in Caughey, McGillivray, 295-97.

46. Bowles, to the Spanish ambassador at London, dated Adelphi, 26 Jan. 1791, MS copy in Public Record Office, London, F.O. America I; printed in Frederick J. Turner, "English Policy Toward America," American Historical Review 7, no. 4, 706-35, 8 (1902), no. 1, 78-86; Jack D.L. Holmes and J. Leith Wright, Jr., trans. and eds., "Luis Bertucat and William Augustus Bowles: West Florida Adversaries in 1791," Florida Historical Quarterly 49 (1970), 49-62.

47. Wright, Bowles, 41-42.

48. Panton to Miró, in Caughey, McGillivray, 295-97.

49. Guy Carleton, first lord Dorchester, to W.W. Grenville, July 26, 1790 (nine enclosures). The enclosures are the Creek and Cherokee petitions to the king and the Bowles and Dorchester letters referred to in the last two paragraphs.

50. Sheffield Register, Nov. 5, 1790.

51. Ibid., Nov. 12, 1790.

52. Ibid., Nov. 19, 1790. The identical sentences appear in the London Daily Advertiser of Nov. 12.

53. London Daily Advertiser, Nov. 13, 1790.

54. Wright, Bowles, 51.

55. David Williams, "John Evans' Strange Journey," American Historical Review 54 (1949), 277-95, no. 3, 508-29; Robert R. Rea, "Madogwys Forever! The Present State of the Madoc Controversy," Alabama Historical Quarterly 30 (1968), no. 1, 6-17.

56. Owen, "Discovery of the Madawgwys," 396-97.

57. Gentleman's Magazine 61 (Sept. 1791), 800.

58. McGillivray, Panton, in Caughey, McGillivray, 298-300.

59. Bowles, Representation.

60. Bowles to Lord Grenville, dated Adelphi, Jan. 13, 1791, manuscript in Public Record Office, London, F.O. America I; printed in Turner, "English Policy Toward America," 728-33.

61. Turner, "English Policy Toward America," 708.

62. London *Daily Advertiser,* Mar. 17, 1791.

63. Holmes and Wright, "Bertucat and Bowles," 49.

64. London *Daily Advertiser,* Mar. 30, 1791.

65. Wright, *Bowles,* 55.

66. Turner, "English Policy Toward America," 734–35.

67. Holmes and Wright, "Bertucat and Bowles," 58-60.

68. *Ibid.,* 49-62.

69. Cotterill, *Southern Indians,* 90.

70. Turner, "English Policy Toward America," 734-35.

71. Craig, "Report," 264.

72. Caughey, *McGillivray,* 49-50.

73. *Ibid.,* 310-11.

74. Wright, *Bowles,* 95-106.

75. Proclamation dated Head Quarters, Wekiva, Oct. 31, 1799, MS in the Library of the Thomas Gilcrease Institute of American History and Art, Tulsa (a document pointed out to me by Duane H. King); see Wright, *Bowles,* 117-20, on the Wekiva conference.

76. Wright, *Bowles,* 171.

Early Nineteenth-Century Cherokee Political Organization

V. Richard Persico, Jr.

Cherokee political organization during the early nineteenth century was a combination of traditional elements and newer forms adopted in response to white contact. Although some elements were directly borrowed from the white men, most of the structure was composed of traditional forms of government which had been changed to meet new challenges. The Cherokees found it necessary to alter their political organization in response to white pressure to create a system that the whites could understand. It was also necessary, however, that the body of the Cherokee people be able to understand and deal with their own government. While the outward appearance and functioning of the political organization had changed greatly, it was still based on long-established patterns that were familiar to the average Cherokee.

White men tended to assume that the Cherokee political system worked much like their own. The Cherokee government was sometimes viewed as a monarchy, sometimes as a democracy, and sometimes as a combination of both. In whatever form, the whites usually regarded it as resting on principles similar to Anglo-American notions of government. In order to deal with the powerful whites, Cherokee political organization often took on at least the outward appearance of white forms of government. However, the system frequently appeared differently to whites and to Cherokees.

Cherokee political organization was undergoing a continuous process of change in response to white pressure from the early eighteenth century through the time of their removal. The overall trend was toward a greater centralization of power. This trend reached its climax with the adoption of the Cherokee Constitution in 1828.

The basic political unit of the Cherokees in the early part of the eighteenth century was the town. A town consisted of all the people who used a single ceremonial center. Individuals might live at some distance from the center and still be townsmen. In one instance, the people of two towns, Tellico and Chatuga, were intermingled in a single compact settlement, yet they maintained separate townhouses and considered themselves separate towns.[1] There was no formal political organization beyond the level of the town.

Within each town, a council handled political affairs. This body made decisions regarding relations with other towns, with other tribes of Indians, and, during the early period of contact, with the Europeans. It also dealt with some internal matters such as repairs to public buildings, communal plantings, and ceremonies. Most disputes between individuals and all cases of personal injury or property damage were the affairs of the clans, not of the town. In some cases, when the issues in dispute between the clan sections of a town were unclear, the town, acting through its council, may have been called upon to arbitrate the matter in order to preserve local harmony. The council decided upon any situation that involved the welfare of the town as a whole.

The town council was composed of the entire population of the town, but was dominated by three groups of elder men. The most important group consisted of the town priest-chief and his assistants. A second group of seven elders, one from each clan, formed an inner advisory council. The remainder of the senior men, designated "beloved men," formed the third influential group. In the council house, the seating arrangement reflected the structure of the council. The priest-chief and his assistants sat in the center with the advisory council. The rest of the people, organized into clan sections, sat around the sides of the house. In front were the beloved men, with the younger men behind them and the women and children in the rear. Anyone could address the council, but the elders dominated the proceedings.[2]

93

When a matter was brought before the council, deliberation was carried on in a calm and orderly fashion until a unanimous decision could be reached. This often required several days of discussion. Matters of importance were known prior to the meeting, and clan members would consult among themselves in an attempt to form a group position. Elder men could use their influence and joking privileges to unify the younger men of their clan behind a single position. The seven members of the advisory council then brought the crystallized sentiments of their clans to the meeting for discussion. The various positions were stated and restated, with occasional adjournments for further clan caucuses, until a consensus was reached. Because the leaders had no real power to coerce others into accepting their decisions, unanimity was essential. If, after much maneuvering, the sentiments of any one group could not be accommodated, it was expected to withdraw to avoid open conflict. In such cases, groups which withdrew were not bound by the decision reached.[3]

The need for unanimity in councils and the lack of coercive power by the leaders were reflections of a central theme in Cherokee culture. Harmony and the avoidance of open conflict were highly valued in interpersonal relationships. A good man was one who did not create discord. Instead, he was cautious in his dealings with others, taking care not to be too forward with his own interests. If a conflict became unavoidable, he was expected to withdraw both emotionally and, if possible, physically. The desire to create and maintain harmony was a strong guiding principle in Cherokee politics.[4]

Because the issues of war and peace affected the entire town, they were determined by the council. When war was decided upon, its conduct was turned over to the town war organization. The various officers of the war organization were primarily concerned with generating popular enthusiasm, recruiting warriors, and insuring success through rituals of purification. In accordance with the harmony ethic, the war leaders did not have strong coercive powers. Warriors apparently could withdraw anytime from a raid up to the actual moment of attack. In order to carry out a successful raid, however, the war party leaders must have had some coercive power. Gearing suggests that this was opposed to the ideal of harmony and would have been out of place anywhere except in a war party. The extent to which a war leader on a raid could have exercised this power is unknown, but appears to have been highly restricted. Town leaders would not have had any such power in formulating town policy.[5]

Beyond the level of the town, the Cherokees of the early eighteenth century recognized no higher authority. The Cherokee tribe consisted of a number of politically independent towns held together by a common culture, language, and history. No formal political mechanism existed on the tribal level. Although each town was independent, there is no record of their ever making war against each other. The sentiment that fellow Cherokees should not fight each other was reinforced by the presence of members of all seven clans in each town. This kept intervillage killings, the major cause of war with other tribes, an affair of the clans, not of the town. At times, several towns might act in unison under the leadership of an unusually influential and charismatic individual. Such unions, however, were temporary and usually formed in response to some crisis. Any town could decide to withdraw from the actions of the others at any time. Aside from such social pressure as could be brought to bear, each town acted independently of the others.[6]

As contact and trade with the Europeans increased, the Cherokee political organization came under increased pressure to change. The Europeans tended to treat the Cherokees as a single political entity—a "nation." They seem to have been aware of the fact that towns could act independently, yet they sought a centralized authority with which to deal. Colonel George Chicken's journal of 1725 provides an example of this tendency. Chicken's mission was to deliver a message from the government of South Carolina to the leaders of the upper Cherokee settlements. When the headmen of Ellijay expressed reluctance to travel to the Overhill country to hear the message, Chicken wrote, "I then Informed them after a Sharp Manner that I would not talk with them in their own town, and as the head men of the Lower Settlements had waited upon their King, so I Expected they would wait

95

upon their King he being of their own Choosing and Approved of by the English that they might be altogether and then there would be no Excuses from any of them in saying that they had not heard the Talk which was usual among them."[7] Chicken's actions seem to be directed at supporting a king by delivering the message only at his council, while recognizing that a town whose leaders were not present at an assembly would not be bound by its proceedings. The reference to the English approval of the king suggests that he was a town leader who was set up as king by the English because of his influence, or perhaps his pliability.

In general, the Europeans appear to have used their concept of a feudal state in an effort to understand Cherokee politics. In such a state, the nobility can act somewhat independently but must acknowledge their king as leader. The English, in particular, sought to establish and stengthen the position of king in order to deal more easily with the Cherokees. Thus, at times, figures appear in the records who are said to function as monarchs. Moytoy of Tellico and his successor, Ammonscossittee, were viewed by the English as kings who could force compliance with their orders. These men were foremost among the leadership of the tribe from 1730 through 1750, but it is unlikely that they functioned as monarchs. They were probably merely very influential men who rose to meet a crisis and worked through an expanded council structure. The support and gifts given them by the English would have added to their influence, but at no time could they be considered kings in the European sense.[8]

The Cherokees themselves began to recognize the need for centralization of power as the eighteenth century progressed. The English increasingly treated them as a single political entity, creating the need to respond as such. Action by one town, or even by a single person, could bring reprisals against all of the Cherokees. As the tribe became more dependent upon trade goods, reprisals by the whites became more serious. Centralization of power required that the towns surrender to some form of tribal government much of their independence in dealing with non-Cherokees.[9]

Under English pressure, a centralized tribal government began to take shape. Its primary task was to regulate relations with the whites and with other Indians. A tribal council was formed, based on the model of the town council. Composed of the entire population of the tribe, it had a set of officials who dominated its proceedings. The headmen of the tribal council were usually the same group who directed the council of the most influential town. Unlike their attendance at a town council, the entire population of the tribe could not gather for deliberations. Usually, each town would arrive at its decision on a tribal issue and then send a delegation of its headmen, along with all the other people who could attend, to present this position to the tribal council. Consensus was more difficult to reach and decisions harder to implement than in a town council. If a town or a block of people withdrew from a decision, the implementation of a unified tribal policy became impossible. Except for informal social pressure, no mechanism existed to force compliance with council decisions. Perhaps the most serious weakness of the tribal government was its inability to control the activities of warriors in their attacks on the whites. It was this weakness that led to war with the colonists in 1760. In spite of this defect, the tribal council was moderately successful in coordinating the actions of the towns.[10]

In an effort to gain control over the raiding activities of the young men, around 1768 the tribal council added a group of distinguished elder warriors to its inner circle of prominent men. Formerly, men acting in the capacity of warriors sat in council only when a war was being conducted. At all other times, they were not distinguished from the other beloved men. By including the leaders of the traditional war organization in the decision-making process of the council, a new element of coercion of the sort previously available to war leaders only when on a raid was introduced into the tribal government.[11]

The tribal council's efforts to restrain the young men from making war on the whites failed under extreme pressure. The opening of Kentucky to white settlement and the beginning of the American Revolution led to a split between the older, traditional war leaders and the young warriors. Finding the decision of their elders to keep the peace unacceptable, many young men followed the pattern of withdrawal. Some of these men and their families moved south to form the Chickamauga towns and carried on warfare with the whites until 1794. Until the schism could be healed, the tribal council was unable to halt the fighting.[12]

During the last decades of the eighteenth century, the tribal council assumed the form it would maintain until 1817. To heal the rift in the tribe, a number of the more influential young warriors were included as a group in the inner circle of decision-makers. Their participation made the council's actions more binding on all segments of the people. The remainder of the council structure remained unchanged. All Cherokees were entitled to attend council meetings, and anyone could ask to address the council. The council itself was composed of influential men, young and old, representing all the Cherokee towns. Men were chosen for council seats on the basis of their reputation both among their neighbors and in the Nation at large. Council business was carried on in the traditional manner. Groups would meet to forge unified opinions, present these in the open meeting, and attempt to arrive at a consensus. Withdrawal from a council decision by any group was still possible, but great efforts were made to resolve all differences.[13]

The council meeting held at Ustanali in June 1792 provides an excellent illustration of the workings of the council. Of primary concern at this meeting was the establishment of peace with the whites. White spokesmen presented their proposals and demands in the open meeting. Having heard these, it is recorded, "The young warriors then withdrew from their beloved seat, to consult in private — after some time, sent for the beloved men, and remained with them in private consultation for some time. . . ." Following this conference, a speaker was chosen to present the sentiments both of the young warriors and of the beloved men to the white representatives. A series of such meetings and private conferences continued for five days. Also during this meeting the Cherokee leader Black Fox proposed the admission of two new council members. Of one, he said:

The Dragging Canoe has left the world. He was a man of consequence in his country. He was a friend both to his own and to the
white people. But his brother is still in place, and I mention now in
public that I intend presenting him with his dead brother's medal:
for he promises fair to possess sentiments similar to those of his
brother, both with regard to the red and the white. It is mentioned
here publicly, that both whites and reds may know of it and pay attention to him.[14]

In 1817, Elias Cornelius, a representative of the American
Board of Commissioners for Foreign Missions, addressed the
Cherokee council. Of this meeting, he wrote, "While I was ad-
dressing them they remained attentive. When I had finished they
consulted together, and unanimously approved of what I had
said. They ordered Kunnataclagee (in English 'The Ridge') a distinguished Indian chief, to proclaim to the whole council the result of their deliberation; which he did in the center of a large
circle of Indians in a speech of 15 or 20 minutes in length." The
Ridge opened his speech by saying, "I am going to address the
council of the Cherokee nation; and each representative will inform his own town of our deliberations on the subject. . . ."[15]
From this it may be seen that the council's method of conducting
business had not changed since 1792. During this period, however, greater power had flowed to the central government, and its
sphere of interest had expanded.

Formerly, the role of the central authority had been to deal
with foreign affairs. Internal matters were left to the various
towns except when such matters involved non-Cherokees. Early in
the nineteenth century, the National Council, as it was then
called, began passing resolutions and making laws that dealt with
internal affairs as well. The first such act to be recorded, passed
in 1808, established regulating companies to suppress horse stealing and enforce inheritance laws. By the same act, regulators who
killed another Cherokee in the line of duty were exempted from
blood revenge. In 1810 another act, canceling all outstanding
blood debts between the clans, was adopted.[16] All of these matters
were internal and formerly would have been handled by the
towns and the clans. From this time until the adoption of the

Cherokee Constitution, the National Council continued to expand its powers to regulate internal, as well as external, affairs.

In 1817, a set of articles was adopted that constituted a major change in the structure of the Cherokee National Council. Article I established a thirteen-member executive committee called the Standing Committee. This name would later be changed to the National Committee. Article II charged it with the overall supervision of the affairs of the nation. Its actions were to be subject to the review of the full Council before taking effect. In Article V, the Standing Committee was specifically given jurisdiction over relations with the United States. Articles III and IV dealt with property rights; Article VI, with the procedure for adoption and amendment.[17]

The establishment of a smaller executive committee within the Council was designed to achieve both greater centralization of power and increased efficiency of management. The decision-making process in the Cherokee government had not changed; matters of importance were still discussed until a consensus of opinion was reached. By reducing the number of participants in the initial stages of the debate, a unified position could be reached more quickly. The approval of members of the larger Council could be more easily gained when they were presented with carefully constructed, compact proposals.

After the adoption of the Articles of 1817 the term "National Council" was often used to refer both to the larger house alone and also to the combined houses. To avoid confusion, the term "General Council" will be used hereafter to refer to the union of the National Committee and the National Council as the governing body of the nation. This is the form adopted in the Cherokee Constitution.

In 1820, a somewhat less drastic change was made in the General Council's structure with the division of the Nation into eight districts. Previously, representatives appear to have been chosen either by towns or at large. With the establishment of districts, representation in the National Council would be decided now on a regional basis. No mention is made in the act of Committee representation. Committee members may have been chosen at large by the members of the National Council.[18]

The trend toward greater centralization of power continued as the National Committee was given additional duties. In 1823, it gained the power to review and approve all actions taken by the National Council. Each body now served as a check on the other. From this time until removal, the structure of the General Council would remain basically the same.[19]

Another set of articles was adopted in 1825. Its primary objective was to confirm and to formalize the control of the General Council over the lands and other public property of the Cherokee Nation. Articles I and II stated that all lands and annuities were public property. Improvements on the land belonged to those who had made, or bought, them. Article III reserved to the General Council the exclusive right to dispose of public property. Articles IV and VIII denied the principal chiefs any power to dispose of public property, to make treaties, or to overrule the Council's decisions. Article V prevented individual Council members from acting in an official capacity without prior approval of the Council. Article VI guaranteed citizens the right to hold, and dispose of, their improvements as they pleased, provided they did not sell them to a non-Cherokee. Article VII restricted the courts from acting on cases that had already been decided by the Council. While the Articles of 1825 ostensibly were concerned with property rights, they were, in fact, a statement of the supremacy of the General Council as the governing body of the Nation.[20]

The Cherokee Constitution of 1828 made no significant changes in the structure of the General Council. Although the wording of Article III, which describes the legislative branch of the government, makes it appear similar to the United States Congress, the General Council continued to function much as before. The major innovation of the Constitution was the establishment of a strong principal chief with veto power over Council actions. Some of the power formerly centered in the Council now flowed to the office of the chief, creating a stronger and more flexible central government. With the exception of the executive branch, which was modeled after that of the United States government, the Constitution was not a break with the previous organization of the government. Article IV, section 12 provided that all laws in force at the time of the adoption of the Constitution would remain in force unless changed by the General Council. Many of the provisions of the Constitution incorporated the essential elements of the Articles of 1817 and 1825 along with numerous other acts of the Council.[21]

Although the General Council had assumed a form similar to that of a bicameral legislature by 1817, many of its functions were of the type traditionally carried out by Cherokee councils. The Council acted to settle disputes between individual Cherokees that could not be settled by other bodies. During the Council meeting of 1819, a citizen named Otter Lifter brought a claim against the owner of a runaway slave who had cheated him at horse-trading. The Council decided against Otter Lifter and passed a resolution that a master was not liable for his slaves' financial dealings if these were carried on without his approval.[22]

In 1821, the National Committee appointed a high court to handle some of the cases presented. So many private affairs were submitted for judgment during the Council session of 1823 that the National Committee and Council passed a joint resolution continuing some of them until the next year.[23] Although courts of law had been established in 1820, many people preferred that their claims be settled by the Council. In 1823, the Committee complained to the National Council that private cases which should have been handled by the courts were being acted upon by the Council. The Committee resolved that such cases should be submitted to the courts for judgment in the future.[24] This resolution does not seem to have halted the use of the General Council as a court. Article III, section 16 of the Cherokee Constitution stated, "It shall be the duty of the General Council to pass such laws as may be necessary and proper, to decide differences by arbitrators to be appointed by the parties, who may choose that summary mode of adjustment."[25] In acting as a court, the General Council adhered more closely to the traditional notion of a town council than to the white concept of a legislature.

The General Council acted toward the town councils much as town councils acted toward the clans. Anytime there arose a dispute that involved either two or more towns, or unrelated individuals from different towns, the parties affected were likely to resort to the central authority for judgment. New areas of concern, such as road building and maintenance, which did not exist prior to the nineteenth century, fell under the jurisdiction of the General Council. In this capacity it acted to maintain public works beyond the level of the town much as the towns acted to maintain their own public works. The pattern of the General Council's activities, however, was not entirely set by the older notions of a council. Much of its action was guided both by white patterns of central government and by the increasing need for a firm central authority to coordinate the actions of the Cherokee people.

James Adair, writing in 1775, commented on the honesty of the Cherokees in dealing with each other in the eighteenth century. He noted, however, that this condition was rapidly degenerating and predicted that they would soon need new laws to prevent them from committing new crimes.[26] Adair's prediction came true in the early nineteenth century when the Council acted both to create, and to enforce, new laws. In 1808 the Council acted to suppress horse stealing by creating regulating parties which came to be known as the "Light Horse." These men were charged not only with discovering and capturing criminals, but also, in some cases, with their trial and punishment.[27] The General Council, already acting much like a civil court, sometimes acted as a criminal court as well. In 1819, an act was passed making it illegal to establish a turnpike barrier on a road without the Council's consent. Offenders were to be brought before the two houses of the Council for trial.[28] Several laws regarding criminal actions were passed prior to the establishment of courts in 1820. The punishment for some of these crimes was to be determined by trial, but the body that would hold the trial was not specified.[29] It must be assumed that, in these cases, the Cherokee General Council acted as a court to sit in judgment of violations of the national laws. Under the traditional system, offended individuals and their clansmen would have taken revenge on criminals. Some sources, however, state that the town councils occasionally sat in judgment of public criminals.[30] The pattern for the General Council's actions may be derived from the older role of the town council as a court for the trial of public criminals as well as for civil action.

One of the first acts of the General Council during its 1820 session was the division of the nation into eight districts and the establishment of district courts. The law itself required that a council house be established in each district "for the purpose of holding councils to administer justice in all causes and complaints that may be brought before it for trial." A judge for each district, as well as a circuit judge for each two districts, was to be appointed to determine "all causes agreeable to the laws of the nation."[31] The reference to councils suggests a judicial process somewhat different from that of the whites and more akin to the traditional system. Although information concerning the district councils is scanty, they probably involved the gathering of a large group of people who not only conducted the trial of people accused of crimes but also debated matters of local and national concern. In 1822, for example, the General Council requested that the judges poll the citizens of their districts to determine their sentiments regarding a possible land cession.[32] The appropriation of forty dollars for the support of each district council by the national government also suggests it was composed of a fairly large gathering.[33]

The process by which the judges were to arrive at their decisions was not specified, although other details of the new courts were carefully noted. In a separate act, the boundaries of each district were outlined with such great care that anyone familiar with common landmarks would be in no doubt as to the district in which he lived.[34] This suggests that, while the idea of districts and judges was new and required some explanation, the activities to be conducted were familiar and no explanation was needed.

Criminal actions came increasingly under the jurisdiction of the central government as the nineteenth century progressed. In 1810 an act was passed canceling all outstanding blood debts between the clans. While the punishment of future murderers was mentioned in the act, no new mechanism for trial and punishment was established.[35] It may be that the Light Horse and the

Council took over this task, abolishing clan revenge. A reference in the act to a specific limited situation in which clan revenge could not be taken, however, indicates that the practice was not so much abolished as limited at the time. Exactly when individual and clan revenge for injuries suffered was replaced by court action, if indeed it ever was completely replaced, is difficult to determine.

Many criminal trials followed a pattern in which the punishment was determined by the court in each separate case without specific penalties being established by law. An 1819 law stated that a person who employed another to steal should be punished the same as the thief, "agreeably to the sentence of such a trial."[36] In the 1820 act which established the district court system, the judges and councils were to decide on the punishment for thieves themselves.[37] Another law, passed in 1824, stated that the courts might inflict any punishment short of death upon a convicted robber.[38] Penalties for crimes apparently were left up to the court until an act was passed establishing maximum and minimum sentences for specific crimes.

The role of the principal chief remained relatively obscure during much of the early nineteenth century. Both Little Turkey and his successor, Black Fox, exercised a great deal of influence in the Council, but at times they were overshadowed by other influential men. The principal chief had influence, honor, and respect, but apparently his power depended upon the number of other influential men he could persuade to back him. During the period prior to 1817, most of the power rested with the National Council. With the passage of the Articles of 1817, the office of the principal chief began a rapid decline in power that was not reversed until the adoption of the Cherokee Constitution in 1828. While the office was retained, all the power to negotiate with the United States was given to the Council.[39] The National Committee now became the most powerful body in the nation, and its president became the most powerful individual. This situation was reinforced by the Articles of 1825. Two years later this situation was reversed when the office of the principal chief was remodeled in the Cherokee Constitution in imitation of that of the president of the United States.[40] After the adoption of the Constitution in 1828, the principal chief had more power than at any previous time since the creation of the office.

Because the attention of most observers was focused on the national government, relatively little was recorded concerning the political organization of the Cherokee towns during the early nineteenth century. However, the role of the town, while reduced, remained important to the average Cherokee, and something of its operation can be reconstructed.

The Cherokees' settlement pattern, and therefore the physical structure of their towns, underwent a change at the beginning of the nineteenth century. Previously they tended to settle in relatively compact villages. The necessity for defense and the primitive nature of their gardening encouraged settlement within a fairly restricted area, although there were probably some Cherokees who lived apart from others. Compact towns would have facilitated the working of the town council. The end of warfare, both with the whites and with other Indians, and the adoption of plow agriculture, which opened new areas to cultivation, resulted in a more scattered population. In 1818, a missionary complaining of the difficulty of assembling groups to hear his sermons reported that "there is no place near us where a large audience can be collected. As the people do not live in villages, but scattered over the country from 2 to 10 miles apart."[41] Towns, however, had not disappeared, for the Cherokees regarded a town not as a place, but as a group of people sharing the same ceremonial and council center. An 1822 list of Cherokee towns prepared by missionaries noted that the town of Hightower, for example, had a population of over two hundred and was perhaps fifty or sixty miles in length. Not all towns were so extended, however; some remained relatively compact.[42]

The new settlement pattern weakened the power of the town councils. People could not gather easily on short notice to deliberate matters of public concern. Decisions were more difficult to forge by means of public opinion. With a dispersed population, interests and problems presumably became more sectional, than local, in nature. Problems involving people from different towns but living in the same area could not have been dealt with by a single town council. As previously noted, for a time such situations were handled by the General Council; later, district courts and councils took over the job of managing sectional affairs. All these changes weakened the town councils and contributed to the increasing centralization of power within the Cherokee Nation.

During the early nineteenth century there appears to have been some competition for power between the central authority of the General Council and the councils of the various towns. This conflict was present, no doubt, in the earliest days of the tribal council, when the independent towns were forced to surrender part of their freedom of action in order to successfully deal with the white men. As the General Council increased its power and its sphere of influence, more strength flowed from the towns to the central authority. Some of the towns resisted this flow. The preamble of the Articles of 1817 reads, "Whereas 54 towns and villages have convened in order to deliberate and consider the situation of our nation, in the disposition of our common property of lands, without the unanimous consent of the members of Council and in order to obviate the evil consequences resulting in such course, we have unanimously adopted the following form for the future government of our Nation."[43] There are no other recorded instances of the towns actively opposing the central authority until 1828, when White Path led a popular reaction against the new constitution from the council house of his town.[44] Even so, it is likely that some friction existed during the intervening period.

The central government may have attempted to undercut the local councils in order to consolidate its control over the Nation. After establishing district courts and councils in 1820, the General Council withdrew financial support of the district councils in 1825.[45] The courts were arms of the central government and were continued. Presumably the district councils also continued, but at local expense. Article V of the Articles of 1825 stated that members of the General Council were to have no authority to convene councils in their districts or to act officially on any matter while the General Council was in recess.[46] Although the above evidence of seizure of power is admittedly slight, undoubtedly the

107

central government would have profited by further weakening the local councils.

The trend toward centralization of the Cherokee political system culminated in the adoption of the Cherokee Constitution in 1828. The central government, in its three branches, was in full control of the Nation. It was even able to halt a conservative movement against the adoption of the Constitution.[47] Local leaders had influence only in local matters unless they were also elected to the central government. The Cherokee Constitution was modeled after that of the United States with the three branches somewhat redesigned to conform more closely to Cherokee government patterns. The Cherokees, however, were to have little time to develop their government further.

Following the adoption of the Cherokee Constitution, agitation for the removal of the Cherokees increased. The central government responded well to this emergency, but with only temporary success. The turmoil that took place within the Cherokee Nation during the final years before removal occupied most of the attention of the new government. Cherokee politics entered a new phase with the opening of the third decade of the nineteenth century. The period of centralization which began with the earliest European contact had ended.

NOTES

1. Williams, ed., *Early Travels*, 98-99, 152-53; Fred O. Gearing, *Priests and Warriors*, 5, 21-23.

2. Gearing, *Priests and Warriors*, 21-24; James Adair, *Adair's History of the American Indians*, ed. Samuel C. Williams (Johnson City: Watauga Press, 1930), 460.

3. Gearing, *Priests and Warriors*, 39-42; Adair, *History*, 460; Timberlake, *Memoirs*, 60, 89, 91.

4. Gearing, *Priests and Warriors*, 30-36, 43; John Gulick, *Cherokees at the Crossroads* (Chapel Hill: Institute for Research in Soc. Sc., Univ. of North Carolina, 1960), 134-38.

5. Gearing, *Priests and Warriors*, 47-54; Adair, *History*, 167-78; Timberlake, *Memoirs*, 93; William H. Gilbert, "The Eastern Cherokees," in Bureau of American Ethnology, *Bulletin no. 133* (Washington, D.C.: GPO, 1943), 348-53.

6. Reid, *Law of Blood*, 75, 154; Gearing, *Priests and Warriors*, 79-83.

7. Williams, ed., *Early Travels*, 97-98.

8. Gearing, *Priests and Warriors*, 88; Reid, *Law of Blood*, 25-27.

9. Gearing, *Priests and Warriors*, 85-88.

10. Gilbert, "Eastern Cherokees," 321-25; Gearing, *Priests and Warriors*, 89-98.

11. Gearing, *Priests and Warriors*, 99-102.

12. *Ibid.*, 102-5.

13. *Ibid.;* Gilbert, "Eastern Cherokees," 363-67.

14. *U.S. Congress, American State Papers, Class II, Indian Affairs*, 2 vols. (Washington, D.C.: Gales and Seaton, 1832-34), I, 270-73.

15. Robert S. Walker, *Torchlights to the Cherokees: The Brainerd Mission* (New York: Macmillan, 1931), 66-67.

16. *Laws of the Cherokee Nation Adopted by the Council at Various Periods* (Tahlequah, Cherokee Nation [Oklahoma]: Cherokee Advocate Off. 1852), 3-4.

17. *Ibid.*, 4-5.

18. *Ibid.*, 14-18.

19. *Ibid.*, 31-32.

20. *Ibid.*, 45-46.

21. *Ibid.*, 118-30.

22. *Ibid.*, 8-9.

23. *Ibid.*, 32.

24. *Ibid.*, 31-32.

25. *Ibid.*, 122.

26. Adair, *History*, 462.

27. *Laws of the Cherokee Nation*, 3-4; Adelaide L. Fires, ed., *Records of the Moravians in North Carolina*, vol. 7 (Raleigh: North Carolina Hist. Comm. 1922), 3074.

28. *Laws of the Cherokee Nation*, 7-8.

29. *Ibid.*, 9.

30. Gilbert, "Eastern Cherokees," 323.

31. *Laws of the Cherokee Nation*, 11-12.

32. *Ibid.*, 23.

33. *Ibid.*, 28.

34. *Ibid.*, 15-18.

35. *Ibid.*, 4.

36. *Ibid.*, 9.

37. *Ibid.*, 11-12.

38. *Ibid.*, 38.

39. *Ibid.*, 4-5.

40. *Ibid.*, 118-23.

41. Henry T. Malone, *Cherokees of the Old South: A People in Transition* (Athens: Univ. of Georgia Press, 1957), 119.

42. *Ibid.*, 54.

43. *Laws of the Cherokee Nation*, 4.

44. James Mooney, "Myths," in Bureau of American Ethonology, *19th Annual Report* (Washington, D.C.: GPO, 1900), 113.

45. *Laws of the Cherokee Nation*, 11-12.

46. *Ibid.*, 45-46.

47. Mooney, "Myths," 113.

Cherokee Planters: The Development of Plantation Slavery Before Removal

Theda Perdue

The Cherokees, unlike weaker tribes along the Atlantic coast, physically survived contact with whites, but cultural imperialism proved to be almost as deadly as military conquest. In order to avoid total extermination at the hands of the European invaders, this powerful inland tribe abandoned or altered their "savage" customs. The Cherokees adopted many aspects of western civilization and hoped to make themselves more acceptable to whites by becoming "civilized." As a southern Indian tribe, the Cherokees had extensive contact with a white slaveholding society which set the standard by which Cherokees measured their progress toward "civilization." Consequently, the Cherokees in their flight from "savagery" established a system of plantation slavery. Because traditional Cherokee culture acted as a leavening agent, Cherokee planters avoided much of the rigidity and cruelty displayed by the white slaveholding society.

The Cherokees quickly modified and transformed indigenous bondage in an effort to adapt to the presence of Europeans. Originally the Cherokees enslaved prisoners of war, and bondage primarily entailed exclusion from the kinship system. Deprivation of kinsmen was an extremely serious liability, since kinship determined both political position and social relationships and provided protection through the exercise of blood vengeance. Bondage was not necessarily a permanent situation, however, because the possibility of adoption into a clan and subsequent incorporation into the tribe existed.[1] In contrast, racism precluded the entrance of blacks into white southern society. Originally, slaves seem to have performed no real function in the Cherokees' economy, where the division of labor was sexual; in fact, the Cherokees' lack of regard for material wealth and the absence of a profit motive contrasted sharply with the capitalistic economy of the antebellum South in which black slaves played an essential role.[2] Not until a well-developed commerce, an inequality of wealth, and a central government stimulated production did Cherokee society become able to support a large number of slaves and to utilize their labor effectively.

Although Europeans did not immediately foist the white man's version of slavery on the Cherokees, their economic system gradually undermined the indigenous concept of bondage. The traders, who inspired and directed much of the transformation, found a ready market for European goods and exchanged them for the Indians' deerskins and war captives.[3] Traditionally, there had been no European type of demand for slaves in the Cherokee economy, but the rapid development of dependence on foreign manufactured goods made slaves very desirable possessions. As a result, warfare escalated, and enslavement came to be viewed in an entirely different way.

Before the advent of a demand for captives, Cherokees went to war only to avenge a wrong committed against them by another tribe. The aggressors usually sent a delegation to offer retribution, and because a military offensive was a very serious matter, the Cherokees would deliberate carefully over their enemy's proposal. Sometimes the tribes worked out a peaceful solution, but on other occasions the wronged party replied that "crying blood is quenched with equal blood" and sounded the war signal. Since the sole object of warfare was to avenge "crying blood," Cherokees placed no premium on the capture of enemy warriors. The victors usually killed the wounded in the field, dismembering and scalping them so that the warriors would have trophies to demonstrate their valor. The warriors' aim was never to leave the battlefield until the number of enemy slain equaled the number of their own tribesmen lost in a previous engagement. An early-eighteenth-century writer reported that, "having accomplished this, they returned home with their scalps, and by some token let their enemy know that they were satisfied." Cherokees did not conceive of war

111

as a continuing, long-range effort but rather as no more than a retaliatory raid of only one battle followed by the warriors' return.[4]

The traders began to incite intertribal warfare in order to profit from the sale of captives. James Adair, an eighteenth-century trader, confirmed the warmongering activities of his colleagues: "The Indians are not fond of waging war with each other, unless prompted by some of the traders; when left to themselves, they consider with the greatest exactness and foresight, all the attending circumstances of war." The traders generally succeeded in their efforts, for by the early seventeenth century Cherokees, no longer viewing captives as mere by-products of retaliatory raids, engaged in warfare for the sole purpose of obtaining prisoners to sell to the whites as slaves.[5]

The traders also introduced economic inequality into Cherokee society, since their way of life displayed tempting examples of affluence. These entrepreneurs possessed, according to one Cherokee, "a great deal of yellow and white stone, of black people, horses, cows, hogs, and everything else our hearts delight in," and they constructed large houses, barns, and stores "like towers in cities, beyond the common size of those of the Indians."[6] For a few years after traders came to live among the Cherokees, a gross inequality of wealth was exhibited only between Indian and white, but intermarriage and the full acceptance of mixed-blood offspring into the tribe resulted in an inequality of wealth within Indian society as children inherited their fathers' estates. This economic inequality provoked envy and spurred an acquisitiveness among Cherokees that was alien to their culture.

As long as the demand for Indian slaves continued, and incessant intertribal warfare was in the white interest, one of the easiest ways for an Indian to turn a profit was to sell the captives he took in battle. Cherokees regarded these prisoners of war as mere commodities to be traded for guns, ammunition, strouds, hoes, and hatchets, since their economy had not yet reached the point at which slave labor could be utilized effectively. When whites embarked on a policy of pacification and civilization, the slave's role changed from product to producer. The termination of warfare and the abandonment of the traditional way of acquiring slaves came at a time when the adoption of the white man's agricultural implements and techniques by Cherokee farmers resulted in a demand for additional workers. Since Indian captives were no longer available, Cherokees had to find another source of labor. The aspiring planters looked to their white southern mentors for guidance and, not surprisingly, began to employ African bondsmen in the cultivation of their fields.

The Cherokees experienced something of an economic depression between the end of the American Revolution and the time when the government commenced its civilizing efforts. Under the impact of compulsory peace and land cession, Cherokee resources dwindled. The Indians could no longer capture slaves, and they had severely depleted their hunting grounds in an effort to satisfy the European demand for deerskins. In this distressing situation the Cherokees gratefully received George Washington's proposal for relieving the economic crisis. The president of the United States, noting that some Cherokees already kept livestock, recommended that others follow their lead. He pointed out that the Cherokees' fertile land would easily grow corn and wheat that could be sold to the whites as well as consumed by the Indians themselves. Furthermore, he urged the Cherokees to grow cotton and flax both as cash crops and for their own use, and he encouraged Cherokee women to learn to spin and weave. Finally, Washington instructed the government's agent to the Cherokees to procure looms, spinning wheels, plows, and other implements and to hire people to instruct the Cherokees in their proper use.[7]

Washington selected Benjamin Hawkins, the scion of a wealthy North Carolina family, as the man to supervise the civilization of the savages. In his position as superintendent of Indian tribes south of the Ohio River, Hawkins tried to set an example for his wards by establishing a plantation complete with black slaves on the Flint River. On his initial visit to the Cherokees, Hawkins discovered that the tribe avidly sought the tools of civilization. The Terrapin, whose farm was fenced and well stocked with cattle and hogs, hopefully inquired when the Cherokees might expect the plows and other implements promised by the government. A

113

group of women at Etowah told Hawkins that "they would plant cotton and be prepared for spinning as soon as they could make it, and they hoped they might get some wheels and cards as soon as they should be ready for them."[8]

Under the direction of Hawkins and his successor, Return J. Meigs, the Cherokees advanced rapidly along the road to civilization. In 1826 Elias Boudinot, one of the most prominent leaders of the Cherokee Nation, documented his people's amazing progress in *An Address to the Whites:*

> In 1810 there were 19,500 cattle; 6,100 horses; 19,600 swine; 1,037 sheep; 467 looms; 1,600 spinning wheels; 30 wagons; 500 ploughs; 3 saw mills; 13 gristmills & c. At this time there are 22,000 cattle; 7,600 horses; 46,000 swine; 2,500 sheep; 762 looms; 2,488 spinning wheels; 172 wagons; 2,943 ploughs; 10 saw-mills; 31 gristmills; 62 blacksmith-shops; 8 cotton machines; 18 schools; 18 ferries; and a number of public roads. In one district there were, last winter, upwards of 1,000 volumes of good books; and 11 different periodical papers both religious and political, which were taken and read.[9]

As the Cherokees accumulated the material evidence of civilization, they realized that traditional tribal methods of safeguarding property no longer sufficed and implemented changes that curtailed individual freedom and consolidated and centralized political power. Indigenous Cherokee law distinguished between two kinds of real property—hunting grounds and fields.[10] Cherokees owned the hunting grounds communally, and each man was equally bound to defend this property from any encroachment. Not even a chief could sell this land because "no Indian, however great his influence and authority, could give away more than his own right to any tract of land, which, in proportion, is no more than as one man to the whole tribe."[11] On the other hand, Cherokees originally considered an individual's house and fields to belong to him personally, or to his lineage, and the owner could dispose of his holdings at will. The attempts by whites to gain control of Cherokee land soon forced the Nation to apply the rules of communal ownership to this property as well. The first step in the evolution of the concept of inalienable property substituted the possession of an estate in occupancy for the posses-

114

sion of a fee simple. By this arrangement a Cherokee still owned, and could sell, any improvements he made on the property. Ultimately, however, it became necessary to prohibit sale of improvements in order to discourage migration to the West.[12]

A corollary to the Cherokees' growing concern over the protection of realty was their desire to safeguard investments in human property.[13] The republican government of the Cherokee Nation rested largely in the hands of slaveholders; over half the signers of the Constitution of 1827 owned bondsmen. The preponderance of slaveholders among the Cherokee founding fathers is even more remarkable when one considers that they comprised less than 8 percent of the heads of households in the Nation.[14] Undoubtedly these planters realized that an economic system based on the use of slave labor required police power and effective government in order to function properly.

The enforcement of their stringent laws required a far more powerful central government than the Cherokees' loose confederacy, which was devoid of any coercive authority. Adair reported, "Every town is independent of another. Their own friendly compact continues the union. . . . The Indians, therefore, have no such titles or persons, as emperors, or kings; nor an appellative for such in any of their dialects. . . . They have no words to express despotic power, arbitrary kings, oppressed or obedient subjects." Adair, however, recognized the limitations of the Cherokees' almost anarchical system of government when dealing with the problems of a civilized existence: "In their former state of simplicity, the plain law of nature was enough; but, as they are degenerating very fast from their ancient simplicity, they, without doubt, must have new laws to terrify them from committing new crimes, according to the usage of other nations, who multiply their laws, in proportion to the exigencies of the time."[15] Beginning in 1730, when Sir Alexander Cuming "nominated Moytoy commander and chief of the Cherokee nation, and enjoined all the warriors of the different tribes to acknowledge him for their King, to whom they were to be responsible for their conduct," Cherokee political history is the chronicle of the centralization of power in response to white pressure for Cherokee land and to the need for regulating the behavior of their own people for the protection of increasingly maldistributed property.[16] The process culminated in 1827 when the Cherokees organized a republic under a constitution patterned after that of the United States government.

Laws controlling the activities of slaves actually preceded the Constitution of 1828. An act passed by the National Committee and Council in 1820 prohibited the purchasing of goods from slaves and provided that anything bought from a slave that proved to be stolen property had to be restored to the rightful owner in fact or value. The law proscribed masters from allowing their slaves to buy or sell liquor and imposed a fine of fifteen dollars on violators. Later laws forbade both the marriage of whites and Indians to slaves and the freeing of slaves for the sole purpose of marriage; they also prohibited slaves from owning property.[17]

The Cherokees enforced their slave code in two ways. First of all, the laws offered an incentive to the prosecutor to seek out offenders and bring them to justice by providing that one-half the fines collected accrued to that official. Secondly, corporal punishment was administered by "patrolers of the settlement or neighborhood in which the offense was committed, and every settlement or neighborhood [was] privileged to organize a patrolling company."[18]

Several features of the Cherokee slave code demand attention. The paucity of laws governing the behavior of masters and slaves stands in stark contrast to the multitude of provisions in the slave codes of the white antebellum South.[19] Noticeably lacking are laws dealing with insubordination and rebellion. Furthermore, the majority of punishments are reserved for the masters, not the slaves. The laws penalized the person who bought goods from slaves, masters who allowed their slaves to buy or sell liquor, and whites or Indians who married slaves. Even the hysteria which usually accompanied any suggestion of white women cohabiting with slaves is missing, and white or Indian women who committed this indiscretion suffered fourteen fewer stripes than males found guilty of the same act.[20] The discrepancies between the slave code of the Cherokee Nation and the codes of the society which many Cherokees were trying to emulate can only be explained in terms of the enduring power of Cherokee cultural traditions. Originally,

116

a captive depended totally on the warrior who had taken him, and the master had absolute power over his bondsman. When a Shawnee captive refused to accompany his Cherokee master Black Dog, for example, the warrior promptly killed him with a tomahawk, and John Lawson reported that the Indians used the word "slave" for anything "which is obsequiously to depend on the master for its Sustenance."[21] The government of the Nation only reluctantly interfered with a matter which Cherokees customarily dealt with on an individual basis and at a social level. As a result, the master alone continued to be responsible for his own actions and for the actions of his slaves. Thus the slave code aptly demonstrates the position occupied by the Cherokee slaveholder in the two decades before removal. The Cherokee planter, driven by the desire to make a profit, amass a fortune, and protect his financial investment, attempted to imitate the plantation society of the white South, yet could not entirely escape his Cherokee heritage.

Slaveholders controlled the government of the Cherokee Nation partly because they had created it, but also because their wealth and situation gained the respect of fellow tribesmen and enabled them to deal more effectively with whites. The slaveholders' advantage over nonslaveholders in relationships with whites stemmed from intermarriage as well. Only 17 percent of the people living in the Cherokee Nation in 1835 had any white ancestors, but 78 percent of the members of families owning slaves claimed some proportion of white blood. Contact with a white parent or grandparent gave these people a head start toward "civilization." Moreover, the Cherokee slaveholders seem to have identified linguistically with white society. Among the people (including infants and small children) living in slaveholding families, 39 percent could read English, while only 13 percent were proficient at reading Cherokee. In the case of nonslaveholding Cherokees, less than 4 percent were capable of reading English, but 18 percent could read Cherokee.[22] Literacy in English clearly gave the slaveholders a tremendous advantage at a time when troubles with the whites were mounting.

According to the Census of 1835 the slaveholders cultivated more acres, produced more corn, and owned most of the nascent

117

industries in the Nation. Slaveholders each farmed an average of seventy-five acres, which yielded an average of 1,040 bushels of corn; nonslaveholders averaged eleven acres and 141 bushels of corn. The slaveholder produced more than he could use himself, and the profit made by the sale of the surplus gave him capital to invest in various enterprises. The 75 percent of the mills and the 42 percent of the ferries owned by slaveholders represented these kinds of investments.[23]

The image evoked by a discussion of wealthy southern planters is popularly one of moonlight, magnolias, white columns, and hundreds — even thousands — of slaves. The moon probably shone as bright and the magnolias smelled as sweet in the Cherokee Nation as anywhere else in the South, and a few mansions with white columns dotted the landscape, but no one in the Nation owned vast numbers of slaves. Joseph Vann had 110 slaves in 1835, but only 2 other planters held the title to more than 50 slaves. Of the 207 slaveholders, 168, or 83 percent, owned fewer than 10 slaves.[24] Even the large slaveholders lacked the trappings of wealth generally associated with white planters. George Waters, who owned 100 slaves, lived in a hewed log house which assessors valued at $250 after removal. Waters' loss, one of the largest in the Nation, totaled only $7,346.50 and included items such as seven "negro cabins," a smokehouse, cribs, fencing, cow pens, a millhouse, and a ferry.[25]

The number of slaves did not necessarily indicate the financial worth of Cherokees. Samuel Mays, the master of 5 slaves, lived in a house appraised at $700 and owned several farms with houses, a fishery, and a ferry valued at $11,935. John Ross, David Vann, and John Ridge owned 19, 13, and 21 slaves respectively and possessed estates that were fairly typical of the large slaveholders. The white men lived in two-story weatherboarded houses with brick chimneys and glass windows and had lumber houses, loom houses, improved fields, orchards, smith shops, mills, and ferries.[26]

Although the small slaveholders owned the same kinds of improvements that the large slaveholders enjoyed, their houses were simpler, farms and buildings less numerous, and nonagricultural assets fewer. Edward Adair lost an estate valued at $2,292 which included a house worth $700, a barn, separate kitchen, smoke-house, a house for his seven slaves, orchards, and a grape arbor. Poorer—and perhaps more typical of small slaveholders—were Green Fox Baldridge and Watie. Watie's loss amounted to $477. He owned a double cabin with two chimneys and a small house for his two slaves, as well as a smokehouse, stable, corncrib, two fields, and fruit trees. Baldridge's slave must have lived in the loft of his master's one-room cabin, because the Baldridge appraisal did not list a "negro house." The $250 valuation of his estate included a kitchen, crib, two stables, two fields, a springhouse, and fruit trees.[27]

The material possessions of Cherokee planters give us a clue about how they lived but provide little insight into their thinking concerning either the institution of slavery, their bondsmen as human beings, or themselves as masters. Although a newspaper does not necessarily reflect the views of its readers, the ideas which a newspaper presents shape, in part, the thinking of its readers. For this reason, the articles published in the *Cherokee Phoenix and Indian Advocate* under the editorship of a slave-holder suggest how at least some Cherokees felt about slavery.

The *Phoenix* frequently addressed itself to the question of the international slave trade and came out in solid opposition to its continuation. The newspaper exposed the techniques employed by traders to evade existing laws and vehemently condemned them.[28] One article, entitled "A Scene in Africa" and reprinted from the American Colonization Society's *African Repository,* vividly protrayed the cruelty of the capture of slaves in Africa and their transportation to the New World: "Here every day for centuries, has the human body been bound in chains, the ties of kind fellowship, of nature's strongest affection, ruthlessly sundered, and hope which smiles in death, made to perish by living agony. . . . My God! who can describe the miseries of those crowded to death in the dungeons of a slave ship?"[29] Articles lamenting the condition of slaves after they arrived in this hemisphere also appeared: "Thus it seems that to only one port in the Brazils, and in the course of two years, 77,350 human beings were transported from their own country and placed in a situation as debasing to

119

the human mind, and infinitely worse as regards physical sufferings, than the ordinary condition of the brute creation."[30]

The *Phoenix* concerned itself with the matter of slavery in the District of Columbia not by taking a direct stand, but by reprinting resolutions introduced and memorials presented to Congress for the gradual abolition of slavery in the capital of the United States. The editor of the *Phoenix* seemed to favor gradual, compensated abolition and voluntary manumission everywhere, and a notice that William Brown, a Tennessee judge, had freed his fifteen slaves in his will offered a subtle hint to Cherokee slaveholders.[31]

Any mild disapproval of slavery voiced by Cherokees should not be construed to mean that they espoused a theory of racial equality. Whites had long assured native Americans that they were simply savage versions of themselves and that Indians did not resemble Africans in the least.[32] Indians responded to this argument by adopting the racism of the whites. As early as 1793 Cherokees expressed racial hostility. Little Turkey, in a letter to Governor Blount of Tennessee, described the Spaniards as "lying, deceitful, treacherous people, and . . . not real white people, and what few I have seen of them looked like mulattoes, and I would never have anything to say to them."[33] When the Cherokees founded their republic in 1828, they excluded blacks from participation in the government. The founding fathers granted all adult males access to the ballot box except "negroes, and descendants of white and Indian men by negro women, who may have been set free." The Constitution restricted office-holding to those untainted by African ancestry: "No person who is of negro or mulatto parentage, either by the father or mother side [*sic*], shall be eligible to hold any office or trust under this Government."[34] The Cherokees sought to discourage free blacks from moving into the Nation and enacted a statute warning "that all free negroes coming into the Cherokee Nation under any pretense whatsoever, shall be viewed and treated, in every respect as intruders, and shall not be allowed to reside in the Cherokee Nation without a permit."[35]

As Cherokees gradually adopted plantation slavery, they acquired the notion that marrying blacks was not the proper thing to do. This attitude manifested itself in the aforementioned law forbidding whites or Indians to marry slaves or to free slaves for the purpose of matrimony.[36] The legislature did not see fit, however, to extend the law to cover marriage with free blacks. Furthermore, people evaded the law and the Council gave dispensations to those who did so.[37] The Census of 1835 confirms that a small group in the Nation readily admitted having African ancestry.

Although no Cherokees sent their freed slaves to Africa, the colonization movement must have had many supporters in the Nation, because endorsements of colonization appeared frequently in the *Phoenix*. One article expressed the hope that "the exile, sufferings, and degradation of the Africans, may be succeeded by their return, felicity and honor." The paper noted approvingly that the Kentucky Assembly had passed a resolution favoring colonization and that Virginians had organized a state colonization society. The *Phoenix* closely followed the activities of the American Colonization Society. The obituary of "Mr. Ashmum, the friend of Africa & late agent of the American Colonization Society," was reprinted from the *New Haven Journal,* and the *Phoenix* happily announced the appointment of Ashmum's successor. The paper noted the society's success in recruiting colonists for Liberia and reported on the arrival of repatriated Africans.[38]

Cherokee planters allowed their slaves to establish the African Benevolent Society, affiliated with the American Colonization Society. William Chamberlain, a missionary of the American Board of Commissioners for Foreign Missions at Willstown who supervised the founding and operation of the slave association, reported to the national office that the society was "composed entirely of Slaves having Cherokee masters" who met "on the evening of the first Monday in each month to pray for the blessing of God on the colony at Liberia and on the ACS." The slaves anticipated "making out enough to carry one emigrant to Liberia" but never realized their goal. The members of the Wills Valley African Benevolent Society made remittances to the national treasurer in 1830 and again in 1831 of twelve and eight dollars respectively. The contribution in 1831 would have been more substantial, according to Chamberlain, but "some busy persons succeeded in prejudicing

121

many of the members against the object and in persuading them to spend their money another way."[39]

The African Benevolent Society, as well as several other institutions, gave slaves in the Cherokee Nation an opportunity for an organized social existence apart from the plantation. Missionaries in the Nation tirelessly ministered to the slaves and found more converts among the bondsmen than they did among their masters. The Moravians, preceding other denominations, located their mission close to the Springplace home of James Vann, the largest slaveholder in the Nation. Although Vann was infamous for his drinking bouts and disdain for religion, he offered the missionaries assistance in building a school and sent one of his slaves to help with the heavy labor. The missionaries held their first service for slaves on Vann's plantation; also, since some of Vann's Negroes usually stayed around the mission premises every night, the missionaries resolved to read aloud something instructive in their hearing.[40] The Moravians permitted no segregation of races at the church services, but the Cherokees probably desired none, since masters and slaves often enjoyed social events together. When no one showed up for the first Easter service at Springplace, for example, the missionaries, going in search of their congregation, found the black bondsmen and their Cherokee masters getting drunk together.[41]

The American Board followed the Moravians, but they built a far more extensive network of schools and churches throughout the Nation than did their predecessors. American Board missionaries welcomed into the church "people of color, who give satisfactory evidence, that within a few months past, they have been converted to God." Worship services were not segregated: "On the Lord's day, the sacrament of the supper was administered. A congregation of more than 100 collected of Cherokees, Africans, and some whites. . . . Five of the natives joined in the communion. . . . Two blacks also joined, one of them a freed man, the other a female slave."[42]

American Board churches held "Sabbath schools" for both black and red parishioners. Sometimes the missionaries conducted separate schools for the two races: "A Sabbath school is held in the

morning for Cherokees, and in the afternoon for the black people."
Other Sabbath school teachers reported integrated instruction: "I
have generally taught a Sabbath school for the blacks, and occasionally several adult Cherokees." Jeremiah Everts described the
success of one of the schools: "A Sabbath school for the instruction of blacks, has been kept up since last summer. The improvement which a number of them have made, is truly wonderful. A
man of thirty years, who only knew the alphabet when the school
commenced, can now read a chapter, or a psalm, very decently.
A boy of fifteen, who did not know a single letter, can now read
very well in the Testament. Several others have begun to read the
Bible."[43]

Cherokee planters seemed to have had no objection to their
slaves receiving instruction in either religion or in reading. Some
masters actively encouraged and aided the work of the missionaries among their slaves. The Ridge, upon hearing from a missionary how the slave traders captured Africans and transported
them to America to be sold, assembled his slaves so the minister
could preach to them.[44] Masters allowed their bondsmen to travel
long distances, apparently without supervision, to attend church
and school. One missionary reported that, of the blacks in the
Sabbath school, "the greater part come six miles or more to meeting; some fifteen or twenty on foot; and none less than two miles
and a half."[45]

Cherokees also permitted the children of their slaves to attend
the mission schools along with their own children. A problem
arose, however, when the state of Georgia, whose slave code prohibited the instruction of blacks, began trying to enforce its laws
in the Cherokee Nation. In 1832 the Georgia state guard invaded
the classroom of Sophia Sawyer, a missionary of the American
Board, and informed her that she was in violation of the law because two black children sat in her class. The guard threatened to
have her arraigned at the next term of court if the instruction of
the children did not cease.[46]

Not only did Cherokee masters grant their slaves considerable
freedom to participate in social, religious, and educational activities, but they probably treated their slaves much better, on the

average, than did their white counterparts. The one obvious exception to this generalization was James Vann. Vann was good and generous when sober, but his frequent and immoderate consumption of alcohol aroused great cruelty. Vann's slaves reacted to the abuse he gave them in kind. On one occasion a group of slaves attacked their master and robbed him.[47] Vann responded by burning one of the participants alive; upon hearing that another slave was plotting against his life, Vann shot him on the spot.[48] However, Vann's brutality and his slaves' insubordination appear exceptional. The absence of advertisements for runaway slaves in the *Phoenix* probably indicates that slaves did not become so dissatisfied that they ran away.[49] One slave who had belonged to a Cherokee and was sold to a white man from whom she escaped insisted that she belonged to a nonexistent Cherokee in the hope that someone in the Nation would redeem her.[50]

Although not as harsh among Cherokees as among whites, slavery constituted a form of property, and Cherokee law protected property rights. The court often ordered slaves sold in satisfaction of debts and judgments and in settlement of estates. The *Phoenix* carried announcements of approaching sales. According to one notice, the marshal, to satisfy a judgment against James Petit, would sell on a certain date corn, fodder, cattle, and also a slave named Gabriel, priced at $500. In another advertisement the *Phoenix* listed Joe, his wife and child, corn, fodder, horses, cattle, hogs, oxen, wagon, loom, rifle, and furniture as the items to be sold in the execution of a will.[51]

Thus the Cherokees faced a perplexing dilemma. Slaves were property and a form of wealth, but traditional Cherokee economics shunned both the accumulation of property and the acquisition of wealth and ridiculed the production of anything in excess of basic needs. A plantation system using slave labor necessitated some sort of centralized control and police power, but traditional Cherokee government bordered on anarchy, and enforcement of behavioral rules was strictly an individual or family matter. Although Cherokees recognized only human beings and possessed no sense of racial identity before extensive contact with whites, the enslavement of one race by another inevitably produced a feeling of racial superiority among the masters. Cherokee culture, in an effort to resolve this dilemma, modified the system of bondage adopted from the whites, and the result seems to have been the amelioration of many of the harsher aspects of plantation slavery. Absolute, indisputable proof of this theory is not available because the only people truly capable of giving us this proof, the slaves themselves, left no accounts. However, Henry Bibb, who belonged to a Cherokee after removal to Oklahoma, resolutely affirmed, "If I must be a slave, I had by far, rather be a slave to an Indian, than to a white man."[52]

NOTES

1. Cherokees captured the Frenchman Antoine Bonnefoy in 1741, and a clan elected to adopt him. His account in Williams, ed., *Early Travels*, 150-55, includes a description of the adoption ceremony. Bonnefoy shared a cabin with one of his kinsmen and reported, "I had the same treatment as himself." David Menzies, not so fortunate, experienced the horror of being rejected by a clan. He survived torture and published "A True Relation of the Unheard-of Sufferings of David Menzies, Surgeon, Among the Cherokees, and of His Surprising Deliverance," *Royal Magazine* (July 1761), 27-29.

2. Timberlake, *Memoirs*, 68: Benjamin Hawkins, *Letters of Benjamin Hawkins, 1796–1806*, vol. 9, Georgia Historical Soc. Collections (Savannah: *Morning News*, 1916), 21; William Bartram, "Observations on the Creek and Cherokee Indians, 1789," *Transactions of the American Ethnological Society* 3 (1853), 30-32. Cherokee myths reflect a sexual division of labor. In "Kana'ti and Selu; Origin of Corn and Game," Kana'ti, the first man, is responsible for the presence of game in the world and Selu, the first woman, is the source of corn. James Mooney, *Myths of the Cherokee and Sacred Formulas of the Cherokees* (*19th* and *7th Annual Reports* of the Bureau of American Ethnology; rpt. ed. Nashville: Charles Elder, 1972), 242-48.

Several sources note the absence of a profit motive and the Cherokees' disdain for material wealth. John Brickell, *The Natural History of North Carolina* (Dublin, 1737; rpt. Louisville, Ky.: Lost Cause Press, 1960), 289; Adair, *History*, 462; John Lawson, *A New Voyage to Carolina*, ed. Hugh T. Lefler (Chapel Hill: Univ. of North Carolina Press, 1967; original ed., 1709), 206. In spite of attempts by historians such as U.B. Phillips and Eugene D. Genovses to demonstrate that slavery was primarily a paternalistic social system, evidence indicates that southern planters were successful capitalists. Lewis C. Gray, *History of Agriculture in the Southern U. S. to 1860*, 2 vols. (New York: P. Smith, 1933, 1941); Alfred H. Conrad and John R. Meyer, *The Economics of Slavery* (Chicago: Aldine, 1964); Robert William Fogel and Stanley E. Engerman, *Time on the Cross: The Economics of American Negro Slavery*, 2 vols. (Boston: Little,

1974). The best study of white racism during this period is Winthrop Jordan, *White over Black: American Attitudes Toward the Negro, 1550–1812* (Chapel Hill: Univ. of North Carolina Press, 1968).

3. The major work dealing with the southern Indian trade is Verner W. Crane, *The Southern Frontier, 1670–1762* (Durham: Duke Univ. Press, 1928). Also useful are David H. Corkran, *The Cherokee Frontier: Conflict and Survival, 1740–1762* (Norman: Univ. of Oklahoma Press, 1962), and John Richard Alden, *John Stuart and the Southern Colonial Frontier, 1774–1775* (Ann Arbor: Univ. of Michigan Press, 1944). Almon W. Lauber, *Indian Slavery in Colonial Times Within the Present Limits of the United States* (New York: Columbia Univ. Press, 1913) contains valuable information but ignores the effects of the use of Indian slaves by whites on native societies.

4. Adair, *History,* 407-9, 415-16; Hewatt, *Historical Account,* 69. An outstanding work that clearly illuminates the role of revenge is Reid, *Law of Blood.*

5. Adair, *History,* 407.

6. *Ibid.,* 443, 463.

7. George Washington to the Cherokee Nation, 1796, printed in the *Cherokee Phoenix,* Mar. 20, 1828.

8. Hawkins, *Letters,* 10, 21-24.

9. Elias Boudinot, *An Address to the Whites* (Philadelphia: W.F. Geddes, 1826), 8. Boudinot became the first and most distinguished editor of the *Phoenix.* He devoted much of his time and literary skill to trying to convince whites that the Cherokees were "civilized."

10. Reid, *Law of Blood,* 140-41.

11. Hewatt, *Historical Account,* I, 67.

12. Reid, *Law of Blood,* 133; *Phoenix,* 6, May 21, 1828, Nov. 26, 1828.

13. Traditionally, slaves or war captives, as well as other forms of chattel property, were owned by individuals and not by lineages nor the tribe as a whole. Lieutenant Timberlake recorded that prisoners taken in war became the property of their captors. In 1760, when Cherokees attacked the garrison evacuating Ford Loudoun during the Cherokee War and captured Capt. John Stuart, Attakullakulla, a pro-English chief who considered Stuart to be a particular friend, "hastened to the fort, and purchased him from the Indian that took him, giving him his rifle, clothes, and all he could command." Bonnefoy referred to the warrior who seized him as "the savage to whom I belonged" and "my master," and when Bonnefoy's master sold him, it was a transaction between individuals. Timberlake, *Memoirs,* 111; Hewatt, *Historical Account,* II, 239; Bartram, *Travels,* 151-52.

14. *Phoenix,* Mar. 6, 1828; Cherokee Census of 1835, National Archives, Washington, D.C.; microfilm, Federal Records Bureau, East Point, Ga. Of the signers, over half owned slaves when the Census was taken in 1835.

15. Adair, *History,* 459-60, 462.

16. Hewatt, *Historical Account,* II, 4. This was absurd, of course, because Moytoy could only be responsible for his own actions. For a study of the process of centralization, see Gearing, *Priest and Warriors.*

17. *Phoenix,* Apr. 10, 1828.

18. *Ibid.,* Apr. 10, 24, 1828.

19. Kenneth M. Stampp, *The Peculiar Institution: Slavery in the Ante-Bellum South* (New York: Knopf, 1956), 192-236.

20. *Phoenix,* Apr. 10, 24, 1828.

21. Reid, *Law of Blood,* 192, 193; Lawson, *New Voyage,* 210.

22. Census of 1835.

23. *Ibid.*

24. *Ibid.* Anyone owning more than 10 slaves was considered a large slaveholder.

25. *Ibid.* Original Valuations of Various Counties in Georgia, National Archives, Washington, D.C.; microfilm, Georgia Dept. of Archives, Atlanta.

26. Valuations. Assessors valued Ross' estate at $10,000, Vann's at $7,075.40, and Ridge's at $6,532.55.

27. Valuations.

28. *Phoenix,* July 15, Feb. 4, 1829.

29. *Ibid.,* Mar. 6, 1828.

30. *Ibid.,* Sept. 17, 1828.

31. *Ibid.,* Mar. 6, Jan. 28, 1828; Nov. 13, 1830.

32. Thomas Jefferson, *Notes on the State of Virginia* (Boston: Lilly and Wait, 1832), 59-70; Jordan, *White over Black,* 89-91, 475-81.

33. U.S. Congress, *American State Papers,* Class II: *Indian Affairs,* 2 vols. (Washington, D.C.: Gales and Seaton), I, 461.

34. *Phoenix,* Feb. 21, 1828.

35. *Ibid.,* Apr. 13, 1828.

36. *Ibid.,* Apr. 24, 1828.

37. In 1824, for example, Shoe Boots petitioned the National Council to recognize the legitimacy and citizenship of his three children by a black slave. The Council granted the request on the condition that "Capt. Shoe Boots cease begetting any more children by his said slave woman." Captain Shoe Boots to the National Council, Oct. 20, 1824 (certified copy from the *Book of Record,* 1837), Cherokee Nation Papers, Univ. of Oklahoma, Norman.

38. *Phoenix,* Mar. 6, 1828; Feb. 25, Mar. 25, 1829; Sept. 28, Oct. 8, July 21, 1828; Jan. 28, 1829.

39. William Chamberlain to R.R. Gurley, Mar. 19, 1830; June 7, 1831; *American Colonization Soc. Records,* ser., vols. 20, 30, Library of Congress, Washington, D.C.; microfilm, Univ. of Georgia Library, Athens.

40. Edmund Schwarze, *History of the Moravian Missions among Southern Indian Tribes of the United States* (Bethlehem, Pa.: Times Publ., 1923), 63, 70-71, 79.

41. Clemen de Baillou, "Diaries of the Moravian Brotherhood at the Cherokee Mission in Spring Place, Georgia, for the Years 1800-1804." *Georgia Historical Quarterly* 54 (1970), 573.

42. American Board of Commissioners of Foreign Missions, *First Ten Annual Reports of the American Board of Commissioners for Foreign Missions, with Other Documents of the Board* (Boston: 1834), 194-96, 284.

43. *Ibid.,* 36, 193, 287.

44. Marion L. Starkey, *The Cherokee Nation* (New York: Russell and Russell, 1972, original ed., 1946), 56.

45. American Board, *Reports,* 93.

46. *Phoenix*, Mar. 17, 1832.

47. Adelaide L. Fries, *Records of the Moravians in North Carolina*, 7 vols. (Raleigh: Edwards and Broughton, 1947), VI, 2799.

48. Schwarze, *Moravian Missions*, 81.

49. The *Phoenix* carried advertisements placed by whites for runaways and by Cherokees for stray horses and cows, wives who had deserted their husbands, and stolen slaves; but in over six years of publication not one notice for an escaped slave belonging to a Cherokee appeared. The absence of advertisements for runaways in the *Phoenix* stands in marked contrast to the numerous such notices in white periodicals. For an indication of the number and scope of the latter, see Gerald W. Mullin, *Flight and Rebellion: Slave Resistance in Eighteenth-Century Virginia* (New York: Oxford Univ. Press, 1972), 39.

50. *Phoenix*, Dec. 31, 1831; Feb. 4, 1832.

51. *Ibid.*, Nov. 4, 1829; Dec. 11, 1830.

52. Henry Bibb, "Narrative of the Life and Adventures of Henry Bibb, an American Slave," in *Puttin' on Ole Massa*, ed. Gilbert Osofsky (New York: Harper, 1969), 141. WPA interviews of old slaves tend to give the same view of a milder slavery under Indian masters: George P. Rawick, ed., *The American Slave: A Composite Autobiography*, 18 vols. (Westport, Conn.: Greenwood, 1972).

Chaos in the Indian Country:
The Cherokee Nation, 1828-35

Kenneth Penn Davis

The major parts of the Cherokee removal saga are well known. After years of successive treaties ceding Indian lands to the United States, four events combined in 1828 to bring the question of removal into open and heated debate. First, the Indians began to publish their own newspaper, the *Cherokee Phoenix*. This was followed by the discovery of gold within the Indian Nation and by the election of Andrew Jackson as president. Spurred by these events, the state of Georgia passed laws incorporating the Cherokee lands as counties of the state.

The publication of the *Phoenix* brought to public attention the establishment in the previous year of a Cherokee republic, based on a written constitution. Pressed by the land hunger of its citizens, Georgia had continually urged the federal government to remove the Indians, a process the state officials felt had been promised in 1802 when Georgia gave up her claims to western lands. The idea of an organized Indian republic within the state boundaries enraged many Georgians. The discovery of gold intensified this desire for the Cherokee land. Since Andrew Jackson was known to favor removal, his election was the final encouragement for Georgia to pass laws appropriating the Indian land and providing for lotteries to distribute it to state citizens. Now the die was cast and a ten-year struggle began.

In 1830 the United States Congress passed an Indian removal bill which many felt Jackson would use against the Cherokees, even though it did not specifically sanction forced movement of the red men. The case finally found its way to the Supreme Court in the well-known *Worcester* v. *Georgia* suit. True to form, Jack-

129

son failed to enforce the decision, which was favorable to the Indians. Eventually the federal government signed the Treaty of New Echota with a minority faction of the tribe in December 1835. Though final removal was not forced until 1838, in the end the tribe was unable to change the government's decision or to resist its pressure.[1] This part of the removal controversy is well known. But while maneuvering went on between the various governments, what was happening within the Cherokee Nation?

The period from 1828 to 1835 in the Cherokee Nation was an era of legal moves by federal and state governments, of gold rush and land boom, of treaty proposals and counterproposals, of delegations to Indian councils—in short, a time of confusion. It was no less a confusing and desperate period for the Cherokee people themselves. The federal Indian agents were at this time attempting to influence the Cherokees to remove. Various agents of state governments, individual white settlers, and gold miners all moved into the Nation almost at will to pursue assigned tasks or selfish motives. As the tribe polarized around John Ross, the elected chief, and Major Ridge, who favored removal, the individual Indians became more and more confused about their rights and probable future.

The Cherokee National Council quickly reacted against the extension of the Georgia laws. Individual members of the tribe were forbidden to enroll for emigration westward (as allowed under the 1828 treaty). Those enrolling lost all privileges as Cherokee citizens. In addition, any person who negotiated to sell was subject to the death penalty.[2]

It did not take long for troubles to develop between the Indians and the whites who were entering the Nation. In early February 1830 Governor Gilmer was informed that a number of Indians had attacked and burned houses occupied by whites who had recently moved into the territory. The whites had taken over improvements abandoned by Cherokees who, despite the new laws of the Nation, had moved west of the Mississippi. About twenty-five houses were burned by the raiding party, which was reportedly organized by Chief John Ross. In retaliation the whites captured several of the Indians, killing at least one.[3]

No doubt some of the whites involved in this altercation came into the Nation seeking gold. News from the goldfields constantly described the easy riches to be obtained, and miners continued to pour into the Indian territory. The *Cherokee Phoenix* reported early in 1830 that several hundred people were mining gold on the Hightower River. Governor Gilmer of Georgia, who felt that neither whites nor Indians had the right to use the mineral resources of the state, reacted by ordering all gold mining halted. As a result of the chaos in the goldfields, Indian agent Hugh Montgomery requested the aid of federal troops. The soldiers, under a Captain Brady, ordered all mining to cease. Indian miners refused, declaring they were working on their own land. Finally, in October 1830 Gilmer asked President Jackson to remove the troops. The Georgia legislature would soon be in session, and the governor felt the state lawmakers could handle the situation without federal troops. Captain Brady was ordered to withdraw his men on November 8.[4]

Citizens of the Cherokee Nation, as well as its leaders, spoke out against the state of Georgia. Residents of the Aquohee district of the Nation issued a strongly worded protest which was reprinted in *Niles' Register*. In addition to challenging the extension of Georgia laws, these Cherokees attacked efforts by the state to bribe Indian citizens.[5]

Throughout this time of confusion in the Cherokee Nation, federal agents attempted to carry out the orders and wishes of the chief executive and the War Department. Since Jackson and his officials were not always sure how they wanted to handle the Cherokee situation, the task of the agents was never easy. The job was further complicated both by the demands of the various state officials and by the problems of individual Cherokees. The agents did, however, make an effort to fulfill their duties and encourage the Indians to remove.

Despite the efforts of federal officials, not much was accomplished in 1830 toward enrolling Cherokees for emigration. What was done was handled by Cherokee agent Hugh Montgomery. On June 9 Thomas McKenney of the Bureau of Indian Affairs wrote Montgomery that President Jackson had decided to suspend the enrolling of emigrants in small parties, although Indians would be allowed to remove themselves. Details are lacking, but apparently some emigration did go on, for Montgomery wrote on several occasions during the following summer concerning payment for improvements and the buying of rifles for emigrants. On November 18, however, Jackson ordered Secretary of War Eaton to halt all Cherokee emigration until the whole tribe was ready to remove.[6] This order from the president was probably based in part on a negative report on removal received by the secretary of war. One person who had traveled through the Nation stated that Ross and the General Council were not interested in removal.[7]

The year 1831 opened in the Cherokee Nation much as had the previous year, with reports of white intrusions. According to the *Cherokee Phoenix* of January 8, a company of twenty-five unidentified men had entered the Nation to arrest some Cherokees, including one Moses Beanstick. In the course of their journey they chased and shot at two Indian boys. Finally, instead of arresting Moses, they arrested his brother Joseph Beanstick, for whom they had no warrant. Despite this illegality, the men carried Joseph with them to Carroll County.[8]

The action of white intruders and Georgia officials also adversely affected the publication of the Cherokee newspaper. In February the editor, Elias Boudinot, apologized for the small size of the paper. Since Georgia laws allowed only those white men into the Nation who were loyal to that state, the *Phoenix* was having a hard time finding printers. Later in the year Boudinot was called before Colonel Nelson of the Georgia state guard and told to quit printing material which was slanderous to the state of Georgia. Boudinot was threatened with a whipping if he refused, according to the *Phoenix*.[9]

In addition to this harassment from Georgians, the Cherokees were pressured by federal officials who were also using every device to discourage them. In the summer of 1830 President Jackson ordered Indian agent Montgomery to cease paying the annuity to the Cherokee leaders. The annuity, granted by earlier treaties with the Cherokees, was not to be paid directly to each individual of the tribe because Jackson seemingly wanted to avoid giving the leaders use of the annuity money. The Cherokees protested this ruling and ordered John Martin, treasurer of the Nation, to apply for the money. According to the Cherokee figures, each member of the tribe would receive a grand total of fifty cents if the money were divided among individuals. When the Indians refused to take the annuities on an individual basis, the money was deposited in a Tennessee bank, to be released only when the tribe agreed to apportion it out to all its members.[10] This annuity controversy continued over the next several years.

At about the time he was changing the method of annuity payment, Jackson also reversed his stand on Cherokee emigration. At the urging of Governor Gilmer, the president ordered the enrollment lists reopened. On September 1, 1831, Benjamin F. Curry of McMinnville, Tennessee, was appointed superintendent of removal for the Cherokee Nation.

The magnitude of Curry's job was indicated in the instruction given by the secretary of war. He was placed in charge of the entire removal operation, which included enrolling the Indians, appraising their property, paying and supplying them according to the treaty specifications, and handling their transportation and subsistence for the first year after removal. The Treaty of 1828 provided that each family head enrolling for removal was to receive a rifle, a blanket, a kettle, five pounds of tobacco, and an additional blanket for each member of his family. Curry was authorized to appoint someone to handle appraisal of property improvements. Items to be appraised included buildings attached to the land and such stock as was not practical for the Indians to take with them. Payment for this property would be made when the Cherokees arrived west of the Mississippi. Although transportation and subsistence were under Curry's direction, an army officer who served as disbursing agent actually handled the money.[11]

Captain William L. McClintock was appointed in November as the first disbursing agent for the Cherokee removal. He arrived at Calhoun, Georgia, site of the Cherokee agency, on December 10, 1831. Although opposition to removal was extensive there, Curry made some progress. He enrolled 360 for removal, calculating that about one-third of these would handle their own emigration, since some of the more well-to-do Indians preferred removing themselves. As might be imagined, Curry also preferred this method.[12]

McClintock immediately set about determining the cost of items needed for removal. The pork, flour, and corn required would have to be delivered to Curry at the agency. Wagons for such transportation were available at $2.50 to $3.00 a day. For the movement west, flatboats could be rented for $50 to $60 apiece; in this respect McClintock was lucky, for he discovered sixteen government-owned flatboats already on hand. The captain found that he could rent a shallow-draft steam boat at $125 a day. By adding two keel boats to be towed behind the steamer, McClintock figured the cost would run between $150 and $160 a day, but would accommodate 500 Indians with their baggage. For those wishing to take the commutation allowance, Curry set the figure at $15.50 per person and $6.50 per horse.[13]

Curry informed McClintock to prepare for the removal of 500 emigrants by the middle of January 1832. The latter estimated that rations could be provided for 7½¢ each. This figure was based on flour costing $4.50 to $5.00 a barrel and pork costing $7.00 to $7.50 a barrel. He also found a cheaper steamboat — one which would carry the Indians for $1.50 a head plus 20¢ per 100 pounds of baggage.[14]

The first removal was planned for the spring of 1832. From the beginning, however, there were difficulties. In January McClintock reported trouble getting supplies because items were not readily available. Curry, in the meantime, had problems with some of his personnel. He had hired David Reese and Reuben Thornton as enrolling agents, but they turned out to be singularly useless. Curry thought, because they were Georgians, they did not command the confidence of the Indians. Both men resigned by mid-February, and Curry received authorization for his appraisers, J.M.C. Montgomery and Jacob Scudder, to help with the enrolling.[15]

In addition to supply and personnel problems, Curry also experienced opposition from the Indians. He commented in a letter to Secretary of War Lewis Cass that the biggest opposition to removal came from "reservees." These Indians had accepted reservations under the Treaty of 1819 and were thus supposedly citizens of the United States. Curry asked if they could not be removed as intruders in the Cherokee Nation.[16] The superintendent of removal was no doubt technically correct that the reservees had given up their rights as Cherokee citizens. It seems likely, however, that the Indians never understood this interpretation of the white man's treaties. Since they had a very hazy understanding of individual land ownership anyway, and since their reservations were probably within, or closely adjacent to, the Cherokee Nation, it seems likely that the reservees had never intended to give up their Cherokee citizenship but only sought confirmed ownership of their land. The question of the status of reservees was to plague Curry for several years.

Federal agents also had to contend with the confusion in the Cherokee Nation resulting from various Georgia laws. In March 1832 the *Cherokee Phoenix* reported the Nation was overrun with Georgia surveyors who were carrying out the stipulations of the state lottery laws. The *Phoenix* editor estimated that each of ninety-two districts was being measured by a company of surveyors; a total of about five hundred and fifty men were involved. The improvement rental law also proved to be a problem for the Cherokees. In one instance an Indian widow was dispossessed of her land and property by a white who had rented the supposedly abandoned improvement. As it turned out, one of her sons had emigrated earlier and had given up rights to the property without permission from anyone else in his family.[17]

Despite difficulties of this nature, Benjamin Curry finally began to collect the Indians for the first emigration by mid-March 1832. He reported unforeseen delays resulting from serving bail warrants and paying off debts of the emigrants before movement could begin. Curry found it necessary to build cheap shelters at the agency to provide protection from the weather for the emigrants while they all gathered.[18]

On April 10, 1832, Superintendent Curry finally got the first removal party under way. The 500 emigrants included 180 full bloods and mixed breeds, approximately the same number of black slaves, and 50 whites — undoubtedly men who had married into the tribe. The group departed in nine flatboats and arrived at Florence, Alabama, on April 18. Three days later Curry reported, without explanation, that his party had been reduced to only 380 members. The group embarked on the steamboat *Tom Yeatman,* navigated the Tennessee by April 23, then following the Ohio, Mississippi, and Arkansas rivers westward, arrived at the western Cherokee agency by mid-May. Immediately there were fresh problems.[19]

Curry had promised the emigrants that they would be paid for their abandoned improvements once they arrived in the West, but on arrival they found that the western agent, George Vashon, knew nothing of the payment. The Cherokees were understandably upset. Immediately both Vashon and Curry wrote their superiors, hoping to clear up the matter. There was also a problem in regard to the Negro slaves. Because Curry had originally viewed slaves as property, he had not included them in the estimates of subsistence to be provided for the first year in the new land. He discussed the problem with Vashon, and they agreed to ask for subsistence for the slaves. Even with these problems, Curry felt the removal trip had been a success and heartily recommended the water route west as the easiest and cheapest mode of transportation.[20]

Curry's experience was probably partly responsible for new regulations which were issued on May 15, 1832, to agents handling emigration for the various tribes. All supervision of removal was taken over by the office of the commissary general of subsistence. Special agents like Curry were to supervise removal of specific tribes, but each agent had to receive higher approval of the people he employed, and the agents had to make weekly reports on their operations. Disbursements were still to be handled by an assigned army officer. Transportation methods were specifically detailed; baggage was to be limited to 1,500 pounds for each fifty emigrants. Each emigrating party had to be certified by two copies of a master roll, one of which went to the War Department, the other to the agent in the western territory. Supplies were to be contracted for, and the quality of goods was stipulated. Provisions were likewise detailed. The daily ration was one and one-fourth pound of fresh beef or pork (or three-fourths pound of salt pork) and three-fourths quart of corn (or corn meal, or one pound of wheat flour) to each person, and four quarts of salt for every one hundred persons. Property appraisal had to include the amount and kind of land cleared, buildings erected, and stock held. Stock was to be branded when received, to prevent fraud. Each detachment moving West had to be accompanied by a conducting officer who was to keep a journal of the day-to-day progress of the journey. Officials authorized to handle the removal were listed; their pay, from that of a special agent at $2,000 a year to that of interpreters at $2.50 a day, was stipulated.[21]

By the time Curry returned to the Eastern Cherokees in June 1832, however, federal officials were less interested in removal procedures than they were in the Cherokee Council to be held in July. Elisha Chester had been appointed representative of the United States government to carry removal treaty proposals to the Council. Enthusiastic in carrying out his duties, Chester traveled throughout much of the Nation before the Council convened, attempting to inform tribesmen and tribal leaders alike of the necessity and advantage of removal. Chester's letters even inquired into the possibility of removal to Oregon country or to some other area beyond the Rocky Mountains. Since at that time the United States had only an indefinite claim to the Pacific coast territory, his over-enthusiasm seems almost childish in retrospect. He was undoubtedly disappointed that the Cherokees were not generally interested in removing.[22]

Chester placed part of the blame for the Indians' reluctance to remove on the actions of General Daniel Newnan. Congressman Newnan, like many fellow Georgian officials, apparently felt impelled to meddle in the Cherokee controversy. In April he contacted members of the Eastern Cherokee delegation in Washington and proposed a meeting with federal commissioners. The Newnan letters, later printed in the *Cherokee Phoenix,* led many Indians to believe the government was trying to conclude a secret treaty with a few unscrupulous Cherokees.[23] In part, Chester was

137

no doubt right about Newnan's adverse effect on Cherokee affairs. There were, nevertheless, other forces at work among the Indians.

According to reports by various officials within the Nation, three factors were responsible for the slowing of removal in the summer of 1832. First, most Cherokees wanted to await developments at the July Council meeting. A second factor was the *Worcester* Supreme Court case. Although the decision favorable to the Indians had been handed down in February, in June there was as yet no indication that it would not be enforced. The final important influence against removal at this time was the upcoming presidential election. It was suggested by many that Jackson would be defeated by Henry Clay, who would then provide justice and relief for the Cherokees.[24] Thus the Cherokees bided their time, hoping for a more favorable turn of events.

Therefore, as the time for the Cherokee Council approached, the attention directed to the meeting prevented any success at removal procedures, and appraisal of property and enrollment of emigrants were suspended until the Council was over.[25] Finally, on July 23 the assembly met and predictably voted against removal. Since the Indians were not interested in removal, Chester suggested that emigration be halted. He felt it drained off those Cherokees most favoring a removal treaty. Superintendent Curry disagreed, however, arguing that emigration was gradually moving the Indian population to the West. He also urged once more the removal of the reservees. Chester, unwilling to give up, continued his quest for a removal treaty. He informed Acting Secretary of War John Robb that he would remain in Georgia with a view to attending the October Cherokee Council meeting.[26]

Apparently Chester's approach prevailed. Even though a few Cherokees continued to remove themselves, Benjamin Curry called a temporary halt to the enrollment process in early September, believing that only the reelection of Andrew Jackson would again encourage removal. His superiors seem to have agreed, for later that month Curry received instructions to stop enrollment until further notice.[27]

138

Lack of interest in removal was not the only problem the federal officials had to face in the summer of 1832. During most of June and early July Indian agent Hugh Montgomery, together with United States troops under General Armistead, traveled throughout the Nation, ordering out gold miners and other intruders. Other white men were reported to be promising the Cherokees relief from both the state and federal governments, if the Indians would rent their gold mines.[28]

At the same time that the government agents were having difficulty organizing an orderly removal, the Indians began to disagree among themselves. One of the most noteworthy events of the summer was the resignation of Elias Boudinot as editor of the *Cherokee Phoenix*. Although initially opposed to removal, personally, Boudinot felt that the paper ought to air both sides of the controversy. He finally concluded that removal was inevitable and urged negotiation of the best treaty possible. In the meantime, John Ross, who was attempting to unite the Nation against removal, insisted that the *Phoenix* should speak out solely for the rights of the Indians. As a result, Boudinot resigned, believing he could not continue to espouse the policy of Ross and the other leaders. The former editor soon became a leader in the proremoval faction, while Elijah Hicks, Ross' brother-in-law, was subsequently appointed editor of the *Phoenix*.[29]

As autumn approached, the Cherokee leaders prepared for their October Council meeting, while the federal officials dealt with the few remaining emigrants who had signed up to move before the enrollment was halted. On September 24, 1832, Lieutenant F.L. Dancy, the new disbursing agent, arrived in the Nation.[30] A month later he reported removal had been progressing slowly in anticipation of action by the October Council. Chester attended the Council but had little success in persuading the leaders to remove. Quite to the contrary, the Council elected its leaders *ad infinitum* in case future elections would be prohibited or invalidated by new Georgia laws. Ross was appointed head of a delegation to proceed to Washington for another attempt to secure the rights of the Nation.[31]

With the Indians' attention once again focused on the proposed Washington trip of the Cherokee delegation, federal officials did not succeed in processing many of them for removal. Lieutenant Dancy had used up all the funds assigned to him and had departed for Washington by December 10. Superintendent Curry complained that, since there were still a few Indians who had signed up to remove, he needed additional funds. Even counting these, the 1832 immigration report listed only 628 Cherokees who had removed. A final pessimistic note was added to the year's record on December 28 when Curry reported the murder of a white family named Bowman. Several years earlier, Mr. Bowman had been witness to a murder which involved an Indian. Because the extension of Georgia laws to the Cherokee country threatened to reopen the case, apparently the Bowmans were killed to eliminate any incriminating testimony.[32]

As the new year began, violence continued to manifest itself. On January 4, 1833, the *Augusta Courier* reported a fiery confrontation between whites and Indians over some improvements in the Nation: two white families were "massacred by the enraged savages," and the Georgia state guard was in pursuit of the murderers.[33]

Such conflict was bound to occur as more and more white people pushed into the Indian Nation. The lottery had been in operation since the previous October, and whites were beginning to take possession of their property. The editor of the *Cherokee Phoenix* complained that the Nation was becoming "wedged" with settlers and land hunters.[34] In the gold diggings, the boom town of Auraria illustrated the frantic influx of whites by the fantastic growth it attained in its short history. In April 1833 the *Western Herald* reported that the town had grown to include 100 family dwellings, 18 to 20 stores, 12 to 15 law offices, 4 or 5 taverns, and a population of 1,000 people. As before, fabulous reports of riches continued to be heard.[35]

In view of difficulties within the Nation and the plan of the Ross delegation to visit Washington early in 1833, it is not surprising that Benjamin Curry did not accomplish much with regard to removal. Lieutenant William Day did arrive, however, to serve as disbursing agent for the few Indians yet to remove under terms of the old emigration list.[36]

In the meantime the Cherokee delegation arrived in Washington, where it remained from early January into March 1833 negotiating with federal officials. The delegation had little success. Secretary of War Lewis Cass offered them no new hope. Emboldened by his reelection in November, Jackson was by this time determined to give the Cherokees no advantage. The delegation once again brought up the question of annuities. Cass replied that the president had not changed his position on the annuity question and the funds would be distributed only to individual Cherokees, not to the leaders. When the Cherokee leaders suggested that the federal government might purchase the Georgia claims to the Indian Nation's lands, Cass flatly refused.[37] The delegation left Washington with little to show for their efforts.

The inevitable intrusions and protests continued in the Nation. One North Carolinian complained of whites from surrounding states destroying timber and taking gold from the Tarheel lands. The Indian commissioner again ordered Hugh Montgomery to remove intruders. In the meantime he had to deal with an Indian whose slaves had been stolen from him.[38]

As always, the approach of the spring meeting of the Cherokee General Council was accompanied by many rumors. One story claimed John Ross and other leaders had been offered a bribe by the federal officials. Curry denied this and charged that the Indian leaders were trying, through court action, to delay removal until Jackson had left office.[39] As Superintendent Curry prepared to represent the United States government at the May Council meeting, he took time to express concern over the poor and destitute of the Cherokee Nation. He sought, and obtained, permission to use annuity money to support these indigent tribesmen until such time as they could be removed.[40]

The Cherokee leaders met at Red Clay in the Indian Nation and on May 20 passed a resolution once again protesting intrusion on the rights of the Nation. Although a minority group of twenty-five issued a proremoval resolution, it was clear that the General Council had not changed any of its former views.[41]

141

The factionalism within the Nation was now clearly evident, however. As a result of the Council meeting, the government changed its policy and began to enroll those Indians who favored a removal treaty. If such a treaty should be successfully completed during the following fall or winter, then those enrolling would move with the tribe; otherwise, they would be removed in the same manner as earlier groups. This policy was designed to take advantage of, and encourage, Cherokee factionalism. One member of the proremoval faction became somewhat overbearing in his efforts to help the government. John Walker, Jr., made all sorts of wild reports and officious suggestions and took it upon himself to correspond at will with Secretary of War Cass, Elbert Herring, the Indian commissioner, and other officials. Although he encouraged removal, Walker himself would not enroll. He even had the audacity, finally, to ask to see Curry's correspondence with the Bureau of Indian Affairs. He was refused, and from this point on his activity seems to have diminished, but while it lasted it served as another illustration of the problems faced by Indian and federal officials alike as the situation in the Nation worsened.[42]

In July it was reported that two Indian women had been attacked. One of the "fortunate drawers" in the Georgia lottery had attempted to rape the women and then had whipped them both. When they presented their story to civil authorities, the women were told that it was illegal for them to testify against a white man.[43]

Despite difficulties, Curry, Montgomery, and their personnel continued to work for removal. J.M.C. Montgomery and William Davis, who had earlier been laid off, were reappointed property appraisers. This property evaluation was no small task. Thousands of such appraisals had to be made, listing every minute item which the Indians could not take west with them. A typical evaluation was that made for one William Hendrex, a mixed-blood, whose address was listed as Long Swamp, Georgia. The federal appraiser made the following assessment on Hendrex's property:

One dwelling house, $55.00, one double stable, $20.00	$75.00
Two cabins @ $20.00, two corn cribs @ $10.00 and $15.00	65.00
One other cabin @ $20.00, 4 lots @ $10.50, $3.00, $2.00, $3.00	38.50
Twenty-two apple trees @ $1.00	22.00
Ninety peach trees @ 75¢	67.50
Thirty-three acres of low ground @ $8.00 per acre	264.00
	$532.00[44]

When Lieutenant J.W. Harris, the new disbursing agent, arrived on September 21, 1833, the enrollment was proceeding and the Cherokee General Council was planning to meet again in October. Harris reported that most of the Indians would require government transportation for the fall removal. The appraisers were carrying out their job, but had been warned to beware of fraud. Reports had been received that some Indians were building new improvements merely to receive additional money on removing. Some had taken over buildings erected by whites. The appraisers were instructed to pay only for the improvements built by Indians for "bona fide use and occupation."[45]

The Cherokee General Council met at Red Clay in the Nation during the last week in October 1833. The meeting produced no new course of action, and once again a delegation led by John Ross was appointed to visit Washington. The Indian representatives were to make another attempt to get the federal government to redress the grievances of the Nation.[46]

Lewis Cass, however, remained adamant in the face of the demands by the Indians. When requested by the Cherokee leaders to release $3,500 of the tribe's annuity money for use by the delegation, Cass refused.[47]

With the federal government increasingly indisposed to help the Cherokees, the cause of the red men seemed to grow progressively hopeless. In 1834, as the government dealt more and more with the proremoval faction, the *Cherokee Phoenix* expressed the fear that a treaty would be negotiated with this minority faction. Even murder could be overlooked, it seemed, if the perpetrator favored removal. One account tells of a Cherokee enrolling agent who was protected by Georgia law when he killed another Indian in a fight over removal.[48]

In May 1834 enrollment was once again suspended. Probably a more noteworthy event, and one which further foreshadowed the fate of the Nation, occurred on May 31, 1834, when the *Cherokee Phoenix* halted publication after six years of controversial existence. Editor Elijah Hicks cited his own poor health and lack of funds for the "temporary" halt in publication. He hoped to raise some money and begin publishing again in July or August. Unfortunately, his plans never materialized.

Difficulties within the Nation persisted and, as has been seen, the fate of the Cherokees was sealed in late 1835. Never giving up hope, the Cherokee leaders contemplated reissuing the *Phoenix* as late as May 1835. These good intentions came to an end, however, when the Georgia state guard seized the press of the *Phoenix*. Later in the year the *New York Star* cited the action by the guard as interference with freedom of the press "after the pattern of Charles X, ex-king of France."[49] The *Star* protest, like many other factors in the Cherokee removal tragedy, had little effect on the final fate of the Indian Nation. The end of the *Cherokee Phoenix* symbolized and anticipated the end of the Cherokee Nation east of the Mississippi River. The time of real trouble, however, was yet to come, for the Cherokees continued to believe that they would not be forced to abide by the Treaty of New Echota. They nourished these false hopes for some two-and-one-half years until they were forced to move west in 1838.

NOTES

1. For more detail on the general removal controversy, see Grant Foreman, *Indian Removal* (Norman: Univ. of Oklahoma Press, 1932) or Grace Steele Woodward, *The Cherokees* (Norman: Univ. of Oklahoma Press, 1963).

2. *Laws of the Cherokee Nation* (Tahlequah, Cherokee Nation: Cherokee Advocate Off. 1852), 139-40, 136-37. The death penalty for ceding or selling lands was an old custom which this law confirmed. The 1828 treaty allowed voluntary removal.

3. J.B. Pendleton to George R. Gilmer, Feb. 6, 7, 1830, in *Cherokee Indian Letters, Talks and Treaties, 1786–1838*, 3 vols., WPA Project no. 4341, Georgia State Archives, I, 210, 202; Allen G. Fambrough to Gilmer, Feb. 8, 1830, *ibid.*, I, 203, 204, 205-7.

4. *Cherokee Phoenix*, Feb. 24, June 26, 1830; Henry Niles, *The Weekly Register of Documents, Essays and Facts* 27 (Nov. 28, 1829), 213; *ibid.*, 39 (Nov. 6, 1830), 181; *ibid.* (Dec. 11, 1830), 263-64; *Senate Doc. 512*, 23 Cong., 1 sess., 1834, II, 21, 60.

5. *Phoenix*, Sept. 11, 1830.

6. *Cherokee Letters*, I, 215-18; *Senate Doc. 512*, II, 16, 23-24, 61, 171-72, 197-98, 186-87.

7. *Senate Doc. 512*, II, 49, 98-99, 178-81.

8. *Phoenix*, Jan. 8, 1831.

9. *Ibid.*, Feb. 19, August 12, 1831.

10. *Ibid.*, July 23, 1831; P.G. Randolph to Hugh Montgomery, June 18, 1830, in *House Doc. 102*, 21 Cong., 2 sess., 1831. Randolph conveyed Jackson's order to Montgomery.

11. Andrew Jackson to Gilmer, July 15, 1831, in *Cherokee Letters*, II, 275; Lewis Cass to Montgomery, Aug. 15, 1831, *ibid.*, 285-86; Cass to Benjamin F. Curry, Sept. 1, 1831, *Senate Doc. 512*, I, 334-37.

12. George Gibson to William L. McClintock, Nov. 8, 1831, *Sen. Doc. 512*, I, 51-52; McClintock to Gibson, Dec. 7, 1831, *ibid.*, 748-49; McClintock to Gibson, Dec. 16, 1831, *ibid.*, 749-50.

13. McClintock to Gibson, Dec. 16, 1831, *ibid.*, 749-50.

14. McClintock to Gibson, Dec. 20, 1831, *ibid.*, 751-52.

15. McClintock to Gibson, Jan. 20, 1832, *ibid.*, 752-53; Curry to Elbert Herring, Jan. 25, 1832, *ibid.*, III, 152-53; Reuben Thornton to Cass, Feb. 10, 1832, *ibid.*, 201; David Reese to Cass, Feb. 14, 1832, *ibid.*, 207-8; Curry to Herring, Feb. 17, 1832, *ibid.*, 208; J.M.C. Montgomery to Cass, Feb. 18, 1832, *ibid.*, 209-10.

16. Curry to Cass, Feb. 20, 1832, *ibid.*, 211-12.

17. *Phoenix*, Mar. 21, 31, 1832.

18. Curry to Herring, Mar. 11, 1832, *Senate Doc. 512*, III, 257.

19. Hugh Montgomery to Cass, Apr. 12, 1832, *ibid.*, 286-87; McClintock to Gibson, Apr. 18, May 2, 1832, *ibid.*, I, 760-61; Curry to Herring, Apr. 21, 1832, *ibid.*, III, 305-6.

20. George Vashon to Cass, May 16, 1832, *ibid.*, I, 916-17; Curry to Herring, June 21, 1832, *ibid.*, III, 377-79.

21. Lewis Cass memo, Dept. of War, May 15, 1832, *ibid.*, I, 343-49.

22. Cass to Elisha Chester, May 11, 1832, *ibid.*, II, 817; Chester to Cass, May 30, June 9, July 1, 1832, *ibid.*, III, 365-66, 372-73, 389, 390-92, 397-99.

23. Daniel Newnan to Cass, Apr. 21, 1832, *ibid.*, 303-4; Newnan to Cherokee delegation, Apr. 24, 1832, *ibid.*, 304-5; Cherokee delegation to Newnan, Apr. 25, 1832, *ibid.*, 305.

24. J.M.C. Montgomery and William M. Davis to Cass, June 16, 1832, *ibid.*, 374-75; William Hardin to Cass, June 8, 1832, *ibid.*, 375-77; Curry to Herring, June 21, 1832, *ibid.*, 377-79; Davis to Cass, June 24, 1832, *ibid.*, 381-83.

25. J.M.C. Montgomery to Cass, Aug. 1, 1832, *ibid.*, 411-12.

26. Chester to Cass, Aug. 11, 1832, *ibid.*, 421-24; Curry to Herring, Aug. 14, 1832, *ibid.*, 429; Chester to John Robb, Aug. 16, 1832, *ibid.*, 431-33.

27. Curry to Cass, Aug. 4, 1832, *ibid.*, I, 620; Curry to Herring, Sept. 4, 1832, *ibid.*, 460-61.

28. Hugh Montgomery to Cass, July 12, 1832, *ibid.*, 399-400; Wilson Lumpkin to Cass, Sept. 22, 1832, *ibid.*, 460-61.

29. *Phoenix,* Aug. 11, 1832; Henry T. Malone, *Cherokees of the Old South* (Athens: Univ. of Georgia Press, 1956), 167-68.

30. McClintock had asked to be recalled in May because of the "objectionable" nature of his job.

31. F.L. Dancy to George Gibson, Sept. 24, Oct. 26, 1832, *Senate Doc. 512,* I, 654-55, 656-57; Chester to Cass, Sept. 29, Oct. 27, Nov. 6, 1832, *ibid.*, 513-14; Hugh Montgomery to Cass, Oct. 31, 1832, *ibid.*, 513.

32. Dancy to Gibson, Dec., n.d., 1832, *ibid.*, I, 658; Curry to Gibson, Nov. 29, 1832, *ibid.*, 630-31; Curry to Herring, Nov. 30, 1832, *ibid.*, III, 540-41; Curry to J.H. Hook, Sept. 29, 1832, *ibid.*, I, 626-28; Curry to Herring, Dec. 28, 1832, *ibid.*, III, 569.

33. Cited in *Niles' Register* 43 (Jan. 12, 1833), 319.

34. *Phoenix,* Jan. 19, 1833.

35. *Western Herald,* Apr. 16, 1833, cited in *Niles' Register* 44 (May 4, 1836), 152.

36. Gibson to Curry, Jan. 4, 1833, *Senate Doc. 512,* I, 204-5; William Day to Gibson, Jan. 4, 1833, *ibid.*, 659-60.

37. Ross to Cass, Jan. 8, 28, 1833, Feb. 14, 1833, *ibid.*, IV, 13, 63-65, 97-100; Cass to Delegation, Feb. 2, 20, 1833, *ibid.*, III, 588-90, 599-600.

38. Joel Vannay to Governor David L. Swain, Jan. 29, 1833, *ibid.*, IV, 101-2; Ross to Cass, Mar. 8, 1833, *ibid.*, 133-34; Herring to Ross, Mar. 14, 1833, *ibid.*, III, 613; Hugh Montgomery to Herring, Mar. 7, 1833, *ibid.*, IV, 132-33.

39. John Walker, Jr., to Hugh Montgomery, Apr. 5, 1833, *ibid.*, 169; Herring to Hugh Montgomery, Apr. 22, 1833, *ibid.*, III, 673; Curry to Herring, Apr. 20, 1833, *ibid.*, IV, 186-87.

40. Herring to Curry, Mar. 21, 1833, *ibid.*, III, 618-19; Curry to Herring, Apr. 26, 1833, *ibid.*, IV, 188-89.

41. Ross to Cass, May 22, 1833, *ibid.*, IV, 408-10; Curry to Herring, May 23, 1833, *ibid.*, 411-16.

42. Robb to Curry, June 22, 1833, *ibid.*, III, 721-22; Robb to Lumpkin, June 22, 1833, *ibid.*, 722; Hugh Montgomery to Herring, June 18, 1833, *ibid.*, IV, 478-80; Walker to Herring, July 26, 1833, *ibid.*, 485-86.

43. *Phoenix,* July 27, 1833.

44. Cass to J.M.C. Montgomery and Davis, Sept. 16, 1833, *Senate Doc. 512,* III, 772; Curry to Herring, June 27, 1833, *ibid.*, IV, 444-45.

45. J.W. Harris to Gibson, Sept. 21, 1833, *ibid.*, I, 709; Cass to Montgomery and Davis, Sept. 16, 1833, *ibid.*, III, 772.

46. General Council to Hugh Montgomery, Oct. 31, 1833, *ibid.*, IV, 630–31; Curry to Herring, Nov. 4, 1833, *ibid.*, 644–47.

47. Cass to Hugh Montgomery and Curry, Nov. 26, 1833, *ibid.*, III, 828–30; Herring to Hugh Montgomery, Nov. 28, 1833, *ibid.*, 831.

48. *Phoenix*, Feb. 8, Apr. 5, 1834.

49. *Ibid.*, May 10, 31, 1834; Marion L. Starkey, *The Cherokee Nation* (New York: Knopf, 1946), 331; *New York Star*, cited in *Niles' Register* 49 (Oct. 31, 1835), 138. For the later removal story, see my "The Cherokee Removal, 1835–1838," *Tennessee Historical Quarterly* 33 (Winter 1973), 311–31.

Postremoval Factionalism
in the Cherokee Nation

Gerard Reed

Until the United States, guided by a resolute Andrew Jackson, launched its Indian removal program in the 1830s, Eastern Cherokees maintained tribal unity as well as peaceful coexistence with the United States. Federal removal pressure, implementing the Indian Removal Act of 1830, then fragmented the tribe, for a proremoval, largely mixed-blood faction, the "Treaty" party, emerged after it became obvious Jackson would not enforce the Supreme Court's 1832 *Worcester* v. *Georgia* vindication of Cherokee rights.

Without federal protection, Cherokees defenselessly watched Georgia land-grabbers overrun their lands. A disillusioned Connecticut-educated Cherokee, John Ridge, assailed that "Chicken Snake Genl. Jackson [who] has time to crawl and hide in the luxuriant Grass of his nefarious hypocrisy" but still dared hope the 1832 election might eliminate Jackson and inaugurate the more conciliatory Henry Clay. Still more, Ridge believed only a traitorous faction, skillfully kneaded by Jackson, would ever sign a removal treaty.[1]

Sharing Ridge's opposition to removal, the tribe's National Council scorned the removal treaty proffered in 1832. Hopes that Clay would oust Jackson from the White House died in that year, however, and removal, like the passing seasons, loomed inevitable. Some Cherokees, embracing their fate, drafted removal plans. They simply could not forever endure Georgia's encroachment. A self-styled "Friend of Liberty" described the border ruffians as more savage than "savages" and thought the Cherokees

148

could retain their dignity only by escaping Georgia's "tyrannical laws, orders, and acts."[2]

The first thin fault on the surface of Cherokee unity appeared in 1832 when a delegation of Western Cherokees, who had earlier moved first to Arkansas and thence to Indian Territory, gave the United States a list of possible proremoval men. This tremor of schism scarcely troubled the Nation, but Principal Chief John Ross, insisting upon consensus in troubled times, pounced upon the alleged traitors. He forced Elias Boudinot, who, like John Ridge, had been educated in New England, and who edited the remarkable *Cherokee Phoenix,* to resign his editorial position in order that news could be managed to puff up Cherokee morale. Dissent went underground and slowly undermined the Cherokee community.[3]

As it became increasingly unsafe to live in areas claimed by Georgia, the underground protreaty faction determined to work for the salvation of a people who they thought would perish unless removal was accepted. John Ridge, especially, began to champion removal. Complaining that the Cherokees suffered intolerable "aggressions" and were "robbed & whipped by whites almost every day," he urged John Ross to "establish" the Nation elsewhere. When Ridge discussed the situation with his mixed-blood kinsmen and friends, those favoring removal formed a protreaty party. He persuaded his father, Major Ridge (given that brevet rank by Jackson himself following the Battle of Horseshoe Bend), long a staunch foe of land cessions, to support removal. In 1809, Major Ridge had helped execute a tribesman who had illegally ceded Cherokee land; for this reason he found it difficult to follow his son's leadership. By 1833 the Treaty party openly proposed to liquidate tribal holdings in the East, and their agitation began splitting the tribe.[4]

Determined to force removal, United States agents, after unsuccessful attempts to negotiate a treaty with the tribe's constituted authorities, naturally turned to the Treaty party leaders. Representing only a small fraction of the tribe, 100 Treaty party men accepted and signed the Treaty of New Echota in the final

149

days of 1835. The United States Senate, by a one-vote margin, accepted the pact, and the United States Army, led by General Winfield Scott, drove the Cherokees to Indian Territory during 1838.

Preceding the general removal of the tribe, however, 1,000 Treaty party people moved west, joining some 8,000 "Old Settlers," or "Western Cherokees," who had earlier drifted west and received land in the northeast corner of present-day Oklahoma. With a minimum of difficulty, Treaty party people settled along the Arkansas border and accepted the long-established Old Settler government.[5]

When the bulk of the Eastern Cherokees, driven from their homes, depleted and discouraged by the "Trail of Tears," entered Indian Territory in the winter and spring of 1838–39, problems erupted. Cephus Washburn, veteran missionary in the territory, reported that "at present there is much confusion & controversy. Scenes of violence & blood are transacted very frequently. Several murders have been committed since the new emigrants came in. The whole nation is much divided. There are three political parties, the Old Settlers, the Treaty party, & the Ross party."[6]

Old Settlers expected the Ross people to accept their government just as the Treaty party had done. On June 3, 1839, John Brown, an Old Settler chief, welcomed the emigrants and detailed plans for their assimilation. He stated that the Cherokees were all brothers and would enjoy equal rights and citizenship; he offered aid to emigrants who needed it.[7]

John Ross, leader of the emigrants, wearied and outraged by the ejection of his people from their homes, momentarily accepted Brown's welcome and assimilation plans. In fact, representing the approximately twelve thousand people who had survived the removal, Ross thought the eastern government should be transplanted and immediately imposed upon all Cherokees in the territory.[8] Thus, one week later, when the Cherokees assembled at Tukattokah (near present-day Tahlequah), he called for a united people "on the border of the great plains of the west."[9] He proposed that a nine-man committee (only three of them Old Set-

150

tlers, the rest emigrants) draft plans for a new government, thus ensuring his own dominance in the nation.[10]

Old Settler chiefs naturally rejected Ross's proposal, arguing that the Cherokees were, in fact, already united under the established Old Settler government, which had been functioning for a decade, and that the newcomers enjoyed the same rights and privileges as the Western Cherokees.[11] They failed to see why their government should be abolished just because the emigrants had joined them. Equally intransigent, John Ross insisted that the emigrants should not be forced to accept "laws and regulations" forged before they arrived.[12]

Since neither faction's leaders seemed conciliatory, compromise parties within each group proposed a convention for July 1, 1839, to fuse the tribesmen. Sequoyah, the famous Old Settler who had devised the Cherokee syllabary which made his people literate virtually overnight, and Jesse Busheyhead, an emigrant, headed the compromise factions. Ross quickly denounced the proposal as an Old Settler plot to impose minority rule on his majority, and tensions tightened throughout the territory.[13]

Adding to these tensions, vengeful emigrants lashed out against the signers of the infamous 1835 Treaty of New Echota. Understandably, many Cherokees of the Ross party blamed that treaty and its signers for the agony of removal. At Tukattokah, as the convention failed to unify the tribe, sullen full-bloods discussed their plight and blamed the Treaty party for Old Settler policies as well as for removal. Thus they called a meeting to plan assassinations to satisfy the traditional blood-law of the Cherokees which prescribed death for anyone ceding tribal lands.

Three hundred emigrant Cherokees quietly gathered at Double Head Springs, four miles north of Tahlequah, on June 20. A committee planned that the assassins would be selected by lot. The conspirators filed past a hat and drew numbered slips of paper; those who drew numbers followed by an *x* were the appointed assassins.[14]

Two days later, in the morning's early hours, the assassins killed the three primary leaders of the Treaty party. John Ridge, who

151

had fought against removal until he became persuaded it was hopeless, was "the chief advocate of removal." He died when four men burst into his house and dragged him from his bed into the front yard, stabbing him to death while his horrified, Connecticut-bred wife looked on.[15]

Ridge's cousin Elias Boudinot had continued his scholarly bent in the Indian Territory, helping a missionary, Dr. Samuel Worcester, establish a printing press and translating for him. A reluctant advocate of removal, he nevertheless shared with Ridge the image of a traitor. Since removal he had been living in Park Hill, a settlement five miles south of Tahlequah, building a house for his family. On the fateful morning of June 22, some men approached him as he worked, asking for medicine. As he turned toward Worcester's house, where the medicine was kept, the three assailants attacked and bludgeoned him to death.[16]

Old Major Ridge, long a tribal leader, had lived through the Cherokees' transition from a powerful, independent tribal nation to a dependent domestic nation removed from its lands. Decorated by Andrew Jackson for his bravery at Horseshoe Bend, lacking the education and culture of his son John, he had supported removal only when John had persuaded him it was the Cherokees' only salvation. Since he had helped execute a Cherokee who had ceded tribal land, he considered signing the 1835 treaty the same as signing his own death warrant. June 22 found him riding toward his daughter's home in Arkansas. Trailed by the men assigned to kill him, he was shot from the saddle forty miles from the scene of his son's death.[17]

In one well-planned forenoon, the Ross party eliminated its most articulate opposition. Other signers of the 1835 treaty, including Boudinot's brother Stand Watie, escaped death. Friends and followers of the slain men naturally reacted and further fractured the Nation. Angry Treaty party men congregated around Watie, whose military abilities would later lead him to a brigadier general's rank in the Confederate Army. Five hundred heavily armed emigrants gathered at Park Hill to protect John Ross. General Matthew Arbuckle, commandant of Fort Gibson, blamed

Ross for the assassinations; Ross denied the allegations but refused to prove his innocence by appearing at the fort for an investigation. The Nation edged near the abyss of civil war.[18]

To resolve the crisis, John Ross abruptly reversed his opposition to the compromise convention scheduled for July 1 — just as Old Settlers, who had not been consulted by the convention leaders, determined to boycott it! The second convention of 1839 began on July 1 at the Illinois Camp Ground, where Sequoyah and his handful of Old Settlers drafted a statement of purpose: "to prevent the further effusion of Cherokee blood; . . . to effect a union; . . . to lay the foundation for a code of laws" equitable for all Cherokees.[19] Uncomplicated by the presence of opposition (perhaps only twelve Old Settlers joined Sequoyah, and people of the Treaty party feared to come), the Illinois Camp Ground convention proceeded with unanimity under Ross' orchestration, drafting an act of union acceptable to the emigrant faction.[20]

But the Act of Union signed here failed to unite the Nation. Old Settlers — clearly supported by Gen. Matthew Arbuckle, who had steadily advocated their cause — called a convention of their own later in the month. Since some of the Illinois Camp Ground convention's decrees transparently justified the Ridge-Boudinot murders and encouraged the slaying of more signers of the 1835 treaty by branding them "outlaws," the Treaty party stirred up opposition to the compact and refused to accept its terms.[21]

With little concern for his antagonists, Ross and his majority moved ahead and dominated the Nation. In the first week of September, delegates assembled at Tahlequah to draft a constitution. They accepted the Illinois Camp Ground Act of Union. A few pro-Ross Old Settlers voted to depose their chiefs and acknowledge Ross' supremacy. Delegates to the convention, untroubled by opposition parties, drafted assorted laws and claimed national unanimity.[22]

Despite this assembly's action in the fall of 1839, real tribal unity was but a dream in Cherokee hearts. Hotheads in all factions nourished their anger, and violence crackled like a simmering fire. Arbuckle commented:

There is still much discontent in the Cherokee Nation, which will no doubt lead to frequent quarrels and violence between individuals & small parties; and independent of this, seven or eight of the signers of the Treaty of 1835, are now regarded outlaws, in consequence of not having attended the convention, and there acknowledged their error in having signed that treaty. It is probable these individuals will be killed in a short time, if they do not leave their nation.[23]

Further complicating the situation, anti-Ross Old Settlers met in November 1839 and annulled the actions of the pro-Ross Old Settlers in the September convention. Obviously representing the majority of Western Cherokees, they elected three chiefs and denounced Ross for trying to "depose the Chiefs, putting down the National Council, and . . . endeavoring to annul the original Laws of the country."[24] In the eyes of those who had lived on the land for a decade before the emigrants arrived, the newcomers were clearly usurping, and destroying, an established government.

In desperation, the minority factions (the Treaty party and Old Settlers) worked together in opposition to the Ross party and called upon the federal government to help them. When federal agents like Arbuckle bolstered their arguments, the Ross people decided they had to forge some workable agreement with the minority parties. Thus Ross' followers called for yet another convention, scheduled for January 5, 1840, which would conclusively unite the tribe.[25]

Delegates from the factions to this convention appeared conciliatory. Ross people claimed they would acknowledge the rights of the Old Settlers, and the minority factions were anxious for peace and security from reprisal. All Cherokees wanted bloodshed and fear left behind. Consequently, the delegates revoked the Illinois Camp Ground convention's decrees against the Treaty party and granted its members political equality. Attempting to placate angry Ridge-Boudinot followers, William Shorey Coodey (acting for absent Principal Chief Ross, who was in Washington) said that the infamous Double Springs convention which had plotted the assassinations had been extralegal and unsanctioned by the Ross government. Coodey also tried to appease Old Settlers by describing their considerable role in the new government.[26]

154

Even this convention failed to reconcile the factions fully, however, for anti-Ross people still felt abused and continued to struggle for their rights. The convention did alleviate some fears, but since Old Settler and Treaty party people played no formative role in it, the Cherokees remained tense and uneasy throughout the early months of 1840. General Arbuckle, never an admirer of Ross (perhaps because he feared the chief might eliminate some of the profits he had reaped through his position) circumvented Ross's authority and called another tribal meeting. He indicated that the army would supervise the assembly scheduled for June 10, 1840, and, should the Cherokees fail to settle their differences, he threatened to split the nation geographically, giving each faction land and autonomy within its area.[27]

Facing this possibility, delegates to the Fort Gibson convention decided to unify formally. Eleven Old Settlers and twelve Ross representatives signed an Act of Union on June 26, 1840, which officially united the Cherokees. It was the third "official" union within a year! The emigrants still claimed legal title to their lands in the East, but they agreed to share funds gained from that claim on a per capita basis with Western Cherokees who had shared their land with them. Old Settlers signed with the reservation that a majority of their people must approve the agreement before it would be valid; no vote, however, was taken among the Western Cherokees, and the Ross government simply implemented the Act of Union with United States assistance.[28]

The new Constitution of the Fort Gibson convention virtually duplicated the one formulated by the Ross-controlled assembly on September 6, 1839. Old Settlers truly representative of their faction approved it for the first time. Guaranteed a "just proportion of the officers and representation in the Government of the Nation for the first constitutional term," the Old Settlers promptly selected Andrew Vann as assistant principal chief, and the emigrants naturally picked John Ross as principal chief.[29] Missionary D.S. Butrick hoped "that the national difficulties are now settled, & the hatchet amicably buried."[30] These hopes materialized throughout the summer of 1840 as Cherokees accepted the political settlement, built their homes, and tilled their soil.

155

The minority factions' acceptance of the 1840 Act of Union did not also mean they accepted John Ross' leadership of the tribe, however. Many Treaty party and Old Settler leaders thought the principal chief had mismanaged the Nation's finances and urged his removal. As the elections of 1841 approached, the people had their first opportunity to indicate their position on the factional issues. During the summer the minority leaders effectively campaigned against Ross, emphasizing one issue: money.

They promised, if elected, to distribute the money guaranteed in the 1835 removal treaty on a per capita basis. In exchange for its eastern lands, the United States had promised to pay the tribe $4,500,000. Since everyone would profit if this sum were distributed to individuals, it proved a popular issue, and anti-Ross people threatened to overthrow the Ross regime.

Wily politician that he was, Ross rode out the storm by promising even more dividends than his opponents offered. He managed to shift his people's attention away from the question of removal finances (later investigations indicated possible fraud on the part of the chief and his brother Lewis) to the future treaty he hoped to obtain from the United States.[31]

While in Washington he talked with the new president, John Tyler, explained the past injustices suffered by his people, and secured presidential assurances that a new treaty would remedy many of the tribe's problems. Like most politicians, Tyler promised well, saying:

> Upon ratification of the treaty contemplated, which shall give to the Cherokee nation full indemnity for all wrongs which they may have suffered, establish upon a permanent basis the political relations between them and the people of the United States, guaranty their lands in absolute fee simple, and prescribe specific rules in reference to subjects of the most interesting character to them and their remotest posterity, a new sun will have dawned upon them, in whose brightness their permanent happiness and true glory may be read by the whole world; and I shall rejoice to have been the President under whose auspices these great and happy results shall have been produced.[32]

Given such prospects, Ross naturally persuaded his people to postpone the per capita payment until a more remunerative treaty could be negotiated. Reelected in 1841 on this promise, he returned to Washington to secure the treaty. Sterile months became years as the bureaucratic maze and congressional indifference to the Cherokees' plight rendered the chief's work ineffectual. Furthermore, despite his goodwill, Tyler's impotence as a president virtually without a party made it impossible for him to deliver the promised treaty.

As Ross continually failed to secure the treaty and its financial bonus, agitation against him accelerated in the Cherokee Nation. Old Settlers became particularly upset because they had lost virtually everything, with no compensation. Treaty party agitators effectively blamed Ross himself for the Nation's problems. Commissions from Washington investigated the dissidents' complaints and sought to secure evidence for the settlement of claims under the 1835 treaty, but little resulted from their work.

As the promised treaty remained illusory, factional bitterness erupted into violence. Though many of them were technically unrelated to the factional struggle, each murder or arrest, like those in urban ghettos just prior to a riot, accentuated the factions' animosities. The Nation's authorities seemed powerless to restrain the violence, and such arrests as police did make appeared, to Old Settlers and Treaty party people, politically motivated. Tensions mounted during the 1840s until, in 1845, full-scale factionalism erupted.[33]

From the early days of 1845 until the reconciling treaty of August 1846, the Cherokee Nation reeled as it was buffeted by internal turbulence. Murders were common, armed bands roamed the countryside, and hundreds of Cherokees (especially Treaty party people) left the Nation seeking refuge in Arkansas. Ross' police companies staged a liquidation campaign against the Starr family, of whom some were notorious outlaws, but others innocent of anything except identification with the Treaty party. A number of Treaty party men, armed and ready for battle, collected around Stand Watie, who lost a second brother, Thomas Watie, to the Ross party's vengeance. Watie's force occupied Fort

157

Wayne, an abandoned Arkansas army post on the border of the Indian Territory. Sporadic violence continued, and the threat of civil war hung over the Nation for more than one year.[34]

All Cherokees wanted to avoid war and each faction sent a delegation to Washington in 1845 to enlist federal assistance on its behalf. The grievances of the Treaty party included the 1839 Ridge-Boudinot murders, Ross' failure to pay the per capita treaty monies (and the fraud thereby suggested), and the endemic persecution endured by anti-Ross Cherokees in the nation.[35]

More than any other agent, they blamed the United States for their agonies, saying:

> If there was a crime in the Treaty of 1835, it was more *your* crime than *ours*. We were all opposed to selling our country, east, but by State laws, you, (meaning your countrymen) abolished our government, annihilated our laws, suppressed our authorities, took away our lands, turned us out of our houses, denied us the rights of men, made us outcasts and outlaws in our own land, plunging us at the same time into an abyss of moral degeneration which was rushing our people to swift destruction.[36]

Life for the Treaty party had been hazardous since 1839, and their situation was growing worse. "We cannot stand this state of things," they said. "We are murdered and the laws afford no redress."[37]

Old Settlers also went to Washington in 1845. Their attorneys argued that the United States owed them compensation for the land they had lost in northeastern Indian Territory. Whether one interpreted the 1828 treaty "by *legal rules,* or by the dictates of a *good conscience,*" the United States owed the Western Cherokees something for their lost land base and political power.[38] They further argued that only "through the MURDER of the *chiefs of the 'treaty party,'* and the DEPOSITION of the *'old settlers,'* by a few rebels against the legitimate authorities, backed by Ross and his foreign horde, was the path of power open to the eastern chiefs."[39]

Violence in the Cherokee Nation forced Washington bureaucrats to listen to the minority factions' complaints. William Medill, the new commissioner of Indian affairs, blamed John Ross for the Nation's plight and suspected him of embezzling Cherokee monies;

in his opinion a division of the Nation, as requested by the Treaty party, was "imperatively required."[40] President James K. Polk proposed to take Medill's advice, since "several unprovoked murders have been committed by the stronger upon the weaker party of the tribe, which will probably remain unpunished by the Indian authorities."[41]

Nothing could have aroused the Ross faction to action more quickly, and Ross and his delegation protested the proposed division of the tribe. In Tahlequah, the *Cherokee Advocate* asserted that "the question of a division of the Cherokee country is too absurd to merit a moment's serious consideration."[42] Despite the Treaty party's separatist desires, most Cherokees disliked the idea of a geographic division, and even the minority factions distrusted Polk's proffered program as much as they did John Ross's proposals.

Consequently, the three factions' delegations in Washington began to discuss their differences, hoping to solve their problems before the United States fractured the Nation. Ross still insisted that the United States pay the Cherokees for their removal losses, but he was now prepared to deal with dissident tribesmen.[43] By early August 1846 the Washington delegations had united, had agreed on acceptable treaty provisions, and had gained an "interview with the President of the United States . . . in order that they [might] submit said treaty for his approval."[44]

The proposed treaty was signed on August 6, 1846. It specifically purposed to conclude the Nation's political factionalism so that "peace and harmony may be restored among them." It was resolved that all lands would be held in common, old enmities buried, legitimate claims paid, and minority factions recompensed.[45]

On August 13, 1846, the Senate approved an amended treaty, and the leaders of the three Cherokee factions called on President Polk, who wrote:

> They had settled all the difficulties between themselves, and between the nation and the Government of the U. States. John Ross, the Principal Chief, addressed me & said they were all now in harmony and were satisfied. I told them that I congratulated them upon the happy adjustment of the difficulties which had distracted and divided them

159

for more than a dozen years, and that I was rejoiced to learn that they were returning to their nation to live as brothers and friends. They were all in a pleasant humour and well satisfied. This event in my administration I consider an important one.[46]

Factional delegates seemed genuinely to have resolved their differences. A Washington paper reported that President Polk bade Stand Watie farewell, saying, "I hope, Mr. Watie, that your people have forgiven each other and that all will be well." To this the solemn Watie answered, "I have entered into this treaty of amnesty in all sincerity; I intend to be peaceable, and have no doubt that others who have less to forgive will follow the example which all the leaders have set."[47]

The treaty, with its financial dividends in claims settlements, effectively quieted the factional strife which had plagued the Nation for a decade. It wrought more than a decade of peace within the Cherokee Nation. In the 1850s former factional leaders like Stand Watie concentrated on business pursuits and served in the Nation's government without apparent discrimination or difficulty. Had it not been for America's Civil War, the factional strife might have been buried forever by the 1846 treaty—though memories and feelings, of course, endured.

After fifteen years of peace, however, the Civil War rekindled factional enmity among Cherokees who sided with North or South largely according to factional backgrounds. As the Confederacy organized in 1861, southern emissaries courted the Indian Territory tribes, and a proslave regiment of Cherokees under Stand Watie began operating in the Missouri-Kansas-Indian Territory region.

Watie led a largely mixed-blood, proslavery minority of Cherokees. On the whole, his followers were Treaty party people who still remembered their persecution at the hands of the Ross government during the removal era. Though the slave issue was certainly part of their cause, for a number were prosperous planters, their dedication to the Confederate States had little to do with loyalty to the South as such. The old Treaty party people saw, in the war, a chance to dislodge the Ross regime.

John Ross at first espoused neutrality both for himself and for the Cherokee Nation. Even though he owned fifty slaves and prospered by virtue of their bondage, he derived his power from and believed his people could prosper only through a continued alliance with the United States. He was staunchly Unionist throughout the war.

However, when Union troops abandoned the forts they had maintained in Indian Territory, Confederate forces quickly occupied them. Faced by the occupation forces, Ross realistically abandoned his neutrality and signed a treaty with the Confederate States in October 1861. A full-blood regiment of Ross supporters took the field and operated alongside Watie's mixed-blood regiment.

When federal forces beat Stand Watie's troops at the Battle of Pea Ridge in 1862, Ross quickly guided his people back to an alliance with the Union. Union forces followed up their victory at Pea Ridge with an invasion of Indian Territory. The successful occupation of the Cherokee Nation, coupled with the cooperativeness of John Ross and his people with Union troops, split the Cherokees. Pro-Union Cherokees now battled against pro-Confederate Cherokees; Ross people fought Watie people.

War in the Cherokee Nation became an intratribal conflict between the old factions, and it proved costly. The Cherokees' population was severely reduced (perhaps by 25 percent), the land was ravaged, and the Nation's polity was destroyed. Few people suffered more intensely during the Civil War than the Cherokees —four years of endemic violence springing from factional animosity rather than from issues of war wasted the region and erased the constructive work of two decades.[48]

Victory for the North reestablished Ross's control of the Cherokee Nation. Violent factionalism, fortunately, ended with the war. Stand Watie and John Ross, as well as some other leaders of factions, died soon thereafter, and younger leaders remembered the removal less vividly than did their elders. To a degree, reconstruction buried the factionalism, but bitterness and unforgiven hatreds endured to affect events in the Cherokee Nation until, in 1907, the tribal government was dissolved by the establishment of the state of Oklahoma.

161

NOTES

1. John Ridge to Stand Watie, Apr. 6, 1832, Cherokee Nation Papers, MSS Div., Univ. of Oklahoma, Norman, Okla. (hereafter cited as CNP).

2. *Cherokee Phoenix*, Oct. 1, 1831. This remarkable tribal newspaper offers much information and insight into the developing removal crisis.

3. Woodward, *Cherokees*, 169–72; *Phoenix*, Aug. 11, 1832.

4. John Ridge to John Ross, Feb. 2, 1833, John Ross Papers, Thomas Gilcrease Institute, Tulsa, Okla. (hereafter cited as JRP); Treaty Delegation Argument, June 13, 1846, Letters Received by the Office of Indian Affairs, National Archives, microfilm roll 90 (hereafter cited as LROIA).

5. Treaties between the United States and the Old Settlers are collected in Charles Kappler, comp., *Indian Affairs: Laws and Treaties* (Washington, D.C.: GPO, 1904), II, 206–9, 283–85.

6. Cephus Washburn to David Greene, Mar. 18, 1839, Cherokee Mission Papers, X, Houghton Library, Harvard Univ.

7. Washburn to Greene, Aug. 12, 1839, *ibid.*

8. *Ibid.*

9. "John Ross Address," June 10, 1839, 26 Cong., 1 sess., *House Doc. 129* (Washington, D.C.: GPO, 1840), ser. 365, 48.

10. Ross to John Brown, John Looney, John Rogers, June 13, 1839, JRP.

11. Brown, Looney, Rogers to Ross, June 14, 1839, *House Doc. 129,* ser. 365, 51.

12. Ross and the National Committee to Monfort Stokes, June 21, 1839, LROIA, 83.

13. Ross to Stokes, June 21, 1839, *ibid.;* JRP.

14. Grant Foreman, "The Murder of Elias Boudinot," *Chronicles of Oklahoma* II (Mar. 1934), 23.

15. Sarah B.N. Ridge to Joel R. Poinsett, June 7, 1842, LROIA, 86; Sarah B.N. Ridge Memorial, Dec. 29, 1845, *ibid.,* 90.

16. Matthew Arbuckle to J.R. Poinsett, Dec. 11, 1839, *ibid.,* 84; S.B.N. Ridge to J.R. Poinsett, June 25, 1845, *ibid.,* 86; Foreman, "Murder of Boudinot," 21; Samuel A. Worcester to Greene, June 26, 1839, Cherokee Mission Papers, X.

17. *Ibid.*

18. Stokes to Poinsett, June 24, 1839, in *Report of the Commissioner of Indian Affairs, 1839* (Washington, D.C.: GPO, 1840), 355 (hereafter cited as *RCIA*); Ross to Arbuckle, June 22, 1839, LROIA, 84; Ross to Arbuckle, June 24, 1839, JRP; Washburn to Greene, July 4, 1839, Cherokee Mission Papers, X.

19. George Guess, "Old Settler Statement," July 2, 1839, *House Doc. 129,* 66.

20. John Brown *et al.* to Ross *et al.*, June 28, 1839, JRP; Ross *et al.* to Stokes, *RCIA*, 1839, 365.

21. Arbuckle to Ross, July 1839, JRP; "Treaty Party Statement," Aug. 29, 1839, *RCIA,* 408; "Cherokee Disturbances," 29 Cong., 1 sess. *House Doc. 185* (Washington, D.C.: GPO, 1846), 114.

22. Provisions of Union, Sept. 6, 1839, John Howard Payne Papers, VI, Newberry Library, Chicago; William P. Thompson, "Courts of the Cherokee Nation," *Chronicles of Oklahoma* 2 (Mar. 1924), 65; Ross to National Council,

Sept. 12, 1839, JRP; *Laws of the Cherokee Nation, 1839–67* (St. Louis: Democrat, 1868), 22–43.

23. Arbuckle to E.P. Gaines, Sept. 10, 1839; LROIA, 83.

24. "Old Settler Resolution," Nov. 5, 1839, 26 Cong., 1 sess., *House Doc. 188* (Washington, D.C.: GPO, 1840), 18; LROIA, 84.

25. Stokes *et al.*, "Statement," Dec. 20, 1839, *House Doc. 188,* 35; Arbuckle, to Poinsett, Dec. 26, 1839, *ibid.,* 32.

26. National Convention Revocation, Jan. 16, 1840, LROIA, 84; Coodey *et al.* to Arbuckle, Jan. 17, 1840, *ibid.*

27. Arbuckle to Joseph Vann, May 24, 1840, LROIA, 84; Arbuckle to Poinsett, May 27, 1840, *ibid.*

28. Act of Union, June 26, 1840, LROIA, 84.

29. *Ibid.;* Constitution of the Cherokee Nation, *ibid.*; Arbuckle to Poinsett, June 28, 1840, *ibid.*

30. D.S. Butrick to Greene, Cherokee Mission Papers, X.

31. Gerard A. Reed, "Financial Controversy in the Cherokee Nation, 1839–1846," *"Chronicles of Oklahoma"* 52 (Spring 1974), 82–98.

32. John Tyler to Ross *et al.*, Sept. 20, 1841, Special Files, Bureau of Indian Affairs, microfilm roll 8; *Cherokee Advocate,* Nov. 28, 1844.

33. P.M. Butler to J.C. Spencer, May 4, 1842, LROIA, 87; Albert M. Sea to Spencer, Mar. 14, 1842, *ibid.*; Ethan Allen Hitchcock, *A Traveler in Indian Territory* (Cedar Rapids: Torch Press, 1930), 87.

34. LROIA, CNP, JRP, *passim.*

35. Protest of the Treaty Party, July 25, 1845, LROIA, 90; Geo Paschal and S.C. Stambaugh, "Argument on Behalf of the Treaty Party," *House Doc. 185,* 116–49.

36. "Memorial of the Treaty Party," *ibid.,* 104.

37. *Ibid.*

38. Stambaugh and Amos Kendall to W.L. Marcy, Oct. 4, 1845, *ibid.,* 28.

39. Stambaugh and Kendall to Marcy, Nov. 1, 1845, *ibid.,* 35.

40. William Medill to Marcy, Mar. 31, 1846, *ibid.,* 11.

41. "Annual Message of J.K. Polk," Dec. 2, 1845, in James D. Richardson, comp., *Messages and Papers of the Presidents* (Washington, D.C.: 1897), III, 2262.

42. *Advocate,* Apr. 30, 1846.

43. Ross *et al.* to Edmund Burke *et al.*, July 8, 1846, LROIA, 90.

44. John R. Wolfe to Medill, Aug. 6, 1846, *ibid.*

45. Kappler, *Indian Affairs,* II, 415–18.

46. James K. Polk, *Diary of James K. Polk* (Chicago: A.C. McClurg & Co., 1910), II, 81.

47. *Washington Daily Union,* Aug. 18, 1846, quoted in Morris L. Wardell, *A Political History of the Cherokee Nation* (Norman: Univ. of Oklahoma Press, 1938), 73.

48. William Penn Adair, in "The Indian Territory in 1878," *Chronicles of Oklahoma* 4 (Sept. 1926), 265, estimated the population depleted by 50 percent; letters in CNP, JRP, and *The War of the Rebellion: Official Records . . .* (Washington, D.C.: GPO, 1880–1901), illustrate the devastation.

The Origin of the Eastern Cherokees as a Social and Political Entity

Duane H. King

"Indian Nations before the Whites are like balls of snow before the sun," declared a chief at the treaty of Sycamore Shoals in March 1775. Despite reassurances to the contrary, he was convinced that the white's desire for land was insatiable, and prophesied that the Cherokees would eventually be required to yield all their land and would then be forced to some distant wilderness.[1] The ominous warning was followed by the signing of a treaty by which the Cherokees ceded thousands of square miles of traditional hunting grounds. By 1819 more than two dozen land-cession treaties reduced the once vast Cherokee territory to the adjacent mountainous border sections of North Carolina, Tennessee, Georgia, and Alabama.[2] The remaining land was not much larger, tribal leaders believed, than that needed to support their population, yet the demands by the whites for additional Cherokee land persisted.

In 1828, gold was discovered in the Cherokee Nation near Dahlonega, Georgia. The state of Georgia, inspired by the presidential election of Andrew Jackson, who campaigned on a policy of Indian removal, soon passed a series of repressive laws against the Cherokees. Within a few years, lucky winners of the Georgia land lottery descended upon Cherokee farmsteads to claim the land and improvements from the previous owners.[3] On December 29, 1835, a small number of Cherokees despairingly signed the Treaty of New Echota. The treaty was ratified by Congress on May 23, 1836, in spite of petitions signed by over fifteen thousand Cherokees denouncing it as a fraud.[4] The treaty ceded the entire re-

164

maining Cherokee territory east of the Mississippi in exchange for five million dollars and equivalent holdings in the Indian Territory.[5] The Cherokees were given two years in which to remove. By May 1838, only 2,000 Cherokees had voluntarily emigrated, and 7,000 state and federal troops were sent to the Nation to enforce the terms of the agreement.[6]

Despite the efforts of the United States government to remove the Cherokees, some managed, by one means or another, to remain in their homeland. Most of these were in North Carolina, where about eight hundred Cherokees on the Oconaluftee River and its tributaries and some two hundred further west in Graham and Cherokee counties remained after the troops had left. According to James Mooney, these Cherokees were the "purest-blooded and the most conservative in the nation."[7] Today, the Eastern Cherokees are very much aware that they are the descendants of people who, because of circumstances, were able to avoid the fate of the Cherokee Nation—removal west. Their beliefs about the circumstances which preserved them as a group play an important role in their social definition of themselves.[8]

These beliefs focus on one individual, Tsali. His presumed role in Cherokee history constitutes the most important story in the Eastern Band of Cherokees' oral tradition, and most members of the Band are familiar with at least one of the accounts. Although numerous versions persist, the most recurrent beliefs are the following: The ancestors of the present-day Eastern Cherokees fled to the mountains in 1838 in order to escape removal. Considered outlaws, they were hunted by the United States Army. One family that was captured was headed by a man named Tsali. Provoked by continual prodding by the soldiers, the members of the family turned upon their guards, killing one or more, and made their escape. General Scott, angered by the incident, but weary of chasing the Cherokees, offered a compromise. If those responsible for the deaths of the soldiers were punished, all others hiding in the mountains could remain in North Carolina. When the message was delivered by Will Thomas, Tsali and his sons voluntarily surrendered and sacrificed their lives for their people. As

165

the ultimate humiliation, other Cherokees were forced to execute the prisoners. Had it not been for Tsali's sacrifice, no Cherokees would be in North Carolina today.

This story is not only ingrained in the oral tradition, but it is also reinforced by the reservation's only outdoor drama, which has re-created the tragedy six nights a week throughout the summer months since 1950. Unfortunately, however, the account cherished by the majority of the Eastern Band and accepted by the several million tourists who have witnessed the play is at best a romanticized version of an important period of Cherokee history.

The historical record substantiates only the central facts of the story. Some Cherokees did, indeed, flee to the mountains to escape removal. Two soldiers of the 1st Dragoons were killed on November 1, 1838, by Cherokees, after which the army left the mountains without taking any additional fugitives. The circumstances surrounding these events, however — circumstances which are more essential to the story than the central facts — are almost entirely refuted by historical documentation.

The sequence of events at the time of removal is best understood in light of the predicament of the Eastern Cherokees prior to this period. In 1819, the Cherokees ceded to the United States a large tract of land which included the present Qualla Boundary.[9] Although most of the Cherokees residing in the ceded territory in North Carolina moved into the remaining tribal land, some did not. Among the latter were several signers of the 1819 treaty who were recipients of 640-acre reservations under the terms of the treaty. Accordingly, they relinquished their Cherokee citizenship and became citizens of North Carolina, having been deemed "persons of industry and capable of managing their property with discretion."[10] On June 26, 1829, three chiefs, Yonaguska, Long Blanket, and Wilnota[11] and fifty-seven other "Citizen Indians" put their marks on a document appointing John L. Dillard their attorney and empowering him to transact all business for them, stating, "We are totally ignorant of the English language, and as much of the laws and customs of this our adopted country by reason whereof we are often imposed on, cheated and defrauded by some of the people of this country, who seem to . . .

166

disregard the moral and natural rights of others."[12] They also acknowledged that they had separated from the Cherokee Nation and had become citizens of the United States. Thus, in the period leading up to removal, these people became marginal not only to the whites who began to settle around them but also to the developing Cherokee Nation, then centered in North Georgia.[13]

Until the year 1830, according to Will Thomas, these people were as intemperate as any other Indians on the frontier.[14] Suddenly, however, Yonaguska, himself an alcoholic, became convinced that alcohol would destroy him and his people. Recovering from a twenty-four-hour trance during which he was mourned for dead, Yonaguska assembled his people and presented the message which he said was given to him in the spirit world. He declared that intemperance was the cause for the extermination of Indian tribes in the neighborhood of the whites, and cited the Catawba Indians as an example of the damage alcohol could do; then every man of Qualla Town was forced to sign an oath written in Cherokee swearing to abstain from the use of "spirituous liquors."[15]

Thomas attributed their state of improvement at the time of removal to abstention from alcohol, and their model citizenship was defended by legislators in open debate both in Raleigh and in Washington.

In addition to coercing his people to join his temperance movement, Yonaguska also encouraged them to resist inducements for removal west. He asserted that the Cherokees were safer among their barren rocks and mountains than on land that the white man might find profitable. He believed that the Cherokees could be happy only in the country apportioned to them by nature.[16] He advised them to remain in North Carolina, considering that state better and more friendly disposed to the Indians than any other. If they went west, he feared that they would soon again be surrounded by white settlements and eventually "be included in a state disposed to oppress them."[17]

Opposition to removal was also high among the Cherokees living on tribal land in North Carolina. Efforts to enroll these Indians for removal were not successful. In 1833, the Reverend Evan Jones and his son presented John Ross with numerous depositions from Cherokees of the Valley Towns on the upper Hiwassee who had been unduly harrassed by the federal enrolling agent Benjamin Currey.[18] John F. Schermerhorn, government negotiator for the removal treaty, was also unsuccessful in dealing with the Carolina Indians. In replying to an inquiry a decade after the treaty was signed, he reported that no Cherokees from North Carolina were present at the Council of New Echota. He also stated:

> After the treaty at New Echota had been signed, I visited the North Carolina Indians in order to explain the treaty to them and obtain some of their signatures to it; but through the influence of the Baptist Missionary, who was under the influence of Ross — I did not succeed in getting any of them to sign the said Treaty; although several expressed themselves in favor of the treaty, but were deterred by the threats of personal violence from the Ross party for putting their names to it.[19]

Of invaluable service to the Cherokees wishing to remain in North Carolina was William Holland Thomas. Thomas, the adopted son of Yonaguska, spoke Cherokee and was a successful trader among the Indians both before and after the removal. Although it is still not clear whether he was motivated primarily by business interests or by his friendship with the Indians, he was responsible for a number of positive accomplishments for the benefit of the Eastern Cherokees.

About the same time the Treaty of New Echota was submitted to Congress for ratification, the president invited Thomas to Washington to examine the provisions of the treaty.[20] Thomas was particularly concerned about ambiguous wording in an article of the treaty which made provisions for individuals wishing to remain in the East. He was able to obtain, in lieu of a supplement to the treaty, a clarifying agreement with the Cherokee delegation supporting removal. This agreement acknowledged Thomas as the representative of the towns of "Qualla, Alarka, Aquona, Stekoah and Che-o-ih," noting that these "settlements expected to remain east." In essence, the agreement specified that the Cherokees not emigrating would be entitled, proportionate to their numbers, to all benefits of the treaty. The agreement was endorsed by the two senators from North Carolina, W.P. Mangum and Bedford Brown.[21]

On July 4, 1836, Thomas submitted the agreement with the Western Cherokee delegation to the War Department for recognition. On July 18, C.A. Harris, commissioner of Indian affairs, replied to Thomas, "I am instructed to inform you that the Cherokees in North Carolina have an interest proportionate to their numbers in all stipulations of that treaty."[22]

On July 28, 1836, the War Department Office of Subsistence instructed the superintendent of Cherokee removal to prepare enrolling books and to indicate "the choice of the signers as to the time of removing under the treaty or whether they would prefer to become citizens."[23] Actually, however, the choice for most Indians was made by the United States Army. On August 1, 1836, General John Ellis Wool, director of removal at that time, reported from Valley Town, North Carolina: "The feelings and dispositions of these Indians are altogether adverse to removal. I have had two meetings on the subject without any decision. On Wednesday next, we are to have another, when I expect a large number to be present; it will then be determined whether they will go peaceably or by force. If they hesitate, I will take them. Under any circumstances I shall take hostages."[24]

General Wool soon ordered into confinement some of the headmen for the purpose of inducing the others to come in and surrender their arms; they were doing so by the second week in August 1836.[25] Later he repeated the tactic at Cheloce, about thirty miles from Valley Town, by imprisoning a chief named Roman Nose as a means of forcing his people to surrender their arms.[26] General Wool was not pleased with his assignment, stating that he "would be glad to get rid of it as soon as circumstances permit. . . . If I could . . . I would remove every Indian tomorrow beyond the reach of the white men, who like vultures, are watching, ready to pounce upon their prey and strip them of everything they have or expect from the government of the United States."[27] Brig. Gen. R.G. Dunlap, commander of the Tennessee militia, also had misgivings about his assignment and threatened to resign rather than execute "at the point of a bayonet" a treaty opposed by the majority of the Cherokees.[28] In December 1836 the Oconaluftee Cherokees sent a memorandum to the North Carolina legislature to determine whether or not the state objected to their remaining in the state under the provisions of Article XII of the Treaty of New Echota. Acknowledging the past kindness shown them by the state, the Cherokees asked for legislation to protect them after the rest of the Nation had been removed. On January 21, 1837, the General Assembly ratified an act designed to prevent frauds upon the Cherokees. The law required that all transactions exceeding ten dollars in value which involved persons of Cherokee blood to the second degree be made in writing and signed by two creditable witnesses. The law had the same intent as the agreement the Cherokees themselves drew up in 1829.[29]

In a speech delivered before the United States House of Representatives in May 1838 concerning a bill appropriating funds for preventing and suppressing Indian hostilities, Congressman James Graham of Haywood County, North Carolina, reported that the Indians in his district were "temperate, orderly, industrious, and peaceable."[30]

When forced removal began in June 1838, the Oconaluftee Indians in Haywood County remained undisturbed, while their neighbors living on tribal land were among the first to be rounded up by federal troops. By mid-July General Eustis reported to General Scott that all the Indians in the North Carolina district had been sent in. On July 21, Scott ordered Eustis and the regulars under him, the 1st and 4th Artillery regiments, to the Canadian frontier.[31] In early August, after those troops were too far away to be recalled, Scott learned that numerous Indians had eluded the troops and were hiding in the mountains. From August until November 1838, Scott maintained small detachments of mounted regulars in the mountains to search for the fugitives.[32] Most of the fugitives had previously lived on the periphery of the tribal land in North Carolina. At least two of the families, Euchella's and Tsali's, lived within sight of Fort Lindsay near the mouth of the Nantahala River within the tribal boundary.[33] Scott estimated the total number of fugitives to be about three hundred men, women, and children, who were joined by forty or fifty runaways from the principal depot at the agency.[34] Assisting the army in search of the fugitives were the Oconaluftee Cherokees. Lieutenant C.H. Larned, reporting to General Scott from Fort Cass at the Calhoun agency, expressed concern that the fugitives brought in by the Oconaluftee Citizen Indians "had all been permitted to escape and rejoin their friends in the mountains."[35] One small girl who made the escape with her family related their plight to her descendants many years later. They escaped during the night and waded in the river so their trail could not be followed. Subsisting on roots and nuts, they traveled only at night and hid under bushes by the water during the day. They arrived at their hideout in the North Carolina mountains cold, wet, and hungry, with badly bruised, numb feet on the seventh night of their escape.[36]

Describing the fugitives, General Scott wrote, "Those wild Indians have refused, again and again, to comply with the urgent entreaties of both the Cherokee and United States authorities. They disregard one as much as the other. They have obstinately separated themselves from their nation, and resolved to live in their savage haunts independent of all government and authority."[37]

By late October the army, with the aid of Cherokee scouts, had succeeded in capturing "140 of those wild Indians," and Scott ordered down the last detachment with its prisoners.[38] This twelve-man detachment of the 1st Dragoons was commanded by Second Lieutenant A.J. Smith. Having captured fifteen fugitives at Pickens Courthouse in South Carolina, they were returning to Fort Cass by way of the Little Tennessee River. Reaching the mouth of the Tuckaseegee River on October 30, 1838, they received information that other fugitives were in the area.[39] Smith then split his command, sending the sergeant and seven men ahead with the prisoners already captured, while he and three soldiers, accompanied by Will Thomas, searched for the fugitives.

The fugitives were Tsali and his family. When their camp was discovered, eight members of the family were present; four came in later. All surrendered without resistance. Of the twelve captured, five were males, two of whom were armed with good rifles. Although twenty Indians supposedly belonged to the camp, Lieu-

171

tenant Smith, having received orders to return to his post at Fort Cass, departed without pursuing the others. He was also informed that the Indians captured in South Carolina had escaped the night before (Oct. 31) through the negligence of the sergeant. Smith had hoped to overtake his other command that day (Nov. 1) but found the Indians reluctant to travel.[40]

Tsali's youngest son, Washington or "Wasitani," later told that a soldier struck his mother with a horsewhip for stopping to care for her infant.[41] To make better time, Smith ordered two of his men to dismount and give their horses to the women and children. Tsali's wife and her infant were placed on a white horse. Wasitani asserted that as the horse started, his mother fell, catching her foot in the stirrup and releasing the infant. The infant apparently sustained a fractured skull and died.

According to Wasitani, it was this incident that provoked his family.[42] Although there is no mention of this in the army record, Smith did report, "I suspected all was not right; & frequently cautioned the men to be on their guard."[43] He also told of confiscating a long dirk from one of the Indians shortly after sunset. Soon afterward, another Indian removed a small axe from his clothing and planted it in the brain of the dismounted soldier at the rear of the party. The soldier fell lifeless at the feet of Lieutenant Smith's horse. The corporal leading the procession was mortally wounded by a blow from a rifle butt and died that night (Nov. 1). The other soldier was stunned by a blow from a tomahawk. Lieutenant Smith was seized by three of the Indians, but his horse, terrified by the warwhoops, broke instantly into a full gallop with Smith, no doubt, hanging on for dear life. He later wrote, "I, fortunately escaped unhurt & owe my life in a measure to the spirit and activity of my horse."[44] Tsali and his family took the other horses and fled into the mountains which rose abruptly from the road. Smith soon joined his other men and returned to the scene but was unable to pursue the Indians because of darkness.

Wasitani recalled that first the fugitives went to the home of Standing Wolfe, leaving the dead infant on the way without burial. After explaining the situation to Standing Wolfe, a Citizen Indian, they continued their journey. The next day, after traveling a long distance, they came upon a farm owned by a white man. One of the younger males, who could speak English, was sent to the house to ask for bread. The farmer, who followed the youth back to the group, gave them food and invited them to hide under a rock overhang near his home. They enjoyed the white man's hospitality for two days before moving on to a less accessible area.[45]

In the meantime, General Winfield Scott was determined to defend the national honor by making sure the murderers were punished. Of the two regiments he had retained to chase the fugitives, the 3rd Artillery was already near Augusta, Georgia, on its way to fight the Seminoles, and the 4th Infantry had been awaiting the return of Lieutenant Smith's detachment before following the emigrants to Arkansas, where they would relieve the 7th Infantry, which was bound for Florida.[46]

After the violence, however, Scott ordered the 4th Infantry back to the North Carolina mountains "to punish the murderers, to quiet the few white families in that region, & to bring in as many fugitives as practical."[47] In the orders to the commander of the 4th, Colonel William S. Foster, Scott emphatically declared: "The individuals guilty of this unprovoked outrage must be shot down. . . . You will summon (if you think useful or necessary) the fugitives to come in, & after or before the summons, fire on any warrior who may disobey you or run from the troops under your command." Scott also carefully pointed out, "The Oconeelufty Indians, in Haywood county, No. Carolina, are not to be considered fugitives, or interrupted, if they continue, as heretofore, peaceable & orderly."[48]

C.H. Larned's company was the first detachment to arrive back in the mountains. He wrote to Colonel Foster:

> I have moved with my company to the Oconoluftee in pursuit of "Little Charley's" gang which comprises all the murderers. My waggons I have directed to follow with all expedition but as I have but two days bread and meat and no sugar or coffee I shall be compelled to purchase unless rations are sent me which as there is a good waggon road all the way can easily be done and a depot established on top of

the Smoky Mountain close to one of the principal lurking places of the Indians at which we shall probably find employment for some days.

The rough map on the other side drawn off by Mr. Thomas will show the points and distances of my course and some of the places where fugitives are supposed to be concealed. Orders will reach me if sent to Mr. Thomas' Store on Oconoluftee.[49]

The attitude of the other Cherokees in North Carolina, both fugitive and citizen, toward Tsali and his family was determined by their own precarious situation. The deaths of the two soldiers had brought an entire regiment of troops back into the mountains when they would have otherwise been en route to Arkansas. The fugitives who had eluded the Army previously would once again be pursued. The Oconaluftee Indians, who had worked hard to project an image of model citizenship, suddenly found the Indian name tarnished by circumstances over which they had no control.

The 4th Infantry sought and received help in pursuing Tsali's family from Will Thomas and the Cherokees remaining in North Carolina. At first, the leader of a band of approximately one hundred fugitives refused to help. Euchella, who had previously been a neighbor of Tsali, stated that he, too, had been hunted like a wild deer by the soldiers. His wife and child had starved to death in the mountains and he had buried them by his own hand at midnight. Subsequently, he capitulated, however, and he and his warriors joined in the search.[50]

Within two weeks, eleven of the twelve fugitives were in confinement at the 4th Infantry headquarters at Camp Scott on the Little Tennessee River. A regimental order of November 21, 1838, states: "A board of officers to consist of Captains McCall & Morris and Lieut. Larned will convene immediately to identify the murderers of Perry and Martin, soldiers of the Fourth Infantry, as such as were accessories before, or after the fact, to the murder, of the above named men, as well as, the individuals concerned in the infliction of a dangerous wound upon Getty, a soldier of the Fourth Infantry, and an assault with intent to kill, upon the person of Lieut. Smith of the 2nd Dragoons.[51]

The document lists the accused in custody as "Nan-tay-a-lee

Jake, Nan-tay-a-lee or Big George and Sowan or Sowney." It concludes with the statement, "The witnesses to establish the identity of these Indians are: Lieut. Smith, W. Thomas, & Esqr. Welsh."[52]

Three days later, as the regiment broke camp, Colonel Foster wrote General Scott that of the four male prisoners "three had been executed by the Cherokees themselves in presence of the Fourth Regiment of Infantry in Line of Battle." Tsali's youngest son had been spared because of his youth. From Fort Cass on December 3, Foster wrote to Scott, "I have now to report that "Old Charley" [Tsali] himself was finally captured and executed by Wa-chee-cha & Euchella at noon on the 25th Utimo (of Nov.) the day after I marched."[53] Will Thomas wrote to an associate, Matthew Russel, the day after Tsali was executed: "Gen Scott employed me to assist in taking the Indians who committed the late murders. Four of the murderers were taken and delivered over. Three of whom have since been shot by the nantihala Indians. The remaining one Charley was brought in yesterday by some of the Indians lying out on Nantihala by them tried and shot near the big Bears reserve on Tuckasega."[54]

Colonel Foster, expressing satisfaction with the outcome of his assignment, wrote to Scott: "The honor of the Nation has been fully cared for, as well as the honor of the Regiment to which I belong—at, & over, the graves of our murdered comrades Funeral honors were paid, for twelve days the men of the regiment passed the mountains, crossed the streams, & threaded the valleys of the country, in detachments of from two to sixty men, in search of the outlaws, or as hunting parties, prepared for Battle or for game."[55]

As for the success of his troops, Foster stated, "I captured no fugitives wither from the camp last summer or from the parties now in March for the West." It is evident that the more serious searching for the murderers was done by the Cherokees. Foster reported to Scott that "the thirty one Indians whom I had in my camp, and whom I held until the final termination of the affair—and then released—all belonged to Euchella's band—with him—(& the Oco nee lufty Indians—under the flying Squirrel) their Fathers, Brothers, and Husbands, pursued, captured, & finally punished the outlaws & murderers—in consequence of which, I permitted them to stay in the mountains."[56]

Colonel Foster continued his report by praising Will Thomas "as an Individual deserving the confidence and patronage of the Country—both for himself—& the Oco-nee-lufty Indians over whom he appears to exercise, unbounded influence, for good purposes."[57] On behalf of the Cherokees permitted to remain, he stated: "I hope that Euchella & his band (including Wa-chee-cha) may be permitted to remain with Wm. Thomas & the Lufty Indians, with whom they fraternized in my presence—Permit me also to state that the conduct of the drowning Bear, the aged chief of the Oco nee lufty' was honorable to himself & tribe & useful to me, & I ask that it may be remembered in his, & their favour."[58]

The widely held belief that today's Eastern Cherokees are descendants of those who fled to the mountains and eluded federal troops in 1838 is a distortion and oversimplification of a very complex episode in Cherokee history. In the period leading up to removal, the Cherokees in western North Carolina were geographically and politically marginal to the Cherokee Nation centered in North Georgia. In 1819, at least sixty Cherokee families relinquished their Cherokee citizenship and accepted individual tracts of land ceded to the United States under provisions of the new treaty. Thus, these people became socially distinct from other Cherokees and socially isolated from whites. Fortunately for these people, encroachment and harassment by whites in North Carolina were not as severe as they were in Georgia or Tennessee. The land was not as valuable. There were no large plantations or productive gold mines. The economy was based on subsistence agriculture, heavily supplemented by food taken from the forests and streams. Thus, the North Carolina Cherokees were much more dependent upon natural resources than were the Cherokees in the other regions.

When forced removal began in June 1838, the rugged terrain and their experience as woodsmen afforded some Cherokees on tribal land an opportunity to escape. By late fall of 1838, several groups of Cherokees, in addition to the Oconaluftee Citizen In-

176

dians, remained in North Carolina. One group of about two hundred Cherokees managed to avoid the spotlight during the removal period. Residing about fifty miles west of the Qualla Boundary, they belonged to the settlement of Cheoah. Mentioned by Thomas in 1836 as one of the towns expected to remain, Cheoah apparently clung to the twelfth article of the New Echota treaty, which permitted a choice of remaining in the East. Although this article was deleted prior to ratification, the Cheoah people, for some reason, were not removed by the soldiers of nearby Fort Montgomery in Robbinsville. At the land sale of September 1838, they were able to purchase 1,235 acres for $1,435.48 in the names of three white men, Joil Manney, Lt. John W. Garland, and J.M. Ray McKay.[59]

The only group affected by the capture of Tsali's family was Euchella's band of fugitives from the Nantahala area. Contrary to popular belief, it was not Winfield Scott who made the decision allowing them to stay, but rather Col. William S. Foster, who found it necessary to justify his action in his report to Major General Scott. Furthermore, it was not a voluntary sacrifice on the part of Tsali that permitted the fugitives to remain, but rather the fact that the fugitive Euchella's band, though at first unwilling, eventually tracked, captured, and executed the murderers. James Mooney and several other writers have spoken of the Cherokee role in the executions of some of their own people as the ultimate humiliation imposed upon them by the United States Army.[60] This attitude is not reflected in any contemporary documentation. Although not explicit, the military reports imply that the executions gave the other fugitive Indians a chance to disassociate themselves from the murders and demonstrate their loyalty (or submission) to the federal government. At the same time it allowed the army to avoid being cast in the villainous role of shooting native Americans who loved their land enough to fight for it. Tsali, who was captured and executed after the troops had left, did not become a martyr to his people until long after the event had become obscured by time.

The most blatant contradiction to popular belief revealed by historical documentation concerns the Oconaluftee Citizen Indians. Today it is commonly held that all the Cherokees of North Carolina were considered fugitives in 1838 and were hunted by the United States Army. In the army records, however, the Oconaluftee Citizen Indians were repeatedly set apart from other Cherokees. They were cited for their assistance in bringing fugitive Cherokees to Fort Cass at the Calhoun agency. Scott, in orders to his subordinates, made it clear that these Indians were not to be disturbed. It can be assumed that, since these Cherokees lived on land ceded in 1819, they were not affected by the Treaty of New Echota and were never expected to remove. The Citizen Indians, comprised of approximately seventy households, formed the nucleus of what became the Eastern Band of Cherokee Indians.

NOTES

1. J.G.M. Ramsey, *Annals of Tennessee* . . . (Charleston, S.C.: Walker and James, 1853), 117–18.
2. Charles Royce, "The Cherokee Nation of Indians," in Bureau of American Ethonology, *5th Annual Report* (Washington, D.C.: GPO, 1887) 219–21.
3. *Cherokee Phoenix,* Jan. 19, 1833.
4. Grace S. Woodward, *Cherokees,* 198.
5. Mooney, "Myths," 123.
6. Royce, "Cherokee Nation," 291; Mooney, "Myths," 129.
7. Mooney, "Myths," 129.
8. John Gulick, *Cherokees at the Crossroads* (Chapel Hill: Institute for Research in Soc. Sc., Univ. of North Carolina, 1960), 14.
9. Mooney, "Myths," 157.
10. *Ibid.,* 164.
11. Yonaguska at that time lived on Governor's Island, across from the ancient Kituhwa site; Long Blanket lived where the Cherokee Elementary School now stands; Wilnota lived on Wright's Creek.
12. Original document in Haywood County's *Old Record Book of Deeds,* Bk. B, 547; typescript copy furnished by Carl Lambert of Cherokee, N.C.
13. Gulick, *Cherokees at the Crossroads,* 13.
14. William H. Thomas to James Graham, Oct. 18, 1838, p. 2; typescript copy in Western Carolina Univ. Archives.
15. Mooney, "Myths," 163–64.
16. *Ibid.,* 163.
17. Thomas to Graham, Oct. 18, 1838, p. 2.
18. Woodward, *Cherokees,* 174.
19. Thomas to John F. Schermerhorn, Aug. 28, 1845; Schermerhorn's reply written on the same paper. Published in *Unto These Hills Souvenir Program* (Cherokee, N.C.: Cherokee Hist. Assoc., 1972), 42.

20. George D. Harman, "The North Carolina Cherokees and the New Echota Treaty of 1835," *North Carolina Historical Review* 6 (July 1929), 243.

21. *Ibid.*, 243-44.

22. C.A. Harris to Thomas, July 19, 1936, Western Carolina Univ. Archives.

23. William H. Thomas, "Explanation of the Rights of the North Carolina Cherokee Indians," 25 Cong., 2 sess., *Senate Doc. 120* (1851; rpt. ed. Asheville: Stephens Press, 1947), 156.

24. *Senate Doc. 120*, 24; Milling, *Carolinians*, 367.

25. Milling, *Carolinians*, 367.

26. *Ibid.; Senate Doc. 120*, 25.

27. Foreman, *Indian Removal*, 272.

28. Gilbert E. Govan and James W. Livingood, *The Chattanooga Country, 1540–1951: From Tomahawks to TVA* (New York: Dutton, 1952), 92.

29. Harris to Thomas, July 19, 1836; (quotation from Thomas' personal notes attached to p. 2), Western Carolina Univ. Archives.

30. Thomas to Graham, Oct. 18, 1838, p. 1, quoting Graham's address to Congress, Western Carolina Univ. Archives.

31. Winfield Scott to James Monroe, Nov. 9, 1838, p. 1; typescript copy in the Western Carolina Univ. Archives.

32. *Ibid.*

33. Carl Lambert (personal communication, Mar. 1974).

34. Scott to Monroe, Nov. 9, 1838, p. 1.

35. C.H. Larned to Scott, Nov. 5, 1838, Civil Archives, S1564 no. 2, National Archives, Washington, D.C.; quoted in Paul Kutsche, "The Tsali Legend: Culture Heroes and Historiography," *Ethnohistory* 10 (1963), 332-33.

36. Charles Crowe (personal communication, June 1971).

37. Scott to Monroe, Nov. 9, 1838, p. 2.

38. *Ibid.*, 1.

39. A.J. Smith to Scott, Nov. 5, 1838, Civil Archives, S1566 no. 2, National Archives, Washington, D.C.; quoted in Kutsche, "Tsali Legend," 331-32.

40. *Ibid.*

41. *Ibid.*, 341.

42. *Ibid.*

43. Smith to Scott, Nov. 5, 1838, p. 1.

44. *Ibid.*

45. Kutsche, "Tsali Legend," 341.

46. Scott to Monroe, Nov. 9, 1838, p. 2.

47. *Ibid.*

48. Scott to William S. Foster, Nov. 8, 1838, p. 1, Civil Archives, S1564, no. 1, National Archives, Washington, D.C.; quoted in Kutsche, "Tsali Legend," 334-36.

49. Larned to Foster, n.d., but written about the 2d week of Nov. 1838; typescript copy in Museum of the Cherokee Indian Archives, Cherokee, N.C.

50. Charles Lanman, *Letters from the Alleghany Mountains* (New York: Putnam, 1849), 112-14.

51. Typescript copy of this numbered regimental order is in the Museum of the Cherokee Indian Archives.

52. *Ibid.;* "Esqr. Welsh" apparently was James Welsh, at whose home

Smith's party stopped the night before Tsali's family made their bid for freedom.

53. Foster to Scott, Dec. 3, 1838, p. 2, quoting letter of Nov. 24, 1838; typescript in Western Carolina Univ. Archives.

54. Thomas to Matthew Russell, Nov. 25, 1838; typescript copy in Western Carolina Univ. Archives.

55. Foster to Scott, Dec. 3, 1838, p. 2.

56. *Ibid.*, 3.

57. *Ibid.*

58. *Ibid.*, 3-4.

59. William H. Thomas, Diary no. 3, 1838, p. 5, Western Carolina Univ. Archives.

60. Mooney, "Myths," 157-58.

William Holland Thomas and the Cherokee Claims

Richard W. Iobst

Although the Founding Fathers of the United States spoke with sincerity of "freedom and liberty for all," and promised a full new life to all who might emigrate to America, they spoke of the rights of white men only. The American Indian, once sole inhabitant of a vast continent, had already been largely dispossessed by the late eighteenth century. The great American frontier, beginning in eastern New England and Virginia in the seventeenth century, had gradually been pushed westward into the Ohio and Mississippi valleys. Moreover, those Indians who fought to defend their homes were brutally pushed aside in such encounters as King Philip's War in Massachusetts, the Rappahannock Uprising in Virginia, and the Tuscarora War in North Carolina. No American of the eighteenth or nineteenth centuries gave the rights of the red men serious thought—in fact, few people regarded the Indians as even possessing the requisites of human beings. By the first half of the nineteenth century such writers as James Fenimore Cooper, William Gilmore Simms, and Henry Wadsworth Longfellow might write about the noble American Indian and the glories of the western wilderness, but when it came to equality with the white man they held the Indian as a member of a race apart.

Probably no Indian tribe in America suffered more at the hands of the white man than did the Cherokees who inhabited the mountain regions of Tennessee, Georgia, and North Carolina. Through a series of harsh treaties negotiated after the American Revolution, the Indians yielded valuable territory. These treaties, from the Treaty of Hopewell in 1785 to the Treaty of New Echota

181

in 1835, were the result of two factors: (1) the constant demand for land which accompanied the westward expansion of the United States; (2) the growing weakness of the Indians, which forced them into a state of compliance.

By 1835 the federal government, supported by such officials as former Gov. Wilson Lumpkin of Georgia, determined to remove the 16,542 Cherokees remaining in the East to lands west of the Mississippi. Early in 1835 the Reverend John F. Schermerhorn of Utica, New York, was appointed commissioner to arrange a treaty with the party of Cherokees in Georgia led by Major Ridge and his son John, important leaders who had despaired of further resistance. The treaty, signed on March 14, 1835, called for the extinction of all Cherokee land titles in the East upon the completion of two conditions: (1) the payment of $4,500,000 to the Indians; (2) the approval of the Cherokee Nation meeting in full council. This treaty was rejected by such a council at Red Clay, Georgia, in October 1835. However, a new treaty, endorsed by the Ridge faction, was signed by Schermerhorn and a number of Georgia Cherokees at New Echota, Georgia, capital of the Cherokee Nation, on December 29, 1835. By the terms of this agreement the Cherokees ceded all of their remaining lands east of the Mississippi to the United States in return for $5,000,000 and the right to occupy lands in the Indian Territory [modern Oklahoma] adjacent to those already occupied by the Western Band of Cherokees, called the "Old Settlers."

In spite of strong protests made by the chief of the Georgia Cherokees, John Ross, who was not a party to the treaty, and other leaders, arrangements were made to remove *all* Cherokees living in Georgia, North Carolina, Alabama, and Tennessee. General John E. Wool was placed in command of federal troops overseeing their removal. He was soon superseded by Major General Winfield Scott, who arrived in the Cherokee Nation and established headquarters at New Echota on May 10, 1838. Troops were sent throughout the area to forcibly remove the Indians from their homes and take them to various forts or depots established for that purpose. Most of the Cherokees submitted peacefully, and were sent to Arkansas and Oklahoma either by steamer down the Tennessee River or along the infamous "Trail of Tears," but some of the North Carolina Cherokees fled into the rugged mountains of western North Carolina. Scott decided it would be militarily impossible to capture more of the escaped Indians because the winter of 1838-39 was beginning. These Indians, and certain others who lived along the banks of Shoal Creek in Haywood County, North Carolina, in a settlement called Qualla Town, were befriended by a white man who had been adopted into the Cherokee tribe. His name was William Holland Thomas.

Thomas was born on February 5, 1805, on Pigeon River in Haywood County. He was the posthumous son of Richard Thomas, who came to North Carolina from Virginia in 1803, and his wife Temperance Calvert Thomas, the descendant of pioneer settlers in Maryland. He was connected to the Calverts, Lords Proprietors of Maryland, through his mother and to President Zachary Taylor through his father. His relationship with the Cherokees began when he was employed by Congressman Felix Walker to clerk in a trading post at Qualla Town in western Haywood County. Here Thomas traded goods to the Cherokees in exchange for deerskins and ginseng, used as a medicine in the Orient. While engaged in this activity he was befriended by Yonaguska, or "Drowning Bear," chief of the Cherokees living in the Middle Towns along the Little Tennessee and Oconaluftee rivers. With Yonaguska's support Thomas was adopted into the Cherokee tribe and given the name "Will-Usdi," or "Little Will." In the late 1820s Thomas began to operate three lucrative trading posts at Qualla Town [Walker's old store], at the mouth of Scotts Creek in the present town of Dillsboro, and at Murphy in Cherokee County.

After the Great Removal Thomas went to Washington as the attorney for those Cherokees who remained in the East. His mission was to secure the money due them under the terms of the Treaty of New Echota and to obtain permission for them to live in their native mountains. His motives for this activity were purely humanitarian. According to his son James, Thomas had "almost romantic fondness for the Cherokee Tribe," which "caused him to devote many of the best years of his life to their advancement morally and materially."[1] Thomas himself wrote T. Hartley

Crawford, commissioner of the Bureau of Indian Affairs and one of the officials he dealt with, that the Cherokees should not be forced to emigrate to the West unless they wished to go. After all, he explained, "What is there to make them more unsettled than the white citizens. they too have a right to remove & are offered a bounty to go to Texes but it is scarcely presumable that such as do not intend going are unsettled in consequence of having the offer made to them."[2] People, Thomas believed, should have the liberty of changing their situation whenever they wished. In a letter to Felix Axley, a prominent lawyer in Murphy, North Carolina, Thomas replied to a report that he had alienated some of his best friends by championing the rights of the Indians:

> If my advocating their rights has offended any of my friends . . . I have one consolation that I have faithfully discharged my duty to those people a conscientious discharge of which is worth more to me than the unjust approbation of the world and I had much rather be blamed for doing my duty than neglecting it and when entrusted with defending the rights of white or red man I hope I shall always be found faithful to my trust and act worthy of the confidence reposed in me without regard to consequences. The Indians are as much entitled to their rights as I am to mine.[3]

He told his Indian friends to be patient and law-abiding while waiting to be reimbursed, because "that Being who rules the distinies of nations . . . will turn all things for good to those who . . . put their trust in him." After all, Thomas assured them, "god . . . has as much regard for his red children as his white."[4] Furthermore, there were so few Cherokees remaining in the East that, except on Valley River in Cherokee County, they could not possibly be in the way of the whites.[5]

Thomas based his defense of the North Carolina Cherokees upon the terms of the Treaty of New Echota. This document provided that the Cherokees would be allowed a common joint interest in the country occupied by the Old Settlers, with a small additional tract on the northeast. The Indians would be paid for all the improvements they had made on their eastern lands, would be removed at the expense of the federal government, and subsisted for one year by the federal authorities. The Indian debts

184

had to be deducted from the $5,000,000 which was promised them. The federal government was authorized to build military posts and roads within the territory of the Western Cherokees. All annuities paid to the Indians under earlier treaties would be placed in a permanent Cherokee national fund, the interest from which was to go toward the establishment and upkeep of schools and orphan asylums, and for the general national purposes of the Indians. However, Article VIII of the treaty provided that "such persons and families as, in the opinion of the emigrating agent, are capable of subsisting and removing themselves, shall be permitted to do so; and they shall be allowed in full for all claims for the same twenty dollars for each member of their family; and in lieu of their one year's rations, they shall be paid the sum of thirty-three dollars and thirty-three cents."[6] Article XII stated: "Those individuals and families of the Cherokee Nation that are averse to a removal to the Cherokee Country west of the Mississippi, and are desirous to become citizens of the States where they reside, and such as are qualified to take care of themselves and their property, shall be entitled to receive their due portion of all the personal benefits accruing under this treaty for their claims, improvements, and per capita [improvements]; as soon as an appropriation is made for this treaty."[7] These clauses had been added to the treaty in order to give the Indians a perfect freedom of choice to go or stay, as they wished, "excepting such only as might be deemed incompetent to take care of themselves and property."[8] Unfortunately, Article XII was deleted from the treaty when it was sent to the Senate for ratification in the spring of 1836. Moreover, in 1837 Martin Van Buren became president, bringing a change in public officials and a corresponding change in the interpretation of the treaty.[9] For a time it seemed that the North Carolina Cherokees, never a party to the treaty, might not be paid their claims and might even be forced to emigrate to the West.

The relations of the federal government with the Indian tribes were regulated in the 1830s and '40s by a Bureau of Indian Affairs presided over by a commissioner. This agency was under the general supervision of the War Department, directed by the sec-

185

retary of war. In Martin Van Buren's administration the secretary of war was Joel R. Poinsett of South Carolina. His Indian commissioner was, as previously noted, T. Hartley Crawford. Unfortunately, when Thomas arrived in Washington in the spring of 1839 with a power of attorney to represent the Cherokees, Crawford was absent. No claims arising under the Treaty of New Echota could be considered until he returned. Nevertheless, Thomas was hopeful that, despite the delay, the claims would be paid.[10] Much of this optimism stemmed from an interview with Secretary Poinsett, who proved willing to allow the Cherokees to remain in the East "under the control of the state in which they resided." Moreover, Poinsett would allow the Cherokees their removal and subsistence allowance, a total of $53.33 each, if they wished to remove to the West.[11]

Typically, the slowness of the federal bureaucracy meant there would be some delay in paying the claims of the Indians. After a quick business trip to western North Carolina in July 1839, Thomas returned to Washington to prepare the total amount of claims due the Eastern Cherokees. One of his objects was to procure the removal and subsistence allowance for each of the Indians and place the money in a bank where it could draw interest for them. He estimated that the total monies owed to the Indians remaining in the East was $200,000.[12]

While Thomas waited for a final decision from Commissioner Crawford, another problem arose to plague him. The chiefs of the Western Cherokees in Arkansas protested against the payment of claims to their brethren in the East, believing that the money should be sent to them and held for the Eastern Cherokees until they emigrated. Thomas believed that this group should be defeated because he did not trust John Ross and feared the money would be spent by the Western Cherokees. He outlined a three-point program to accomplish his objectives: (1) the Eastern Cherokees should be permitted to remain where they were, with assurance from the government that they would not be forcibly removed; (2) if any wished to emigrate they should be paid their removal and subsistence allowances; (3) all of their other claims should be paid to them even if they remained in the East. As we have seen,

Secretary Poinsett agreed to the first two points of this program but told Thomas that no decision could be made on the third request until Commissioner Crawford made a full report. In the meantime Thomas urged the Eastern Cherokees to "be industrious honest, and temperate, and to live in peace with each other and their white neighbors."[13]

Thomas retained his confidence that final justice would be done the Cherokees. He felt that the War Department, in its review of Commissioner Crawford's report, would probably give a more liberal construction to the terms of the treaty than was given to it by a special board of commissioners which had been appointed by President Van Buren to administer it. While the claims were being considered, Thomas worked to procure a settlement of his own claim for reimbursement as contractor for the army stationed in the Cherokee country during the Great Removal.[14] He also occupied himself with obtaining the claims of some of his white friends who had rendered similar services.[15] Most of his time was spent, however, in preparing a report on the Indian claims for Commissioner Crawford. This paper, completed by midsummer 1839, included a commutation claim for $50,000 which had previously been believed to be unallowable. Thomas felt that he could gain this claim by remaining in Washington and fighting for it.[16] Summer dragged into early fall as he wrote out arguments in the War Department office from nine in the morning until five in the evening, then worked in his room until ten or eleven at night.[17]

In late July 1839, news arrived from the West which greatly enhanced Thomas' efforts to procure justice for the Eastern Cherokees. Reports indicated that Major Ridge, his son John, and one of their principal supporters, Elias Boudinot, had been brutally murdered by members of the Ross faction among the Western Cherokees.[18] News arrived in late September that Ross also was in danger of his life and was being guarded by 500 of his friends. Moreover, it looked as if a civil war would break out between the Ridge and Ross factions, although federal troops were doing all they could "to prevent the effusion of blood."[19]

In the meantime Thomas did his utmost to secure the Indian

claims and to satisfy the clamor of lawyers such as John F. Gillaspie, George W. Churchwell, Nicholas Peck, William Roan, Felix Axley, George W. Chandler, and Nicholas Woodfin, who claimed compensation for services rendered to the Cherokees in preparing and attending to their reservation claims. He informed Commissioner Crawford, "Some of those gentlemen have prepared and forwarded to me, arguments in support of reservation claims rejected by the Commissioners, which they wish filed in the respective cases for which they were intended. Will you please inform me if you have any objections to the above requests being complied with."[20] These problems caused much anxiety for Thomas, leading him to exclaim, "The great responsibility resting on me taking into consideration the large amount involved, has compelled me to remain and give thereto my constant attention."[21]

Sadly, Thomas began to realize, by late August 1839, that no payments would be made on claims before fall because Secretary Poinsett, who had to make the final decision on Commissioner Crawford's report, was away from Washington for the summer. About all Thomas could do was to prevent the money from being sent to the strife-torn Western Cherokees.[22] He busied himself by writing letters to inform the various claimants of this circumstance, urging them to be patient.[23]

In early September, hoping for the earliest possible settlement of some of the claims, Thomas continued to press Secretary Poinsett's department for payment of the removal and subsistence allowance. If he were paid the money, he could deposit it in the State Bank of North Carolina and give it to the Indians as they emigrated to their new homes in the West. He informed Poinsett, "May I be permitted to make known to [the president] through your Department the desire of the Cherokees still remaining east that so much of said appropriation as they shall be deemed entitled to, be set apart for the purposes for which it was intended." If the president should decide to place a limitation on the time for removal, under the terms of the treaty he should "allow them at best three years which owing to the great excitement and domestic strife prevailing with their brethren who have emigrated, is not considered unreasonable." If it should become necessary to appoint an agent to oversee the emigration, Thomas tendered his services to perform the necessary duties. Secretary Poinsett must quickly arrive at a decision in the matter of the removal and subsistence allowances, however, because the season for emigration was getting late.[24]

To facilitate the government's plans, Thomas even suggested a program for emigration. Under this plan a supplemental census of the Cherokees remaining East would be taken in the counties where they resided. Each head of a family would be required to express his voluntary desire to remain in the East or to emigrate. This new census would list all the Cherokees born since the 1835 census. Thomas explained that all of this could be done under machinery established by Article XII of the Treaty of New Echota.[25]

Because Secretary Poinsett looked with favor upon the claims for removal and subsistence, Thomas optimistically made arrangements to deposit the money in a state bank to draw interest until the Indians should emigrate. He wrote former Governor Wilson Lumpkin of Georgia asking if the Railroad Bank of Georgia would receive at least $50,000 in such funds. He then sent a similar letter to Major Hinton, the public treasurer of North Carolina, inquiring about depositing the funds in the state bank at Raleigh, and added, "None of the principal will be required only as those Cherokees who have become citizens of the state, desire to emigrate and join their people at their new homes west of the Mississippi, therefore none will be wanting before next fall and then it is probable but a very small amount, those people having made their choice to remain it is not presumable that they will change their opinion only as influenced by information received from their friends in the west."[26] Thomas sent a copy of this letter to Governor Edward B. Dudley of North Carolina, praising the state "whose Statute Books have never been disgraced by Legislative enactments, calculated to oppress or distress the poor and unfortunate Indians within her territory."[27]

In spite of this optimism, in the fall of 1839 Thomas still did not know the ultimate conclusion of his efforts to secure the Cherokee claims. As late as October 3, Commissioner Crawford had not completed his report, and Secretary Poinsett was still absent. Until the report was finished and the secretary had reviewed it, very little could be done.[28]

During the delay, Thomas occupied his time writing an explanation of the rights of the Eastern Cherokees, including the claim for preemptions which had been rejected earlier by Commissioner Crawford. As Thomas wrote J.W. King, the decision had been made upon *ex parte* evidence; that is, no evidence was furnished in favor of the claimants. If he failed to obtain this claim, it could be added to the claim for removal and subsistence. Thomas believed that, if the War Department confined the construction of the treaty to the letter, then the preemption claim had to be allowed. It was well worth fighting for because it amounted to at least $60,000.[29] The situation in Arkansas was still favorable to Thomas's cause because the Indians there were "in a state of great excitement and confusion." The federal government had demanded the murderers of the Ridges and Boudinot, and the Cherokees' future in that area was uncertain. It was still inexpedient for the Eastern Cherokees to move west, at least until the difficulties between the Ridge and Ross factions had been resolved. In the meantime, Thomas advised the Eastern Cherokees "to have no correspondence with those west."[30] It would hurt their chances of being fully remunerated under the terms of the treaty and perhaps defeat their desire to "be permitted to remain in the land of their fathers."[31]

Unfortunately, the explosive situation among the Western Cherokees caused Secretary Poinsett to suspend claims payments to all of the Indians on November 12, 1839. Thomas informed a friend, James P.H. Porter of Tennessee: "The government is determined on having punished" the murderers of the Ridges and Boudinot.[32] In the midst of all this, Commissioner Crawford completed his report and submitted it to Secretary Poinsett in late November, but "until [Poinsett's] action thereon but little [could] be known or said respecting it."[33] To make matters worse, Ross and a delegation from the Western Cherokees were expected to try to get all the Indian claims paid to the treasurer of the Nation.[34]

190

Because of these unforeseen developments, Thomas could do nothing. When George W. Churchwell suggested that the rejected claims should be referred to Congress, Thomas replied: "As I have previously suggested to you I deem it inexpedient to lay any of the rejected claims before Congress until after those allowed are paid. If we were to lay them before Congress before payment is made on such as have been allowed a Commit[tee] might be appointed to investigate all the Cherokee business which in all probability would occasion a further delay of at least 2 years."[35]

Thomas felt that the rejected claims should be ignored temporarily, for he hoped to establish principles which would lead to their being allowed at the proper time. If it were once decided that the "life-estate reservees"—those who owned their farms or reservations only during their own lifetimes—could dispose only of their own interest in their reservations and that they could not act against their children's rights to secure fee simple titles, it would naturally follow that all such claims would constitute legal claims against the United States. If the claimants were not finally compensated under the terms of the Treaty of New Echota, Thomas believed Congress would make an additional appropriation to satisfy such claims. He hoped that Churchwell would, in his position as one of the attorneys for the Cherokees, keep such information confidential because "it might be thought improper in me to make such suggestion at this time."[36]

By December 17, 1839, after he had been in Washington for nine months, Thomas could report that he had gained the per capita claim, as well as some others. However, he had been unable to obtain either the Cherokees' removal and subsistence claims or their preemption allowances. Until Secretary Poinsett completed his review of Commissioner Crawford's report, Thomas could not ascertain what would be done with the money due the Eastern Cherokees. Although he had been able to secure some of the Indian claims, this was, in a very real sense, an empty victory. The money had not been released by Secretary Poinsett to pay the Indians. When it was released Thomas planned either to deposit it on interest in the State Bank of North Carolina or to

191

leave it to the individuals to invest in bonds "with such sureties as might be considered sufficient to insure the payment at" the promised time.[37] Whatever happened, Thomas was determined to persevere and not to surrender any claim "until every ground it can be placed on has been tried."[38]

In late December Secretary Poinsett made his decision. The decisions made by the Board of Commissioners, established by the Treaty of New Echota to administer the treaty, would be final. All of the claims were allowed except four. Two of these involved men who had sold their reservations before the conclusion of the treaty and had thereby forfeited their rights to compensation. The other two were claims upon which the commissioners had decided to issue grants. Secretary Poinsett and his attorneys felt that these claims should also be relinquished because no grants could be issued to the claimants except when it was ascertained that they were entitled to receive the value of the claims. The secretary also decided that the last appropriation made for the Indians could be used to pay for reservations which had been allowed.[39] Commissioner Crawford and Secretary Poinsett still adamantly held the position that the Cherokees were entitled to the subsistence and removal claims only after they had removed to Arkansas. Thomas would, therefore, do everything he could to overturn the decision regarding these claims. In addition, Thomas asked Secretary Poinsett to separate the claims of the Eastern Cherokees from those in the West. Poinsett took the matter under consideration.[40]

While he was securing the per capita and spoliation claims under the Treaty of New Echota, Thomas was plagued by many problems. John Ross and his delegation of Western Cherokees arrived in Washington in December 1839 after procuring the consent of a majority of the Cherokees to have the Treaty of New Echota annulled and to make a new one containing a special provision that the money due the Cherokees should be paid to Lewis Ross, the treasurer of the Nation. Although Ross had not been received by Secretary Poinsett because he was still under suspicion of murdering the Ridges and Boudinot and of inciting the Creeks and Seminoles to war against the United States, there was a possibility that his demand for claims money would be met.[41] Furthermore, reports had arrived in Washington that some of the whites living in the Valley River area of Cherokee County had petitioned for the removal of the Indians. Thomas wrote John Simson, a Cherokee chief, that the Cherokees should "entertain no unkind feelings toward them but treat them with the same friendship as if they had not signed the petition." If Simson's people acted in a quiet way, they would have nothing to fear, because God would turn all things for good.[42] He elaborated upon this theme in a letter to two other Cherokees: "The only thing necessary is to demean yourselves as good citizens by being temperate [N]one can long remain who will not conform to this rul in . . . a white population — for you would if even permitted to remain — soon sink into degradation and annihilation like the Catawbas and many other tribes. I therefore as your friend advise you to adhere closely to your temperance rules. Be peacible with each other and your white neighbors."[43]

Thomas also had to defend himself against officials such as Gen. John E. Wool, former commander in the Cherokee country, who had made an attack against his character. Although the matter was straightened out, some animosity remained between the two men.[44] Then, of course, there was the "tardy process" of doing business with federal officials. Thomas wrote H.P. King, his clerk in the store at Qualla Town, that "it requires constant perseverance and the patience of Job to accomplish anything."[45] All these difficulties combined to make Thomas understandably eager to see his "native country" again.[46]

Although the claims were not resolved until a treaty was signed at Washington on July 29, 1848, which allowed the Eastern Band of Cherokees to participate in the benefits of the New Echota Treaty, Thomas had some advantages in conducting his otherwise tedious business. Commissioner Crawford was a pleasant man to work with, and J.K. Rogers, an attorney who provided legal assistance, was an able lawyer. Furthermore, Washington, even in the 1830s and '40s, was an interesting place. At dawn on July 4, 1839, the city celebrated the Fourth of July by ringing fire and church bells and discharging small cannon. At ten o'clock troops paraded through the streets, and an oration was delivered at the Baptist Church, where the Declaration of Independence was read,"accompanied at intervals by a Band of Music."[47] On January 1, 1844, Thomas attended President Tyler's levee, observing, "The foreign ministers appeared in the costumes addopted at their courts — officers in military dress. A band of musicians was stationed near the entrance to amuse the company."[48] During the 1840s he attended a number of Fourth of July celebrations during which rockets were fired in the evening on the Mall near the White House.[49] Faithful in attending church, he noted the sermons and his Sunday afternoon outings in the diaries which present a daily record of his life. He also attended a number of dinners, went on many excursions, including an extended trip through New York and New England in the summer of 1845, and, since he was a bachelor at this time, enjoyed the company of the ladies. Possibly his most important activity was his companionship with the great men of the day. He was on intimate terms with such national leaders as Governor David S. Reid, General Duff Green, and Senators Willie P. Mangum, William Haywood, and Thomas L. Clingman.

During his stay at Washington, Thomas was a witness to many of the outstanding events of the day. On March 4, 1845, he stood in a heavy rain to witness the following incident:

James Knox Polk standing on the East portico of the Capitol with an umbrella held over him delivered his inaugural address. I remained until tired of standing in the rain — returned to my boarding house. There were a large concourse of people said to be greater than that of 1840 — canon continued to fire while the procession was forming and when the President closed his address, which was delivered in a plain manner, without any apparent affectation, his mien seemed suitable to the occasion, and where I stood in the crowd I had an opportunity, of hearing most of what he said. [H]is message was written and only read by him.[50]

During the early 1840s Thomas continued to spend most of his time in Washington trying to separate the claims of the Eastern and Western Cherokees on a per capita basis and attempting to obtain the removal and subsistence allowance for the Eastern Cherokees even if they remained in the East. Commissioner Crawford still refused to pay the latter claim because the Indians had not gone West. In an effort to win his point Thomas took the position, in a letter to President Polk's secretary of war, William L. Marcy of New York, that a supplementary act of Congress of June 12, 1838, which pertained to the removal and subsistence allowance, applied only to those Indians which it was the purpose of the government to remove, "and to accomplish which the Government was authorised to use *coercion.*" Articles VIII and XII of the Treaty of New Echota provided for two classes of Indians. Article XII provided for individuals and their families who did not want to go West to become citizens of the states in which they resided. Thomas contended that those Indians who remained in the East had automatically become citizens of Georgia, North Carolina, and Tennessee. Besides, he claimed, the Cherokee Nation had ceased to exist when it was absorbed by the state of Georgia even before the ratification of the Treaty of New Echota.[51] To support his argument Thomas wrote the Reverend John F. Schermerhorn, the agent who had negotiated the treaty. In reply to Thomas's question of whether or not the Cherokee Indians who resided in North Carolina were present or represented at the Council which concluded the treaty, Schermerhorn replied that they were not. In fact, none of the North Carolina Cherokees gave their consent to the treaty even after a visit by Schermerhorn to persuade them to sign it.[52]

Thomas constantly urged the Indians to move to Qualla Town, located on Shoal Creek in what was then the western portion of Haywood County, and Buffalo Town [Cheoih], located near the site of modern Robbinsville, county seat of Graham County. The other Indians who lived along the Valley River in Cherokee County continued to concern Thomas. He wanted them to move to Qualla Town or Buffalo Town because they were being debased by the whiskey shops which surrounded them. In a long petition to the General Assembly of North Carolina, their white neighbors complained of their too-liberal partaking of spirits. Thomas insisted, "That spirit of contention will be kept up as long as the Indians remain there, and may lead to an opposition to their claims which will defeat most of them."

He asserted that the rights of the people of Qualla and Buffalo towns were entirely different from those of the Indians on Valley River. The Secretary of War had agreed, as early as 1836, that "a settlement of Cherokees might remain unmolested at Qualla and also one at Cheoih or Buffalo."[53] Thomas, moreover, hoped that the new president, Polk, would settle the Indian claims by giving their full proportionate share to the Eastern Cherokees. Unfortunately, once again problems relating to the Western Cherokees caused delay in the settlement of the claims of their kinsmen in the East. One of the commissioners sent to treat with the Western Cherokees was accused of drunkenness and neglect of duty. The commissioner, a General Mason, confirmed these reports by visiting President Polk and Secretary of War Marcy while under the influence of liquor. Mason and the other commissioners were dismissed by Polk, who then began to look with favor upon Thomas' claims for the Eastern Cherokees.[54]

Shortly after Polk came into office Thomas spent nearly a month preparing a twenty-four-page argument which set forth all the treaties made with the Cherokees and all their claims.[55] Polk read Thomas' argument and its accompanying documents and, at Thomas' request, forwarded it to John Y. Mason, attorney general of the United States. Polk propounded the following important questions, evidently suggested to him by Thomas:

> 1st. are the Cherokee Indians remaining in the State of North Carolina entitled under the Cherokee Treaty of 1835 to fifty three dollars and thirty three cents each as a commutation in lieu of having been removed west at the expense of the Government, and did not the United States stipulate to pay all the Cherokees that chose to remain east that sum, and did not the United States pay to the Cherokee remaining in Georgia that sum under the same Treaty.

> 2d If the Attorney General should be of opinion that the Cherokees remaining in North Carolina are not entitled to that sum, then are they not entitled to the land granted to them under the act of 1783, by the state of North Carolina — which embraces all of the Cherokee County and a part of Macon.[56]

Mason waited until September 19 to answer Polk's letter, giving "urgent business" as the reason for his delay. He pointed out that the War Department had paid the Georgia Cherokees the $53.33. However, Mason pointed out that Schermerhorn believed it to be the understanding of both parties to the treaty "that the sum of $53.33 should be paid to each of the Cherokees that remained in North Carolina."[57] Also, Mason explained that the Cherokee chiefs who made the treaty had acknowledged the North Carolina Cherokees' right to remain in North Carolina and become citizens of that state provided they lived in Qualla Town or Buffalo Town; they had agreed "also that the sum of $53.33 was to be assigned by the Government to the use of each of the Cherokees who then belonged to those Towns or might afterwards belong to them."[58] However, Mason believed that Congress would have to pass a law authorizing Polk to pay the $53.33 claim. Mason felt that the lands sold by North Carolina under the Act of 1783 were in the possession of the purchasers. Since Polk had no authority to take the land from the rightful owners, and since Mason believed the question was "one for the judiciary," he deemed it unnecessary to express an opinion about it. Nevertheless, Mason realized the North Carolina Indians had been treated harshly because, while their lands had been sold, they had received no corresponding benefit.[59]

Polk agreed with his attorney general and, in a conference with Thomas, stated that he "was perfectly satisfied that great injustice had been done to the North Carolina Indians."[60] The president wanted to settle all just claims of the Eastern Cherokees but preferred to wait for a delegation of chiefs in the old Ridge-Boudinot faction who were momentarily expected from the West. Thomas agreed to wait for this group because he felt Polk was "in favor of adopting a liberal policy towards the North Carolina Indians" and had no desire to hinder them from remaining where they were.[61]

On February 2, 1846, Thomas visited the War Department and heard Secretary of War Marcy tell the Commissioner of Indian Affairs that Polk wanted to dispose of the Indian claims through a treaty with the Cherokees. At long last it seemed that the claims of the Cherokees for which Thomas had been fighting for ten years would be settled.[62]

197

During the spring of 1846 Thomas wrote a number of arguments to the Senate in support of the Indian claims. He also saw President Polk several times and attended a number of meetings of the Board of Commissioners which Polk had appointed to arrange the treaty. On August 3, 4, 5, and 6 Thomas gave his full attention to the treaty and made an effort on August 8 to add to the treaty an amendment providing that the Eastern Cherokees should receive their portion of the money to be paid to the Cherokee Nation for lands ceded under the Treaty of New Echota. At first it appeared that all of Thomas' efforts would end in failure because the treaty was voted down, but then, while the Senate still seemed to be in a state of uncertainty over the ultimate fate of the treaty, an effort was made to submit his amendment. Gallowatty Thompson, the attorney for the Cherokees, agreed to introduce it. Senator Willie Person Mangum, a strong friend of Thomas and the Eastern Cherokees, was able to get the treaty ratified shortly afterwards. On Monday, August 10, 1846, Congress convened at an early hour. The Senate promptly passed an appropriation bill to supplement this treaty and sent it on to the House. Here Gen. Duff Green persuaded Rep. Daniel Moreau Barringer of North Carolina to offer an amendment to the money bill proposing that the North Carolina Cherokees should receive their due portion of all "the moneys stipulated to be paid by the United States to the Cherokees." After further debate, although the amendment was rejected, the bill passed but did not, for lack of time, receive the signature of the Speaker. Therefore the bill was lost.[63] It was not until July 29, 1848, that both houses of Congress passed a money bill providing for the payment of the subsistence and removal allowance to the Eastern Cherokees. It is difficult to see how the bill could have passed at all without the support and enthusiasm of Thomas.[64]

Thomas had a distinguished career during the 1850s in the North Carolina senate where, as chairman of the Committee on Internal Improvements, he championed the cause of roads and railroads throughout the western counties of the state. He was instrumental in the completion of the Western North Carolina Railroad to Asheville and Murphy in the postwar period. In 1861 he

198

served as a member of the constitutional convention which voted North Carolina out of the Union, but he was opposed to secession, comparing it to the separation of the Methodist Church into northern and southern branches and to the divorce of a man and his wife when they find that living together no longer promotes their mutual happiness.

Never an ardent secessionist, he nevertheless was a good Confederate, serving on a committee on mountain defense in the convention, and later proposing to Gov. Henry T. Clark that the passes in the Iron Mountains should be fortified "as [the] best mode of defending the Carolinas and Georgia." In April, 1862, Thomas organized the nucleus of the Thomas Legion, leading it until May, 1865, when it fired the last shots of the conflict in North Carolina.

Although he later accomplished all these things, the outstanding achievement of his life was securing the Indian claims. It is in this capacity that he rose to true greatness. His fight for the acceptance of the Cherokee Indians into the white community at a time when such a cause was unpopular — even radical — proves that he was a true humanitarian of the nineteenth century. Thomas' struggle to procure the Indian claims provides a unique chapter in the history of western North Carolina, an area hitherto largely neglected by the professional historian.

NOTES

1. Eugene I. McCormack, "Personnel of the Convention of 1861," in James Sprunt, *Studies in History and Political Science.* MS of Mrs. Sarah Thomas Avery, "Sketch of Col. William H. Thomas, p. 2. Copy in possession of author.

2. William H. Thomas to T. Hartley Crawford, Nov. 12, 1839, William H. Thomas Letter Book, 1839-1840, in William Holland Thomas Coll., Hunter Library, Western Carolina Univ. (hereafter cited as "Thomas Letter Book, 1839-1840").

3. Thomas to Felix Axley, Dec. 9, 1839, *ibid.*

4. Thomas to the Cherokees on the Valley River, Cherokee Co., N.C. Jan., 1840, *ibid.*

5. *Ibid.*

6. Thomas to Joab L. Moore, Feb. 8, 1840, *ibid.*

7. Charles J. Kappler, comp., *Indian Affairs. Laws and Treaties,* 5 vols. (Washington, D.C.: GPO, 1904, 1913, 1939, 1941), II, 443-44.

8. Thomas, *Explanation of the Rights of the North Carolina Cherokee Indians, Submitted to the Attorney General of the United States* (Washington, D.C.: Thomas, 1851), 12. See also George D. Harmon, "The North Carolina Cherokees and the New Echota Treaty of 1835," *North Carolina Historical Review* 6 (July 1929), 239.

9. *Ibid.*

10. *Ibid.*, 239, 244–45.

11. Thomas to Nicholas S. Peck, Apr. 22, 1839, Thomas Letter Book, 1839–1840.

12. Thomas to Gideon F. Morris and Cherokee Friends, Apr. 22, 1839, *ibid.*

13. Thomas to Nicholas Woodfin, Aug. 5, 1839, *ibid.*

14. Thomas to Cherokee Friends, Washington, D.C., June 10, 1839, *ibid.*

15. Thomas to John G. Dunlap, July 7, 1839, *ibid.*

16. Thomas to C.O. Collins, July 17, 1839, *ibid.*

17. Thomas to Price, Newlin and Company, July 24, 1839, *ibid.*

18. Thomas to H.P. King, July 29, 1839, *ibid.;* Thomas to A. Fisher, July 24, 1839, *ibid.*

19. Thomas to H.P. King, July 29, 1839, *ibid.*

20. Thomas to Gideon Morris and Cherokee Friends on Valley River and Cheoih, Sept. 25, 1839, *ibid.*

21. Thomas to T. Hartley Crawford, Aug. 7, 1839, *ibid.*

22. Thomas to H.P. King, Aug. 9, 20, 1839, *ibid.*

23. Thomas to Morris and Cherokee Friends on Valley River and Cheoih, Sept. 25, 1839, *ibid.*

24. Thomas to Joel R. Poinsett, Sept. 9, 1839, *ibid.*

25. Thomas to Wilson Lumpkin, Sept. 20, 1839, *ibid.*

26. Thomas to Hinton, Sept. 21, 1839, *ibid.*

27. Thomas to Dudley, Sept. 22, 1839, *ibid.*

28. Thomas to Andrew Taylor, Oct. 5, 1839, *ibid.*

29. Thomas to J.W. King, Oct. 28, 1839, *ibid.*

30. Thomas to John Simson and Friends, Nov. 6, 1839, *ibid.*

31. Thomas to the Cherokees at Qualla Town, Nov. 15, 1839, *ibid.*

32. Thomas to James P.H. Porter, Nov. 25, 1839, *ibid.*

33. Thomas to James H. Bryson, Dec. 4, 1839, *ibid.*

34. Thomas to Silas G. Perry, Dec. 4, 1839, *ibid.*

35. Thomas to George W. Churchwell, Dec. 14, 1839, *ibid.*

36. Thomas to William Bean, Dec. 1839, *ibid.*

37. Thomas to Benjamin S. Britain, Dec. 17, 1839, *ibid.*

38. Thomas to Preston Staritt, Dec. 20, 1839, *ibid.*

39. Thomas to Churchwell, Dec. 28, 1839, *ibid.*

40. Thomas to Jesse and Thomas Raper, Jan. 8, 1840, *ibid.*

41. *Ibid.;* Thomas to William Roa, Jan. 2, 1840, *ibid.;* Thomas to John Simson and Friends, Dec. 20, 1839, *ibid.*

42. *Ibid.*

43. Thomas to John and Enoch Welch, Jan. 8, 1840, *ibid.*

44. Thomas to John E. Wool, Nov. 2, 1839, *ibid.*

45. Thomas to H.P. King, Jan. 17, 1840, *ibid.*

46. Thomas to James R. Love, Jan. 16, 1840, *ibid.*

47. Thomas to Jason L. and Seth Hyatt, July 4, 1839, *ibid.*

48. Entry of Jan. 1, 1844, in William H. Thomas Diary, 1844–1845, in William Holland Thomas Coll., Hunter Library, Western Carolina Univ.

49. Entries of July 4, 1844 and July 4, 1845, *ibid.*

50. Entry of Mar. 4, 1845, *ibid.*

51. Thomas to William L. Marcy, June 2, 1845, in William Holland Thomas Coll., Hunter Library, Western Carolina Univ.; hereafter cited as "Thomas Coll."

52. Thomas to John F. Schermerhorn, Aug. 28, 1845, *ibid.* Schermerhorn made interpolations on Thomas' letter and returned it to him.

53. Thomas to Chiefs and Cherokee People of Qualla Town, Feb. 15, 1845, June 25, 1845, in William Holland Thomas Coll., Addition, Hunter Library, Western Carolina Univ.; hereafter cited as "Thomas Coll., Addn."

54. Thomas to the Cherokees Belonging to Qualla Town No. Carolina, Feb. 2, 1846, with enclosures: Polk to John Y. Mason, June 11, 1845; Mason to Polk, Sept. 19, 1845, *ibid.*

55. This detailed account of Thomas' activities on behalf of the Cherokees during Polk's administration was later printed as Thomas, *A Letter to the Commissioner of Indian Affairs, Upon the Claims of the Indians Remaining in the States East* (Washington, D.C.: Buell and Blanchard, 1835).

56. Polk to Mason, June 11, 1845, Thomas Coll., Addn.

57. Mason to Polk, Sept. 19, 1845, *ibid.*; Mason explained: "As the Executive would have no power to divest those in possession and the question is one for the judiciary I have deemed it unnecessary to embrace my views on it in this communication nor have I deemed it proper to express my opinion on the hard measures which seem to have been dealt out to the North Carolina Indians, whose lands have been sold while they have received no corresponding benefit. I have examined the subject as one of legal construction and have no doubt of my conclusions in that respect."

58. *Ibid.*

59. *Ibid.*

60. Thomas to the Cherokees Belonging to Qualla Town, North Carolina, Feb. 2, 1846, *ibid.*

61. *Ibid.*

62. *Ibid.*

63. Entries of Aug. 3, 4, 5, 6, 8, 10, 1846, Thomas Diary, 1845–1846. Thomas Coll. The Treaty of 1846 may be found in Kappler, *Indian Affairs*, II, 561–65.

64. *Congressional Globe*, 30 Cong., 1 sess., Dec. 6, 1847, June 1, 14, 20, July 14, 28, Aug. 4, 14, 1848, pp. 809, 840, 858, 932, 1030; Thomas, *Letter to Commissioner of Indian Affairs*, 27.

Observations on Social Change
among the Eastern Cherokees

John Witthoft

The earliest definable base from which we can calculate social change on the Qualla Boundary was the immediate postremoval period. It was characterized by the following features: a blending of old and new, native and European methods and beliefs selected mainly for their utility and value, and integrated into a new culture complex; effective subsistence agriculture with abundant stored surpluses; barter economy; full practice of hunting, fishing, and gathering; local and minimal self-government; little need for bilingual skills; local medicine and herbalism at least as effective as the official medicine of that date. Many other features can be listed, but such cultures had partial counterparts in frontier subcultures and represented very effective social and cultural adaptations to environments. They contrasted with missions and other domiciliated communities, were vigorous, were undergoing internal evolution, and provided better contexts for human life than did most cultures of that time. Memories of an old reservation culture represent the golden age of Cherokee nostalgia.

Cherokee agriculture before 1860 was based upon a wide variety of native and introduced crop plants. Important introductions included peaches, wheat, Hickory King maize, field peas, butter beans, lima beans, large summer squash, turnips, yams, cabbage, and potatoes. Population of the Boundary was small, with a maximum of about twelve hundred people, and agriculture was effective. Hogs, cattle, oxen, and chickens were partly free-ranging; oxen were the major work animals. A series of epidemics of foreign plant diseases, parasites, and insect pests, dating between 1870 and 1900, devastated the agricultural economy, practically ending the cultivation of peaches and of wheat, and affecting most other crops.

Barter of foodstuffs, craft objects, and services within the community was the rule. Dependence upon the outside world for fabrics, steel, coffee, paper, pencils, lime, and other imports was largely met by barter. Markets were at a distance, and Cherokee contact with them was mainly through local storekeepers. Whereas many whites in mountain and Piedmont communities organized caravans of "tar-boiler" wagons to convey out their produce in the form of whiskey, butter, horses, cattle, and herbs, the Cherokees dealt with local middlemen and produced little in the way of concentrated valuables. They lacked the land base needed for the development of an export pattern like that of the upper Yadkin Valley, where the produce of agriculture was concentrated into whiskey, horses, and cattle for external markets. Little cash found its way to the Cherokees.

Important Cherokee exports were white-oak baskets woven in both Indian and white styles, buckeye-wood dough trays, pipe bowls carved from stone and from rhododendron root burls, rhododendron hominy ladles, indigo, dried roots and leaves for the raw-drug trade, grain, and the oil extracted from butternut and walnut. These were bartered to local merchants for imported goods and only rarely were sold for cash. Although most of the produce went to nearby Piedmont and Coastal Plain outlets and was consumed within a regional market, some of the pipes and herbs went to extremely distant cosmopolitan centers.

Lumbering was of little importance until after the Civil War; even then it employed very few Cherokees. Most of the accessible prime timber of the Qualla area was quickly removed, and the whole region was in slash long before 1890, with lumber camps operating many miles to the north. After 1900, the cutting of second-growth and undesirable wood for tanbark, pulp, and chemical wood provided day labor for many Cherokee men, and the railroad which served this industry provided jobs for a few. Cash wages became of some importance to the Cherokee community for the first time. In the 1920s and '30s, until the collapse of forest-based industries during the Great Depression, the standard wage paid to the Cherokee workman was thirty-five cents per day. Wages for white workmen on roads in adjoining counties were one dollar per day.

The social organization of the Cherokee economy is of special interest because it followed the formal patterns of a bilateral descriptive-kinship system with patronyms as inherited family names. Households were strongly organized about female centers, with wives and mothers representing the anchors of social life. Women were also the stable economic centers of households; frequently property holders, they normally provided most of the subsistence of the household. Gardening and gathering were conducted largely by women, with varying amounts of aid from fathers, husbands, and children. Some men did an equal share of work in their wives' and mothers' fields and contributed most of what goods and cash they obtained elsewhere to household support. Many men, however, adhered to a different tradition; contributing little labor to agriculture and nothing in other goods to the household, they apparently felt few sanctions to do so despite their support by female labor. Some showed little responsibility for family when young but became major resources in middle age, while even then many remained apart from family responsibility. Some showed more willingness to labor for their mothers than for their wives. Many households included husbands who were temporarily or permanently absent, while others represented stable, permanent, domestic and economic bonds. Apparently local conventions expected little of a man but did reward him for domestic stability. The economic roles of men were quite secondary to those of women. In the usual multigeneration household, elders and women were frequently the economic mainstays. However, no generalization would hold.

Another institution crosscut and complemented the family in economic production. This was the *gadugi* ("work company"), a voluntary association of men and women drawn from one neighborhood. Sometimes both a man and his wife were members, sometimes only one was. The company met almost daily as a group, working for a full day as a labor gang on the land of each member in succession. In case of severe illness of any member, other members did his or her necessary work. The company conducted the funerals of members, absorbing the costs. The company also rented out its labor as a group and it lent money at interest, maintaining a treasury for the use of its membership. I consider the *gadugi* to be the social survival of what had been the Cherokee town, carrying on the economic functions of the town long after its political functions were lost. It served important economic functions in maintaining the productive stability of the female-centered Cherokee household, despite variations in male productivity. The *gadugis* had become formally extinct by 1910, but still met informally as work-sharing groups at least as late as the 1960s, only losing their vigor and fundamental economic importance within the last decade.

The Cherokee extended family has served well in child rearing. In the multigeneration household, care of children was shared by several adults of at least two generations, with the eager involvement of older siblings. Many children were raised by grandparents in the aftermath of domestic tragedy. Unwanted or neglected children were readily shifted to another household where they were loved and cared for. Pregnancy of a young woman at the age of thirteen or fourteen might cause gossip in the "white Cherokee" community, but presented no real problems to the Indians except those imposed by the outside world. Women entering a marriage with children from an earlier episode normally found the new husband eager to accept a foster child but reluctant to accept any actual authority over a child not his own. Death or incapacitating illness of parents merely shifted children into a household in some other part of the kinship net, since the distinction between an adopted child and one born to the family was practically nonexistent, as it has always been both in Indian and in white law. Some genetic mixture in the Cherokee community has certainly been due to willingness to accept foundlings dropped on the Boundary.

The Indian social order, as illustrated by these brief statements of customs of the nineteenth and early twentieth centuries, has been complicated by the insertion of white social orders into a new complex society at Qualla. One social order, that of the

205

white Cherokee, may be seen as an aristocratic caste with a distinct social organization and culture which has been imposed by federal power upon a Cherokee proletariat. It consists of a few families of alleged Indian ancestry whose family names do not occur in the Indian community and whose kinship charts do not interdigitate with the Indian charts. These families represent an endogamous caste within Cherokee society. Their dialect, speech usage, bearing, and extroverted behavior are not those of the Indian community. Some of these families were first known as storekeepers at Qualla after the Civil War, while others, appearing at more recent dates in the sparse surviving records, have a totally unknown history. However, they have now long held prominent positions in Cherokee affairs and represent an economically privileged segment of the Qualla community. Their family names are not represented in nearby white communities of North Carolina, although some of them occur in Tennessee, while others come from Cherokee County, North Carolina. They have come to Qualla by immigration from other regions.

Easily confused with the white Cherokee are certain mixed families which have a local origin, some branches of which have Indian ancestry. Some are descendants of local white families which married into the Cherokee community, bringing local mountain white patronyms with them, while others carry Indian family names and presumably represent the descendants of foundlings raised by Qualla families. Their kinship charts interdigitate with those of the Cherokee people. None of this distinguishes them in any way from the Cherokees, for an odd ancestor from outside would have little significance. What is significant is that different branches of these families have followed different marriage patterns by preference; as a result, some lines appear indistinguishable from white Cherokee in physical appearance, speech, and behavior, while others hold intermediate positions. Those in intermediate positions are apt to be torn between conflicting cultural values. Mixed families occupy varied positions in the Qualla caste system; those of white culture fit into the white Cherokee class and share its power and privileges; others, less Nordic in appearance, occupy somewhat subordinate roles; and members of many branches either hold an intermediate level or live as proletariat. Federal and other bureaucracies have always been eager to deal with Cherokees who are phenotypically, culturally, and linguistically white. Such elements in the Qualla society have therefore always had better access to power, employment, business opportunity, privilege, economic advantage, and formal education. It is the existence of white and quasi-white factions which introduces the concept of class into Cherokee relationships and makes it necessary to examine the total social system as a complex society. The distinctions of class are entirely those of cultural tradition, not of race, although whiteness has always given great advantages in dealing with the outside world and its white power centers. The white Cherokees and their cohorts have played central and crucial roles as agents for the Cherokee people in many of the events of history, even though their roles have been self-assigned. Their existence is a vital part of Cherokee society.

Until the 1940s, Cherokee life maintained its subsistence base in agriculture. Growth of a cash economy had been slight. Federal policies were directed toward family-farm development at a time when the family farm of any sort was becoming noncompetitive with the agri-industries. Cherokees resources could not support a family-farm economy, since available land was adequate only for subsistence gardening. A gradual but real impoverishment of the land had been going on since 1860, partially through erosion and resource destruction, partially through plant disease, partially through white Cherokee land-grabbing, and partially through changes in national economy and business. The white Cherokees and the peripheral members of their class had been the entrepreneurs and the speculators and had often dominated Cherokee politics. A cash economy had not yet come into existence, although standard wages had risen to one dollar per day by 1946—provided any jobs were available. Income from military wages, dependency allotments, military disability pensions, and military life insurance policies brought a new kind of income to Cherokee families. Public assistance funds, beginning in the 1930s, have been an erosional force to Cherokee independence, although they are still less than minimal and have had slight effect on Qualla economy. Many men worked away from home for prolonged intervals in the 1940s, and they and their families had some experience with wage economies. A slight but steadily growing tourist business was conspicuous, but the overall future of the community seemed very bleak.

It appeared to many in the 1940s that the old feudal economy of Qualla and the social order that went with it had altered little and that Qualla was incapable of cultural, social, and economic improvement because of the inertia of its proletarian social order. At the same time, the philosophy of rising expectations was eroding Cherokee economy and character. Changes that had actually been going on were not perceived, and economic forces of enormous consequence were not anticipated, unless by white Cherokee speculators.

Unnoticed changes that had been taking place included shifts in male social and economic roles, in cash economy and credit resources, in drinking patterns, in violence, and in the national ideology. These changes were overlooked, in part, because so many circumstances at Qualla had long been undergoing serious deterioration. In many ways, 1945 seemed like the lowest ebb of promise for the Eastern Cherokees.

Many scapegoats were identified; alcohol and irreligion were the two most often cited. Indeed, moonshining, bootlegging, and alcohol consumption had changed little in thirty years. Nearly universal Cherokee church membership seemed to have had no more effect upon reform than had seventy-five years of local prohibition. Preachers themselves were generally credited with more drunkenness, more sexual offenses, and more adherence to pagan magic than any other segment of the population; the outrage voiced in their sermons seemed in direct proportion to the magnitude of their own transgressions.

Although by 1945, in response to better medicine, population was rapidly increasing, agriculture declined. The fixed land base was being stripped of natural resources. Government employees, tribal employees, businessmen, and those closely associated with them formed a segregated "golden ghetto" quite isolated from any real contact with the common people. Most of the valuable agricultural land of the Boundary had come into the possession of the white Cherokees and of white branches of the mixed families. They held the land as a speculation, expecting huge increases in market value when the land became private property through termination, which ended tribal status and federal supported programs. White Cherokee interest groups, constantly active in Washington, used organized propaganda and political pressure to effect the parceling out of tribal land allotments.

Housing was inadequate, worn-out, and filled with multigeneration families. Almost no construction had been possible for many years; during the Great Depression and World War II, building after building had burned with no resources for replacement. Families had been compacted into the available houses. Sanitation was bad. Public and personal physical health were simply deplorable, despite a Bureau of Indian Affairs hospital. As a result of widespread want, nutrition was often poor, as evidenced in the frequent obesity caused by protein deficiency. Hepatitis was everywhere, cirrhosis was widespread, children were overloaded with roundworms, fleas and bedbugs abounded, lice were epidemic, and tuberculosis was still the Great White Plague. Awaiting reform in their bureau, medical personnel who worked in the golden ghetto mainly held their noses, and their distance, as they still do.

The schools seemed content with a record of constant failure. Girls were thrown out of school as soon as they were married or appeared pregnant, boys as soon as they accepted family responsibilities. Few Cherokees ever completed high school. Abuse of monolinguals was standard in the school system, consistent with its place in the golden ghetto. Cherokees saw education as the only way forward and found it completely blocked to them by a white bureaucracy—a bureaucracy of schoolmarms and athletic coaches.

Tribal rolls were many years out of date, and tribal government, completely dominated by federal agencies, seemed as stultified as the Bureau of Indian Affairs. Tribal government had no significant monetary base to support municipal services and had less than zero status with federal agencies, which were purely colonial in their intent. In short, local representative government was totally crushed under the heel of federal control. Men such as Will West Long, active in local government, became utterly disillusioned concerning justice and the Cherokee word *duyukta,* reflecting the cultural norms and expectations of society.

The Boundary's main problem was that it had been undergoing impoverishment since 1860. Decay of subsistence activities, the increase of population, and isolation from the advancing mainstream of American economic life were major causes of poverty. White Cherokees, integrated into the business network of neighboring communities, had long before moved into an economy of cash and of capital ownership. They utilized a large part of the fluid resources of the Cherokee community, controlling commerce, government employment, the labor market, and the flow of bartered goods and labor. Their entry into the Cherokee world brought poverty with them. If poverty existed in the ante-bellum stage of Boundary life, it was occasional and seasonal, and its force was blunted in late winter or after crop failure by the economic distribution factors of the family. Only a white Cherokee could turn the winter hunger of an Indian family into a land transaction. After 1920, poverty and resultant land deals with white Cherokees became chronic.

The fundamental definitions of poverty, as stated by Booth and others in the 1880s and as redefined in many ways since, are difficult to apply without intensive — and often unethical — research.[1] The "poverty line" of Booth is that level of income and productivity which merely maintains a family's health and laboring efficiency at the minimum costs for nutrition, clothing, housing, and other essentials. It includes no provision for postage, paper, tobacco, transportation, medical expenses, or other nonessentials. A family below this level of income in cash and produce must also show physical symptoms of malnutrition to be graded below the poverty line. Therefore, according to Booth, a combination of low measurable productivity with physical symptoms of malnutrition equals poverty. Few families in the modern American world would qualify for that category.

Such states of poverty exist in many parts of the world today,

210

and were commonplace in the cities of nineteenth-century America. I doubt that any nineteenth-century Qualla family lived in similar conditions, despite the absence of any significant cash income. Many twentieth-century Qualla families have experienced numerous intervals of such hardship.

Since much malnutrition and hardship is experienced by families with incomes above the arbitrary poverty line, Booth and other students came to distinguish between primary poverty, as described above, and secondary poverty.[2] In secondary poverty, malnutrition and want are caused by factors other than low productivity. Secondary poverty results from the diversion of income from subsistence to other costs, thus reducing subsistence expenditures to a level below the poverty line. Illness and medical expenses, improvidence, failure to utilize subsistence resources, gambling, drinking, overextensions of credit, and the support of motor vehicles are among the main contributing causes to secondary poverty. In the classic definition, secondary poverty exists only when nutrition and health are damaged by diversion of income and subsistence to nonessential uses. Malnutrition must be medically determinable. Many Qualla families, like numerous others in America, have suffered frequent intervals of malnutrition — long or short — during the twentieth century. Too often, for some, secondary poverty is still experienced.

However, "poverty" is a term used loosely in popular speech and in the literature of sociology to include all examples of low income, whether or not necessities are threatened, when nonessential expenditures must be limited. Thus poverty becomes merely a measure of relative affluence within an affluent society, and only retains its index of malnutrition when applied to colonialism, to underdeveloped countries, and to lower-class conditions. Much of what we refer to as poverty at Qualla today is lack of affluence, some of it is secondary poverty, and little primary poverty exists. The history of poverty and of household economics provides the deterministic context for social change among the Eastern Cherokees.

Limited craft production, slight job opportunities in lumbering, and some barter in herbs, nut oil, and produce yielded the nineteenth-century Cherokee household a small amount of non-subsistence income, much of which was redeemed in cloth, tools, notions, tobacco, coffee, livestock, and whiskey. As noted previously in this chapter, male economic and domestic roles were poorly defined. Gardening was by tradition a woman's occupation; its heavy labor was shared by her husband and kinsmen, but its daily tasks lay outside traditional male roles. Hunting, warfare, diplomacy, and ball play had dwindled to insignificance, and the defined economic responsibilities of men were slight. The dependence of men upon a woman-centered economy was no longer balanced by an equally strong dependence of society upon men's traditional roles. The household could — and frequently did — function with very minimal participation by husbands. Cash income earned by many men did not find its way into a household economy, but was diverted to personal use in a manner approved by many, condemned by many, and normally tolerated by all. Female independence and pride usually forbore the follies of men, while men often felt their irrelevance to household and family life. The long absences of men in the armies of the Civil War and the prevalence of households with separated husbands demonstrated the relatively slight importance of male economic functions to the life of the people. The wifely self-confidence in female economic production within a subsistence-production and barter system did not boost the male ego. However, many men participated as fully as they could in the work of the household with only occasional lapses from responsibility.

The decline in subsistence production which was accompanied by a much slighter increase in wage-opportunities for men produced tension of great complexity. On the one hand, cash incomes were frequently expended as household funds, and labor came to replace hunting as the substantive male role. On the other hand, cash income could be expended as a surplus. Growing impoverishment, pessimism, and the uncertainty of employment imposed great stress upon the marriage bond. This, in turn, occasioned greater individual expenditure of male cash income in waste and a consequent trend toward secondary poverty. As economic forces and other externals damaged individual relationships, stress on marriages continuously increased from 1880 until about 1950. Wage incomes strengthened many households and reinforced male roles, but they were accompanied by severe injury in many others. The morale of the people became more eroded after 1924; constant threats of allotment, of domination by white Cherokee factions, and of submergence into a lower-class colored labor pool combined with constant declines in subsistence production.

There had been some consumption of alcohol by Cherokees since the first white contact. Those Indians who had remained in the vicinity of Qualla on lands ceded to the United States in 1819 and would become the nucleus of the Qualla community in 1838 lived outside the bounds of the Cherokee Nation's severe temperance laws. Cherokees were scattered through a white frontier where corn whiskey was both an item of everyday consumption and a major product for export. About 1830, a strong temperance movement began at Qualla. Except in Cherokee County, Cherokee use of white liquor was very slight in the period before the Civil War, but, with greater cash income and with decreasing production of a subsistence economy, it gradually increased. The white Cherokees and their white neighbors, on the other hand, brought with them a knowledge of distillation, frontier habits of alcohol consumption, and a ready eye for profit. The more Indian morale declined in the face of diminishing production and other threats, the greater became Indian consumption of alcohol, and the stronger became personal and ideological conflicts about its use.

Prior to World War I, most of the alcohol consumed on the Boundary was carried over well-worn footpaths from white communities (mainly Cosby and Smokemont) on the north and west, but almost as much was produced by white Cherokees within the Boundary area. By 1920, most liquor was produced on the Boundary, and distillers had switched to the more efficient sweet-mash method, which depended upon commercial sugar and yeast as well as upon corn and other grains. The beginning of prohibition made the import of whiskey from other white communities more hazardous and caused expansion of the local moonshine business, with Cherokees for the first time operating their own stills both for their personal use and for sales. Consumption increased steadily as more severe stresses were felt by the Cherokees. Social sanctions against the use of alcohol were becoming more severe, since alcohol was identified by many as a dangerous cause of secondary poverty and as a threat to domestic and community tranquillity. At the same time that some men were experiencing reinforcement of male roles through wage earning, many other people were experiencing threats of role-disintegration through economic decline, scarcity of employment, and other widespread menaces to Cherokee survival. Many persons found some solace in the pleasures of intoxication or in the satisfactions of Armageddon-preaching religion, often rapidly alternating between the two. This lowest ebb in Cherokee hopes lasted from 1924 to 1943.

During the 1920s, copper stills and essential materials for moonshining were sold by local storekeepers on the Boundary; some also retailed and wholesaled liquor as they had done in the nineteenth century. One man, a white Cherokee who lived in the Big Cove, specialized in the manufacture of stills for local and outside sale. His stills were retailed by local storekeepers, who allowed liberal credit. In 1926, at a time when wages on the Boundary were thirty-five cents a day and wages in surrounding communities were one dollar a day, a thirty-five-gallon still retailed at seventy-five dollars. Indians and white Cherokees both tended stills in remote areas, producing for their own use and finding sale of surpluses more profitable than heavy manual labor. The penalty—a term of two to five years in a federal prison—was no more severe for manufacture than for carrying corn liquor from Tennessee. Outside markets ensured good prices, but long absences of men in prison were damaging to households, and Indians were much more exposed to arrest than were whites.

By 1946, production of moonshine on the Boundary had dwindled to a minor industry for local consumption, and I know of no Indians who were still in the retail business. Considerable amounts of "legal" (taxed commercial) alcohol were being brought into the Boundary, and the consumption of moonshine whiskey was dropping. Drinking was, as it is today, the source of much ideological conflict. Personal and family tragedies associated with its use were very apparent. In a rural community where everyone knows everyone else, and where nearly everyone is related, any personal tragedy immediately touches all, and a stranger hears of so much misfortune that it seems to be epidemic.

In the years since 1946, moonshine has completely disappeared from the Boundary, and all alcohol is the taxed variety imported from legal, outside, retail outlets. Liquor consumed today lacks most of the very toxic and damaging ingredients found in white whiskey. A strong trend toward the consumption of beer has developed, with less consumption of alcohol in any form now than at any time in the past century. Thus the Cherokees today show very marked gains both in temperance and in abstinence—symptoms of definite economic increases by the Cherokee community and of stronger role-satisfactions within individuals. Alcohol presents no greater social and economic threat today than it does in other communities of comparable size and stage of economic development, and certainly less than in many.

Ideological conflict and anxiety concerning the use of alcohol are unusually conspicuous to any observer. The degree of anxiety is in no way proportional to the threat, but the long experience of most Cherokee families with past poverty and the intensity of clerical attack upon drinking fill the issue with dread. As in the past, sermons frequently reflect the transgressions of the preacher himself.[3]

In the years since 1945, growth of the tourist industry has produced, directly and indirectly, sources of employment on a scale never anticipated. Jobs pay low wages and most of them are seasonal, but they are jobs. Secondary benefits include the municipal services made possible by business development on the Boundary. The most conspicuous effect of cash economy is fuller participation of husbands in economic responsibility for the household. Sharing the incomes of all employed members of a household as a family resource is now a major force in Cherokee life. It is having deep and far-reaching effects upon male roles, with the reemergence of a full sense of equal responsibility by all as a norm. It is as though the aboriginal role of the male as an equally important

215

member of society has been at least partially restored, with economic gains translated into greater stability, tranquillity, and unity for the extended family. Restoration of role-significance is producing male morale based upon solid accomplishment. Role-inadequacies, which were often compensated for by behavior of rejection in past times of impoverishment, are being corrected. An equal partnership in marriage has now become more possible. With jobs available to men and women, agricultural and craft activities have become supplementary sources of income rather than mainstays. Extension of state unemployment compensation to include many seasonal workers, begun in 1975, may serve to minimize recurrent late-winter hardships and further strengthen family and marriage bonds.

Economic change associated with the "welfare state" is producing comparable effects upon the roles of the elderly. Care and support for aging members has always been a conspicuous goal of the Cherokee family, regardless of difficulties, inconvenience, and financial hardship. Status increases with age among the Cherokees, and few people younger than forty are considered fully capable of understanding and meeting all the problems and hazards of life. In earlier times, care of the aged was frequently a matter of great difficulty, carried out with much sacrifice regarding other family members, since it involved the equal sharing of scant resources in food, housing, and necessary purchases. Rarely resulting in conflict within the family, the stresses of family responsibility were projected elsewhere, and were reflected in witchcraft belief. Elderly members of other families were frequently alleged to be antisocial magicians, and their deaths were interpreted as witch-killings by other magicians.

Accumulated years of cash employment have brought many elderly people into the Social Security system, with its allied benefits. Other government funds for assistance of the aged are now available. The tourist industry has also produced opportunities for many individuals too old for arduous jobs, and a number of persons in their seventies are now seasonally employed. Improved markets for craft products provide good supplementary incomes

216

for some, and many of the most skillful and productive of the Boundary's traditional craftsmen are elderly.

The net effect is that now the elderly are usually more an economic asset than a liability to the family. Grandparents and great-grandparents of Cherokee schoolchildren are frequently as productive as parents, contributing heavily to the economic needs of households and to the raising of children. The traditional high status of the elderly is being reinforced by recent economic change. This reinforcement strengthens the structural unity of the extended family and reduces those stresses in family life often associated with dependent elders. Indeed, in some cases one sees exploitation of elders by less responsible couples in middle age; the exploitation is double-edged, because the roles and status of the exploiters are likewise damaged. In general, however, just as the recent changes in male roles have done, those changes in roles of the elderly are serving to strengthen the Cherokee family as an effective pattern of social organization.

Major goals of the present tribal government are education, housing, and roads. The first lies outside my present attention, because innovative programs in formal education, large capital expenditures for new school facilities, and an adequate teaching staff are very recent. Beside this, my own prejudices against the older educational system are so extreme that I am not capable of rational judgments.

The most visible, and in some ways the most important, changes resulting from cash economy are in housing and associated facilities. A housing revolution is in process among the Eastern Cherokees.

In 1946, one of the most conspicuous defects at Qualla was housing. More than 90 percent of private houses—old log and frame structures that had outlived their life expectancy—were inadequate by any standards. All were jammed with people. At least half were occupied by multigeneration families. Most cooking was done in fireplaces or upon wood-burning stoves. Screened windows and doors were uncommon, and most of the roofs leaked. Water was normally carried from a nearby branch or spring.

217

Sanitary provisions were usually little more than those offered by a slit-trench latrine. Individual space and privacy were at an absolute minimum. Timber fit for traditional log construction was not available. Other building supplies were almost impossible to obtain, and there was little money to buy them. Credit for repairs, renovation, or construction could not be obtained. Housing effectively reflected the failing morale and economy of the Cherokee community at that time.

Attempts to upgrade housing proved extremely difficult. Mortgage moneys from the Veterans Administration or from commercial sources were not available to the Boundary. Progress began in the 1940s with local community action programs, utilizing social structures that already existed, such as the *gadugi,* church memberships, and community clubs. The early projects included screen-making, digging and construction of sanitary privies, water-source improvement, roofing, treatment of log house-walls with used crankcase oil instead of the more expensive paint, and other activities within the resources of neighborhood groups. A Quaker work camp, together with local volunteer groups, started a program of rural electrification. Progress was slowed by scant financial resources.

The Cherokee Tribal Community Services program was established in 1952, with a local sales tax imposed to finance it. Police and fire departments, garbage collection, and the Water and Sewer Enterprise were inaugurated. Local community efforts to improve housing finally led to the establishment of the Qualla Housing Authority in 1962. Leasehold mortgages which legalized financing for home construction and improvements were arranged. Thirty-six low-rental housing units were completed in 1966 as an initial major effort in new housing, and private loans were, for the first time, obtained through federal agencies. In 1967 funding became available through the Bureau of Indian Affairs and the Department of Housing and Urban Development. A mutual-help program was then begun. One hundred eighty houses were completed by 1972, and another one hundred began in that year. Owners are committed to payments spread over a period of seventeen years on new houses expected to last about twenty years. In 1968, Bureau of Indian Affairs funds became available for repairs and reconditioning of existing houses — funds primarily for persons unable to finance participation in the mutual-help program. More than six hundred houses have been built or substantially improved, leaving approximately half the housing at Qualla still in substandard condition, but there now is continuous progress in the building programs. Many mobile homes are also occupied by Cherokee families, and a program to provide sanitation and other facilities for them has begun.

The general effect of the housing programs has been to disperse the extended family into a tiny community, with new houses situated at convenient distances from a rebuilt older home. Consequently, the extended family and the multigeneration household are not fragmented but are separated into reasonably smaller units, still closely attached but with more adequate space, privacy, and facilities. Stresses and frictions within the family are reduced without weakening ties. In every case, water is piped either from a safe and improved spring at a branch-head or from the municipal supply, and sewage disposal is handled either by properly placed and constructed cesspools and drain-fields or by the municipal sewerage and treatment system. The effects of these improvements upon general health, contagion of communicable diseases, parasitism, and emotional well-being of the families are marked, even though economic costs, in terms of mortgage payments, electrical bills, and heating oil, represent a considerable burden for the typical Cherokee family. All of the associated changes seem to be in the direction of strengthening the extended family and reinforcing its economic, social, and child-rearing roles. As in other Indian communities, experience is demonstrating the vital function of housing in the well-being of the people.

Having explored only a few aspects of social change and its contexts among the Eastern Cherokees, I conclude that the pessimism of past decades may have been well founded, but that recent conditions do not justify any sense of hopelessness, nor do they imply any social or cultural degeneration among the Cherokee people. Very real threats to the future well-being of the Cherokees certainly do exist, and others will appear in the unpredictable turnings of history, but current situations offer some promise of continued progress.

One persisting threat to the well-being of the Cherokees is the continued existence of a poorly integrated class structure in which the white Cherokees, non-Cherokee businessmen, and culturally white branches of mixed families occupy an upper-class status of economic and social privilege in the total system which is the Qualla society. This class is poorly integrated into the society in the sense that most of its members show little or no commitment to the goals or welfare of Cherokee society and seem opposed to Indian values and language use. Contributing strongly to political factionalism, they seem motivated primarily by financial gain. In roles of economic exploitation, they play the part of colonists, extracting as much money as possible from the Qualla economy and expending as much of it as possible in outside markets, while participating as little as possible in self-governed community development. Many of them function as though they were living in a boom-or-bust economy. Especially, integration of the white Cherokees and their associates into their necessary place in Qualla society requires that they accept the responsibilities as well as the advantages of their class membership. Their skills, abilities, and knowledge are needed to be used for the good of the whole society, rather than as tools for exploitation of that society. The white Cherokees are Indians beyond any question, having been declared so by law, and they should accept the consequences of that fact, just as the Indians of all degrees of mixed blood have had to do.

The tourist industry upon which the Cherokee cash economy is based may prove to be a precarious foundation, or it may be a lasting business. Since the Cherokee as an authentic Cherokee Indian is indeed the main asset of the tourist business, that business will depend more and more upon Indian visibility. At the present time, the policies of most businessmen at Qualla are to make the Indian totally invisible. The future of their businesses is being seriously damaged by many factors: general employment of non-Indians in public-contact jobs; the import of seasonal labor; decline of quality in Cherokee handicrafts and traditional ways; social downgrading of brown skin and Cherokee speech; sale of

220

imported junk from foreign nations with depressed wage scales; fraud in salesmanship; and pay scales discriminatory against Indians. It is sometimes hard to find either a visible Indian or an Indian-made object in the business districts of Qualla. Such lack of enlightened self-interest is difficult to imagine!

What is good for the Indian community will ultimately be good for business at Qualla, since that business has no other asset than the Indian. The tourist business is today as essential to the Eastern Cherokee as subsistence agriculture once was. On the other hand, any business at Qualla needs the Cherokee people even more that they need it. The Cherokees will long be there, but businesses may not. Ethics of the business community and responsibility of the white Cherokees are closely related problems, both intensely depressing.

At Qualla, I have been watching the emergence of an ancient folk community into the modern world. This community has been waging an uphill fight for every gain that has been made, either in economic base or in ability to maintain its own integrity. The economic base of the Cherokee community, which has been fundamental in the determination of other cultural and social changes, is still feeble, threatened on one side by upper-class forces of exploitation and on the other side by attitudes of great expectations and of dependency. That any Cherokee people have survived the historical interaction of these two opposing forces is a matter for amazement. That people still grow up speaking the Cherokee language and behaving like decent Indian people remains a marvel. The strength of an undefined Cherokee value system has revealed itself through survival; its future remains a matter of intense interest.

NOTES

1. Charles Booth, *Pauperism, a Picture, and the Endowment of Old Age: An Argument* (London: Macmillan, 1892); Booth *et al.*, *Life and Labor of the People in London.* First Series; *Poverty,* 4 vols. (1902; rpt. ed., New York: AMS Press, 1970).

2. Benjamin Seebohm Rowntree, *Poverty: A Study of Town Life* (London:

Macmillan, 1901); Alexander Morriss Carr-Saunders and David Caradon Jones, *A Survey of the Social Structure of England and Wales as Illustrated by Statistics* (London: H. Milford, 1927); Rowntree, *Poverty and Progress: A Second Social Survey of York* (London: Longmans, Green, 1941).

3. Very different conclusions, based upon an abuse of sociological questionnaire technique and upon clerical moralizing about Cherokee drinking, are contrary to present and past reality: Laurence French and Renitia Bertoluzzi, "The Drunken Indian Stereotype and the Eastern Cherokees," *Appalachian Journal* 2 (1957), 332-44.

New Militants or Resurrected State? The Five County Northeastern Oklahoma Cherokee Organization

*Albert L. Wahrhaftig
and Jane Lukens-Wahrhaftig*

From 1965 through 1972, we witnessed a small and brief American Indian social movement which might otherwise have passed unnoticed. In fact, having been drafted as its English-language secretary, I (A.W.) observed it from a position rarely offered to ethnologists.[1] If the history of this movement, the Five County Northeastern Oklahoma Cherokee Organization, were written at some future date, and especially if it were written from newspaper accounts and accessible records in English, rather than from primary documents presently in the hands of Cherokees, it would probably be categorized as an example of the sporadic ethnic militantism which was common throughout the United States in the 1960s.[2] However, the Five County Cherokee Organization was a movement independent of others, undertaken by a tribal people who lived in great geographic and social isolation. It had its own etiology and a recognizably Cherokee structure which was the result of traditional Cherokee social processes. Perhaps, in terms both of its impact on non-Cherokees and of its place in the history of contemporary America, the Five County Cherokees should legitimately be treated as an example of the Red Power movements which were then beginning to surface.[3] Nevertheless, its significance to Cherokees themselves and its meaning as an event in Cherokee history were actually quite different. It was not a response by an ethnic group oriented to, and experiencing deprivation relative to the norms of the general American society but rather was a product of long-standing processes of Cherokee social organization—the same processes, we believe, which led to the formation of the historic Cherokee Nation.

At least 11,000 Western Cherokees in eastern Oklahoma participate in an identifiable and culturally conservative way of life.[4] This traditional Cherokee way of life is firmly rooted in some seventy named settlements scattered among the hollows of the Oklahoma Ozarks (map 1). Each settlement consists of a cluster of people related by kinship who primarily speak Cherokee. Typically, these settlements consist of ten to thirty-five households whose members attend a common ritual meeting place, which may be either a church belonging to the Cherokee Indian Baptist Association or a non-Christian "stomp ground." At present, the Cherokee Indian Baptist Association and non-Christian Cherokee ceremonial societies are the only traditionally recognized institutions beyond the level of kinship and intermarriage which link these settlements.[5]

Cherokee settlements are ancient and have survived as intact social units. At least four Cherokee dialects persist in eastern Oklahoma, and these correspond to the dialects Mooney identified among the nineteenth-century Cherokees in the Southeast.[6] The lack of linguistic leveling is one evidence for the proposition that Cherokee settlements have maintained their integrity since long before Andrew Jackson had the tribe removed from its southeastern homelands. Today some Cherokee settlements are geographically isolated, highly traditional and closed, while others are relatively more accessible and open, but in them all life proceeds within an essentially traditional framework of human relationships and meaning.[7]

The Cherokees who live in these settlements are both poor and economically exploited. Their income is less than half that of neighboring whites who themselves are federally designated as a poverty population. Cherokees are the region's laboring caste. Menial jobs at substandard wages in commercial nurseries, canneries, chicken-processing plants, and strawberry fields are reserved for them.[8] Moreover, residents of Cherokee settlements experience an unrelenting pressure, administered through

224

teachers, social workers, and the public at large, to give up their language and customs. A sociologist recently described them as an "administered people" to whom Oklahoma authorities "represent an awful and irresponsible power,"[9] while an anthropologist who observed a rural school which services a Cherokee settlement concluded, "Day after day, year after year, students must . . . subject themselves to the school's attempts at intrusion, must prepare and present their defenses. . . . Total withdrawal from the school system is the final act in defense of Cherokee feelings of integrity."[10]

Subjected to continual onslaught against both their culture and their resources, Cherokees have concluded that Americans have determined that their distinctive existence as a people should die. This assumption pervades day-to-day discussion of current events in Cherokee settlements and has become incorporated as a basic proposition in ritual discourse on the present state of Cherokee life. It is revealed in these opening phrases from a formal statement by an elderly ceremonial specialist. "This is about Indians. Today they are held down. They are a poor and sorrowful people. They can't get out of it."[11]

The Cherokee tribe, as defined under United States law, is itself an ethnically plural society. The present Cherokee tribal government was created, and is directed, by white Americans of Cherokee descent who are legally recognized as Cherokees.[12] When conflict between Cherokees in traditional settlements and the tribal government imposed on them by whites legally designated as Cherokees occurs, this conflict is passed off as factionalism within the Cherokee tribe.

Eastern Oklahoma contains a unique population of perhaps thirty thousand persons—no figures based on state of residence have ever been compiled—who for generations have been indistinguishable from other Americans in culture, political allegiance, personal loyalty, and area of residence. Because of peculiarities in federal legislation for enumerating Cherokees,[13] these persons are legally recognized as Cherokees; they identify themselves as "having Cherokee ancestry" (although never as "Indians"), and on this basis other Oklahomans accept them as Cherokees. The Cherokee

225

tribe as a legal entity consists both of culturally Cherokee people living in rural settlements and towns and of these culturally white people absorbed within Oklahoma society.

This distinction sounds like, but is emphatically different from, the distinctions which commonly exist in American Indian communities between mixed-blood and fullblood factions (as among the Pine Ridge Sioux, for example[14]) or between conservative and progressive factions (as among the Sac and Fox,[15] the Pueblos,[16] and many other tribes). Elsewhere, factionalism occurs between more and less *acculturated* Indians, whereas in eastern Oklahoma ethnic conflict occurs between a culturally Indian population (within which some individuals and settlements are considerably more acculturated than others) and a long-*assimilated* population identifying with Indian ancestors.[17] The latter situation is common to all of the Five Civilized Tribes in Oklahoma and appears to be unique to them.

The predicament of Cherokees living in traditional settlements is that they are enmeshed in a plural society based on conflict between ethnic sectors[18] — Indians and whites — in which the identity of those sectors is disguised by the presence of a legal identity which defines as Cherokee both persons who are culturally Cherokee and persons who are culturally white. Cherokees living in traditional settlements are thus deprived both of experiencing themselves as a culturally distinctive community and of being treated as such by others.

Conflict in the Cherokee Nation arose just after the Civil War and was at first embedded in factionalism. In time, one faction assimilated, and the other remained Indian. Immediately after the war, longstanding factionalism among Cherokee citizens resulted in a geographic partitioning of the Cherokee Nation.[19] One faction confined themselves to the Ozark hollows, refrained from further intermarriage with whites and even, for the most part, with members of the opposing faction, maintained the Cherokee language and culture, and now survives as the culturally Cherokee population in identifiable Cherokee settlements. The other faction intermarried extensively with the whites who were illegally settling in the Cherokee Nation in increasing numbers and there-

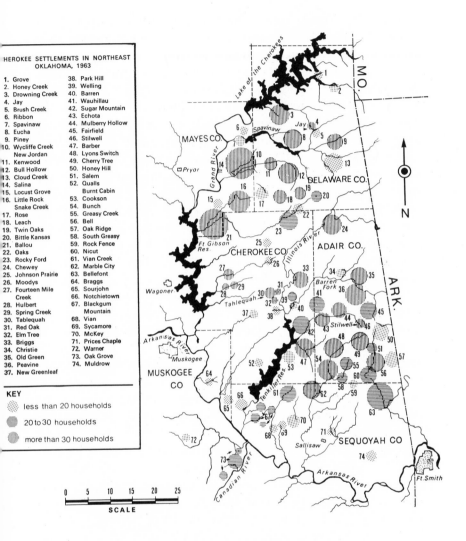

CHEROKEE SETTLEMENTS IN NORTHEAST
OKLAHOMA, 1963

1. Grove
2. Honey Creek
3. Drowning Creek
4. Jay
5. Brush Creek
6. Ribbon
7. Spavinaw
8. Eucha
9. Piney
10. Wycliffe Creek
New Jordan
11. Kenwood
12. Bull Hollow
13. Cloud Creek
14. Salina
15. Locust Grove
16. Little Rock
Snake Creek
17. Rose
18. Leach
19. Twin Oaks
20. Bittle Kansas
21. Ballou
22. Oaks
23. Rocky Ford
24. Chewey
25. Johnson Prairie
26. Moodys
27. Fourteen Mile
Creek
28. Hulbert
29. Spring Creek
30. Tablequah
31. Red Oak
32. Elm Tree
33. Briggs
34. Christie
35. Old Green
36. Peavine
37. New Greenleaf

38. Park Hill
39. Welling
40. Barren
41. Wauhillau
42. Sugar Mountain
43. Echota
44. Mulberry Hollow
45. Fairfield
46. Stilwell
47. Barber
48. Lyons Switch
49. Cherry Tree
50. Honey Hill
51. Salem
52. Qualls
Burnt Cabin
53. Cookson
54. Bunch
55. Greasy Creek
56. Bell
57. Oak Ridge
58. South Greasy
59. Rock Fence
60. Nicut
61. Vian Creek
62. Marble City
63. Bellefont
64. Braggs
65. Sourjohn
66. Notchietown
67. Blackgum
Mountain
68. Vian
69. Sycamore
70. McKey
71. Prices Chaple
72. Warner
73. Oak Grove
74. Muldrow

KEY

less than 20 households

20 to 30 households

more than 30 households

0   5   10   15   20   25
SCALE

Map 5. CHEROKEE SETTLEMENTS IN NORTHEAST OKLAHOMA

227

after became their political allies in establishing the state of Oklahoma and developing its present economy.[20] Because citizens of the Cherokee Nation were the old, legal settlers, while whites were the unlawful newcomers, and because the Cherokees were generally admired as a "civilized tribe," the maintenance of identification with Cherokee ancestry (though not with Cherokee culture) conferred prestige on descendants of these assimilating Cherokees. Further, legal recognition as a Cherokee assured access to a share of the tribe's estate, which was parceled out in allotments prior to the creation of the state of Oklahoma in 1907. For these reasons, a population which might otherwise have been submerged in the wider society instead assimilated with that society both culturally and politically, while still preserving a legal status and identity which was once ethnically based.

In what historian Angie Debo has called "an orgy of plunder and exploitation probably unparalleled in American history," Cherokee land-holdings were reduced from 19,500,000 acres in 1891 to a barren remnant of 146,598 acres in 1971. Debo's meticulous documentation reveals that grafting, that is, speculation in fraudulently obtained lands, was an honored profession, and that Cherokee assets were obtained by operating within the legal framework of the United States and the state of Oklahoma through spurious guardianships, trusteeships, and the like, all of which required collusion among lawyers, judges, bankers, and officials of Oklahoma and the Bureau of Indian Affairs. Both whites and assimilated, legally designated Cherokees profiteered; together they became the backbone of the present Establishment in eastern Oklahoma.[21] During the last quarter-century, these allied populations and institutions have created the contemporary Cherokee government. That government, staffed by legally Cherokee, long-assimilated Americans of Cherokee descent has become the center of eastern Oklahoma's power structure. It operates in a sphere far removed geographically, socially, and culturally from Cherokee settlements and links local businessmen, banks, ranchers, and oil companies into a monolithic establishment.

The programs the Cherokee government administers are directed toward the ultimate assimilation of the culturally Cherokee

228

population into a monoethnic society. The administration of these programs and the multiplier effect exerted by them within the economy of eastern Oklahoma have made them a mainstay for non-Cherokee housing contractors, manufacturers, educators, bureaucrats, and tourist industry entrepreneurs. The Cherokee tribal government's first business manager said of these programs, "The Cherokee tribe is controlled essentially by non-Indians. They don't do anything that will harm non-Indians. Fact, they go even further. They don't do anything that will not *benefit* non-Indians. Of all the programs that the Cherokee tribe has, none were started with the prime objective of helping Indians."[22] Conflict of interest between ethnic groups is built into the structure of the Cherokee government and its activities.

The assessment of this situation among Cherokees in traditional settlements is expressed in these words from a formal address by a ceremonial specialist: "It would seem that someday the Indian could get out from under the harsh laws of the State of Oklahoma. Our forefathers said this can be done.

"For God said, if the Cherokees be destroyed and become extinct, Then that will be the destruction of the whole world. This is the word of the forefathers of our own land."[23]

In ritualistic language, this statement summarizes the view that legal technicalities permit Cherokees to be represented by spokesmen whom they consider impostors not of their choosing, for until 1971 the Cherokee principal chief was a federal appointee who personally appointed his own administrators. To Cherokees, the tribal government is a component of an entirely illegitimate and alien society which exists only by virtue of its unilateral abrogation of federal treaties. The tribal government, in turn, explicitly pledges allegiance to the laws of the United States and the state of Oklahoma and to institutions which in the past and at present sanction the theft of Cherokee lands and assets.

In the early 1960s, Cherokees feared the law and resorted to strong magic from Indian doctors when faced with a summons to appear in court or before public authorities. In their collective desperation, they determined their only sources of support to be God and their treaty-determined relationship with the federal

229

government, for they deemed their oppression in Oklahoma to be a situation that local authorities had conspired to keep secret from responsible federal authorities in Washington who otherwise would remedy it.

Interference with Cherokee hunting and fishing by Oklahoma state game officials who insisted that Cherokees purchase licenses and observe seasonal restrictions, and who impounded game, confiscated firearms, and levied fines, finally induced Cherokees to gather and seek redress of their grievances. Cherokee perception and protest of economic, political, and social exploitation became focused only in reference to this specific and critical issue.

The issue of hunting strikes at the very core of Cherokee existence. It affects all—young men who actively hunt, old men who remember Cherokee national sovereignty and understand life sacredly, and women who not only understand the need for game protein as a crucial supplement to family diet but also appreciate the need for hunting as a validation of male proficiency. Beyond this, Cherokee hunting and the United States–Cherokee treaties which guarantee Cherokee hunting rights are fundamental symbols of the meaning of Cherokee life. Hunting is, in effect, a reality-test of propositions basic to the Cherokee world view. Cherokees believe that their Creator intended them to be permanently a part of the world; therefore, game was placed on earth to sustain them. Through all their turbulent history, hunting has persisted among Cherokees not only as a subsistence activity but also as a demonstration of the Cherokee peoples' covenant with their Creator. Cherokees conceive of the universe as harmonious and ordered, a system in which all populations of plants, animals, and human peoples exist with preordained and reciprocal relationships to one another.[24] Hunting is, therefore, what Geertz has called a "primordial" right—one which derives from the Creator's structuring of the universe and is therefore not subject to modification at the hands of men.[25]

Cherokees understand the meaning of their treaties with the federal government in this context of primordial creation. The treaties are taken as evidence that Americans recognize the inalterable framework of primordial relationships among peoples.

230

Cherokees say that they educated Americans to this, "God's Rule." Their basic thought is succinctly expressed in a memorandum which two Cherokee emissaries drafted to prepare themselves to address white religious congregations in a large midwestern city. They describe the events following 1492 when "13 bunches" of white men "settle on a small piece of Ground" near the ocean:

> Then He Began towards an Independent Nation. . . . They would look Back and wanted to use the Old Constitution which They had cross the water. But This Didn't work. More of them wanted to use or make New Constitution. . . .

> So Then They Invited 7 of the Indian Chief or Leaders But only 5 come. The 5 were asked what Kind of Rules They had Living In peace. They had a Deerskin and on this Deerskin There was Writings With Beads. The Chiefs presented Before the White Man WAMPUM BELT. And on This skin the Writings was picture of Fire and from This Fire a White line leading upward, which represented the Narrow Way to Heaven.[26]

Cherokees see Americans as a people who left their homelands and abandoned their "old rule" and therefore found themselves helpless. Cherokees helped them to write a constitution and extend treaties in order to reintegrate themselves within the framework of "God's Rule," without which no people can survive. The resulting treaties do not create new legal relationships; rather, they recognize preexisting, permanent, and holy relationships which no nation has the power either to make or to break.

The Five County Cherokees were the product of a gradual process of emergence. They were presaged by months, perhaps years, of front-porch discussions between young hunters and old men who together were searching for an appropriate response to the restriction of Cherokee hunting. As the fall of 1965 approached, a consensus evolved. Young hunters, with the sanction and, presumably, with the magical support of old men, would go hunting in a body to see who dared stop them. Initially they planned no more. Before Cherokees take drastic action, however, they must be convinced that they are "acting right," that is, that their proposed behavior is sacredly sanctioned and legitimately within the primordial framework. Accordingly, a delegation approached

231

the traditional Cherokee priesthood by talking to Fines Smith, head of the Keetoowah Society stomp ground on Blackgum Mountain and grandson of Redbird Smith, who resurrected traditional Cherokee ceremonialism at the beginning of the century.[27] As head of a stomp ground with a medicine council at his disposal, Smith could refer their proposal to the supernatural through divination. In the reflective tradition of the Cherokee priesthood, Smith recognized the explosive implications of the proposal. An ex-marine with considerable understanding of white behavior and something of a cultural broker between his own ritual constituency and local whites, he understood that a "hunt-in"—a mass demonstration of protest—was innocently being proposed and, knowing the violence in Ozark white culture, he feared that the plan would end in reprisals against Cherokee participants or, worse, a shoot-out between Cherokee hunters and game officials. Through divination he determined that such action would be sanctioned by God. What remained to be seen was whether this Cherokee proposal would be sanctioned by their other guarantor, the United States government. Smith therefore solicited a meeting with federal authorities, and this was arranged.

On the night of November 20, 1965, about fifty Cherokee Indians gathered in a rural schoolhouse in Cherokee County, Oklahoma. They came to ask a representative of the Department of Commerce's Community Relations Service whether or not the United States government agreed with them that the Cherokees' treaties did indeed guarantee their right to hunt and fish without restriction by the state of Oklahoma. By the end of the evening, the Cherokees extracted an assurance that the Community Relations Service would recommend to them an attorney from outside the state of Oklahoma; they also agreed upon a chairman, secretary, and a schedule of meetings to be convened in each of the five northeastern Oklahoma counties with large Cherokee populations. These meetings were to be followed by a "general assembly" of Cherokees. Though this group bore no distinctive name for months, at their seventh gathering, on January 7, 1966, they decided to be known in English as the Five County Northeastern Oklahoma Cherokee Organization.

In the months that followed, the Five County Cherokees acquired a fluid, open structure which expressed characteristically Cherokee principles of social organization. Initially, a chairman, vice-chairman, treasurer, and Cherokee- and English-language secretaries were chosen by consensus. These moderators and record keepers (with the exception of the English-language secretary) were all traditional Cherokee ceremonial specialists. They were contemporary exponents of the Cherokees' priestly tradition. Fines Smith, the first chairman, was head of one branch of the Keetoowah Society; he was succeeded in office by Andrew Dreadfulwater, head of the Cherokee Seven Clans Society. The vice-chairman and treasurer had records of distinguished service to the Cherokee Indian Baptist Church. These officers were understood to be servants of the Cherokees. No power other than that of convening meetings and keeping records was delegated to them, yet they served a specific function. By virtue of their own religious roles in Cherokee society and of the convention of opening meetings with prayer, followed by a hortatory address by the chairman, they defined Five County meetings as taking place, as it were, on sacred grounds where rules of harmony, consensus, and deep respect for each individual must, by custom, prevail. This placed thought and interaction on a level that transcended kin, community, and personal loyalty.

As time passed, the Five County Cherokees developed into a loose confederation of committees representing counties, individual settlements, and (as in the case of a committee to keep track of losses of Cherokee land through fraud) special-interest groups which crosscut territorial units. These committees exemplified the fluidity which pervades Cherokee social structure. Through them, the Five County Cherokees consistently gravitated toward forming an institution with which any interested Cherokee individual, as well as any settlement, could be free to participate or to withdraw according to the extent that he subscribed to public sentiment voiced at Five County meetings.

Consistent with this principle of freedom to participate or withdraw, the Five County Cherokees maintained an absolute openness. Meetings were convened in any county or settlement that expressed interest. All meetings, wherever held, were open to all Cherokee-speaking people, regardless of age, sex, or residence. There were no agenda. After an opening address in which the chairman invariably reminded Cherokees of the importance of being loving toward one another and recalled to them that whatever their other concerns, establishing Cherokee hunting rights remained first in their list of priorities, and after a reading of minutes of all meetings from the very first, persons simply rose to speak whatever was on their minds. There was no enrollment or registration of members, for the Five County Cherokees did not consider themselves an organization that one joins, but rather an instrument of the Cherokee people as a whole. For that matter, they conceived of the Five County Cherokee Organization as an entity subject to the same sanctions that regulate Cherokee interpersonal conduct: participation to indicate support; withdrawal to indicate disapproval. Said one participant, "I don't know much English, but I had the treaties and laws read to me in Cherokee, and I think I know a little something. . . . I am beginning to see that this group, these young men, are trying to do something for us. This is the reason why I am for this organization. I am glad I can say this. If you believe me, then follow me. If you don't, don't let it get any farther than this."[28] Although a written Declaration of Five County Purposes was speedily drafted, adopted, and distributed so that Cherokees who had heard of the meetings could be given an authoritative statement of what the Five County Cherokees stood for, the Five County Cherokee Organization did not, for its first two years, restrict the fluidity and responsiveness of its structure by adopting either a constitution or bylaws.

Loosely structured meetings, moving from location to location in response to local demand, were the form of the first nonritual institution connecting Cherokee settlements since the dissolution of the Cherokee Nation in 1907. Discussion at the meetings ranged widely, and as these discussions spread throughout the Cherokee country, Cherokees radicalized themselves. Minutes for just the first three meetings (November 20 in Cherokee County, November 24 in Adair County, and November 27 in Delaware County) record deliberations about hunting laws, fradulent sales of Cherokee lands by the Bureau of Indian Affairs, maltreatment of Cherokees in Indian hospitals, fears of reprisals by welfare officials against Cherokees attending Five County meetings, difficulties experienced by Cherokees on welfare, cases of illegal taxation of Cherokee allotments, and failure of officials to respond to petitions drafted and sent fifteen years earlier. Any subject was admissible, and as a succession of Cherokees from previously isolated settlements spoke their minds, Cherokees began to recognize similarities in their treatment by white officials whose interrelatedness became increasingly obvious.

News of the Five County Cherokees soon reached the coalition of white businessmen and legally designated Cherokee tribal administrators who constitute eastern Oklahoma's Establishment. Perceiving the Five County Cherokees' existence as a challenge to their own credibility as legitimate representatives of the Cherokee people, a threat to their power, and a refutation of their assimilationist version of the Cherokees' ultimate destiny, they reacted by spying on the Five County Cherokees, harassing individual participants when identified, and dismissing the Five County Cherokees as a militant organization supported only by a tiny handful of malcontents. They tried to associate the Five County Cherokees with the Black Power movement, with urban rioting, and with other forms of racial agitation. Federal officials, local whites, and Cherokees not yet affiliated with the Five County Cherokees, when subjected to these conflicting definitions, wondered: Were the Five County Cherokees representative of the Cherokee people? Was their membership tiny? Did they even have members as such? Were they militant?

The questions were especially difficult because they assumed a culturally American form of organization, that is, a voluntary association, goal oriented, with individual members the principal units within the social structure, and with policy established by a hierarchy of leaders. The Five County Cherokees, of course, did not fit this model. They represented a rapid and spontaneous resurrection of structural elements of the Cherokees' earlier tribal republic, the Cherokee Nation. The organization was a communication and sanctioning institution uniting Cherokee settlements

235

as principal units. Policy was established within these settlements and expressed during meetings of the organization as a test of consensus. Officials at the apex of the Five County structure were expected to be drudges, performing specialized tasks at the bidding of, and for the benefit of, all Cherokees participating in the consensus articulated through the organization.

At many Five County meetings there were, in fact, only a dozen or so older Cherokees, most of them men. With the model of an American voluntary organization in mind, it did appear that membership in the Five County Cherokees was tiny and did consist of nothing but old-timers. These men were, however, delegates — self-selected or chosen by informal consensus — from a dozen settlements in several counties: the eyes and ears for perhaps four thousand or more Cherokees. When members of a settlement agreed that the Five County Cherokees' consensus about a broad issue suggested a specific course of action for them, they could then proceed with confidence with their own plans as a small community, knowing these actions, in tune with Cherokee sentiment generally and approved by others, might well spark support beyond the limits of their own settlement. They could, on the other hand, express local policy by silently refraining from participation, sometimes even avoiding their own delegate. In this way Cherokees, like many tribal people, voted with their feet and thus influenced decision making at a suprasettlement level.

As the structure of the Five County Cherokee Organization developed, the center of action continued to move toward participating settlements. The first chairman, Fines Smith, was always at the center of the scene. A charismatic orator closely identified with his grandfather, who had catalyzed Cherokee resistance to Oklahoma statehood, Smith epitomized a Cherokee model of passive resistance and personal courage.[29] He was at his best exhorting a crowd, insisting that the Cherokee ideal of interpersonal harmony could be an instrument for alleviating the Cherokees' situation:

> The government took on the responsibility of watching over Cherokee property long ago. Who is responsible now? Are they taking care of us when we are sitting here broke? They are discussing how to

236

take everything away from us. That is how it is. Here in Oklahoma, the Congress, Indian Agent, and Government were all together, figuring how to take everything we own. If they took care of us the right way, where is the Indian land now? Just think. You can see who took care of us. They don't want us to use our eyes to see what is going on.

So now it is way toward evening. There are just a few Indians and communities. Go all out! We shouldn't be scared if we want the truth. A person who wants truth and asks the Lord has nothing to be scared of.[30]

We are all brothers by blood, and we should not hurt each other. God looks at us as Cherokees, and we do not judge anybody. We have not the right to what our Creator did not intend for us. . . . We should move as one thing with the same purposes in our minds or we will fail. If we move as one with the aid of God we will move ahead, and it is now time for that — for ourselves and for our people.[31]

Cherokees were inspired by Smith but found his concept of an appropriate organization uncongenial. His vision was one in which Cherokees would hold massive meetings, "backing up one another" as a total community while they pressed for federal recognition of treaty rights, restoration of confiscated property, and, ultimately, recognition of the culturally traditional Cherokees as the sole membership of a politically autonomous tribe. The expectations of most Five County participants were different. For them, Cherokee autonomy began with their own settlements. Disliking centralized leadership, no matter how charismatic, they created an array of committeemen to coordinate activities in each county and in each Cherokee settlement, making it clear that policy would be decided by these spokesmen. One participant explained, "The Committeemen aren't going to depend on our Chairman, as the committeemen will have to work on this and when we have this thing going then we the committeemen of the Five Counties will decide on the issues involved."[32]

Gradually, a new spokesman, more in tune with Cherokee expectations of organization based on a confederation of settlements emerged, and at the end of January 1967 Andrew Dreadfulwater became chairman; at that time the Five County Cherokees decided to be known in English as the Original Cherokee Community Organization. Whereas Smith had asked Cherokees to come to meetings, Dreadfulwater went to Cherokees. Nearly every

237

night he traveled to the homes of the old men, the consensus leaders in individual Cherokee settlements, to bring news of activities in other Cherokee settlements and to offer encouragement for activities in the settlements visited. He assumed that meetings should be held only when demanded by individual settlements which wished to coordinate their local activities with those of other Cherokee communities.

The impact of the Five County Cherokees roused members of Cherokee settlements from the fifty-year period of dormancy which had persisted since Oklahoma statehood. During that time, Cherokees had been apathetic and settlement institutions had atrophied. With the emergence of the Five County Cherokees, this trend was abruptly reversed. A ceremonial society which had barely maintained its facilities suddenly erected a new combination dance and council house in order to meet actively through the winters; two other settlements, one Baptist and the other non-Christian, began to reconcile their differences with a view toward building a joint Cherokee-language school. In another dramatic reconciliation of Christian and non-Christian Cherokees, the membership of a Cherokee Baptist church and a non-Christian ceremonial society joined forces, built a bandstand on the stomp ground, encouraged Cherokee dance-hall musicians to play country music on weekends, sold hamburgers and pop, and saved the revenues to build a community center for the use of both faiths. Seeing these developments, older people said it was as if Cherokees were "living under the old rule" again.

Starting with the refurbishing of settlements, the transformation of Cherokee life became general. Cherokees began to redefine themselves to outsiders and to demand a voice in institutions outside their settlements. They carried a test case of Cherokee hunting rights to federal court. They picketed the inauguration of a supposedly authentic reconstruction of an ancient Cherokee village, employing Indians costumed in yarn wigs and vinyl buckskin, which the official tribal government had created as a tourist attraction. They drove from Oklahoma to Portland, Oregon, to challenge the credentials of "official" Cherokee tribal delegates at the annual convention of the National Congress of

American Indians. Conquering their long-standing fear of white bureaucrats, Cherokees literally came out of the woods to participate in a committee of Cherokee-speaking people recruited to advise the federal Indian hospital. Cherokee laborers physically drove off token-Indian whites who had been given construction jobs funded by the tribal government and originally intended for impoverished Cherokees. Cherokees documented and archived information concerning recent losses of their land. The diversity of projects was incredible. The Cherokee country was in ferment.

Eastern Oklahomans, especially those in the local Establishment, called the Five County Cherokees "militants," thus associating them with the Black Power proponents and the nascent Red Power movement. This label effectively obscured the fact that the Five County Cherokees had great faith in the American system. Although they attacked as impostors those whom whites considered legitimate Cherokee leaders, the Five County Cherokees continuously acted on the assumption that the return of divinely sanctioned reciprocities between the Cherokees as an autonomous people and Americans could be effected through peaceful litigation in federal courts. They believed federal judges would recognize Cherokee treaty rights and discipline state and local courts which had ignored them; they believed that federal institutions such as the Bureau of Indian Affairs could be educated to "act right"; and in general they believed that their abuses at the hands of Oklahoma whites were forms of misbehavior which federal authorities in Washington would correct if the facts could be made known to them.

A case can be made that it was this moderate political outlook that led the Five County Cherokees to a premature and ironic demise. In 1967, following their understanding of generally moderate political means, the Cherokees hired a lawyer with money provided by a foundation. They expected him to advise them in their encounters with the American legal system and, in addition, to initiate a legal-education program for the Cherokee people. A difficult and paradoxical situation quickly arose—one which was not resolved until many months and several chairmen later. The lawyer, somehow paralyzed by the fluidity of the Five County

Cherokees, became increasingly unable to operate until participants in the Five County Cherokees identified themselves by formal, and presumably binding, registration. Furthermore, as a white man, the lawyer was unwilling to tell Indians what to do. He could not be satisfied until he had pressured the Five County Cherokees into adopting bylaws authorizing the election of a board of directors to give him orders. The more the Five County Cherokees endeavored to establish a relationship that would enable them to utilize the services of their lawyer, the more they inadvertently and involuntarily froze their amorphous social movement into a rigid and closed organization.[33] These changes alienated the Five County Cherokees from residents of Cherokee settlements in whose view something you "sign up for," something in which decisions are made by majority vote rather than by consensus, and something that inhibits an individual's freedom to participate in activities he agrees with while withdrawing from activities he disagrees with is something not Cherokee.

With the adoption of registered membership, bylaws, and elected directors, the Five County Cherokees ceased to be regarded as a forum that conjoined Cherokee settlements. Thereafter, Cherokees regarded them as a kind of benevolent service agency much like the Indian hospital or the welfare office. One Cherokee dismissed the Five County Cherokees by saying, "After 1968 the Five County Cherokees became kind of like the good Bureau of Indian Affairs." All that held them together was competition for salaried organizational jobs funded by the lawyer's grant; in 1973, when the granting foundation became disillusioned with the skeletal organization it was supporting, the funds were withdrawn, and the Five County Cherokees came to an end.

In but two years, in a form that outsiders perceived only as militancy, Cherokees achieved an impressive degree of political unification: both "priests" and "warriors" fashioned roles for themselves which replicated the kind of social structure Gearing identified among eighteenth-century Cherokees just prior to the emergence of their constitutional republic.

In the eighteenth century, according to Gearing, the Cherokee structural pose for dealing with normal times and essentially domestic affairs, known as the "White Organization," took the form of a village council headed by beloved men who, presiding over a body of Cherokees organized by clans, used their powers of persuasion to achieve unanimous decisions. While all Cherokee policy was made in council, the council, while retaining nominal authority, could permit young men to form a war organization. As a "Red Organization," these young men, loosely controlled by older relatives of an age to sit in council, waged war and conducted foreign policy negotiations. Basically, Cherokees expected their young men to restrain themselves until unleashed by their elders, after which they were given license to deal with urgent situations by their own means.[34] This same bifurcation of responsibility between younger men and older men reappeared among the Five County Cherokees.

The Five County Cherokees, as described to this point, were the contemporary White Organization. They functioned as a council which integrated Cherokee settlements, uniting through the persuasiveness of priestly personalities negotiating consensus.

The latter-day Red counterpart to this organization remained in the shadows. It consisted of a network of twenty-five young Cherokee men, pledged to secrecy and prepared to back their elders with force if need be. Their existence was never discovered by non-Cherokees, and few Cherokees knew of them. They were seldom seen at Five County Cherokee meetings. They kept themselves informed of Five County Cherokee activities through reports from older relatives and communicated with one another privately during chance meetings in town and nocturnal visits to one another's homes. They believed that their elders, innocently participating in an organization that antagonized whites in a notoriously violent part of the American South, ultimately would provoke a brutal showdown; therefore, they maneuvered to protect participants in the Five County Cherokees from the consequences of these actions. Fearing that the chairman might be ambushed while traveling back roads to meetings in isolated hollows, one or two of them accompanied him as bodyguards. When Five County Cherokees worried that Delaware County officials might try to buy off the defendant in a lawsuit testing Cherokee hunting rights, they stood guard over him. When the case came to trial in a federal courtroom in Tulsa, and again when Five County Cherokees picketed the opening of an offensive replica of an ancient Cherokee village, a detachment of these young men, armed, stood on the sidelines.

Comparison of the Five County Cherokees with the Cherokees of the eighteenth century makes it evident that there are similarities in social process as well as in social structure. Gearing argues that the original Cherokee Nation was an example of a "voluntary state" formed by a joining together of independent, face-to-face communities exhibiting certain necessary characteristics. One important requirement is that villagers distinguish between tasks coordinated through persons with coercive command, like Cherokee war leaders, and tasks coordinated by voluntary consensus, such as was ensured by Cherokee beloved men, with the greater honor accorded to consensus leaders. Such villages will unify "only under duress which the villages severally perceive," such as retaliatory raids on any Cherokee village by the colony of South Carolina, which held all Cherokees equally responsible for any Cherokee raid against its people. Under such duress, initial unification is guided by the village priesthood or its equivalent—men who are, "through natural bent and through training, most patient, most restrained, most sensitive to the nuances of feeling in others" and who are thus "able to move unthreateningly behind the territory wide consensus they help to create." Once territorial integration is achieved in this manner, Gearing believes, new forms of coercive political relations may appear to further structure a native state. Such social process is initiated, then, when villagers of a certain kind perceive problems which they must deal with in common.[35]

This process reoccurred among the Five County Cherokees. Although contemporary Cherokees suffered other social, economic, and political exploitation, interference with hunting, a right Cherokees regard as divinely given and inalterable, constituted a duress which, as it called into question the very foundation of Cherokee life, no Cherokee could ignore. Non-Christian and Baptist ritual leaders shared the burden of a forum which transcended the settlement level of organization and allowed Cherokees to identify and assign priority to injustices suffered by the Cherokee people as a whole. Gathering on what was, in effect, consecrated ground and overseen by a priesthood, delegates from individual kin-based settlements arrived at consensus. Publicized consensus provided a freedom for individual settlements to act on specific issues as they saw fit, knowing that their local actions would be sanctioned and backed by the Cherokee polity as a whole. Committees were then retrospectively organized to fit into an emerging larger framework of actions initiated by individual settlements.

Cherokees never formally deliberated about the structure and organization of the Five County movement. Once gathered, they simply enacted the harmonious and reciprocally attentive relationships among counties and settlements that they demand of their closest and most-loved relatives. From action based on this habitual and personal model of relationship, literally overnight a framework replicating their former autonomous republic emerged. This resurrection of the Cherokees' earlier political structure did not, then, arise by conscious design. Rather, it is an instance of what Vogt calls structural replication; that is, a situation in which the same set of relationships obtains between successively larger and more inclusive units of social organization, and, presumably, one in which the relationships between larger categories of persons are modeled on the relationships between kin.[36] This kind of organization, occurring first in the eighteenth century during the formation of the Cherokee Nation, again at the very end of the nineteenth century in the form of the Redbird Smith movement,[37] and finally among the Five County Cherokees of the mid-twentieth century, makes it appear that an impetus toward political development in this form is inherent in the social and intellectual structure of Cherokee settlements.

NOTES

1. This paper is based on data collected during Albert Wahrhaftig's fieldwork in northeastern Oklahoma from Sept. 1963 through Dec. 1968 and during brief visits by Albert Wahrhaftig and Jane Lukens-Wahrhaftig in 1967, 1972,

and 1974. Portions of the fieldwork were conducted in association with the Carnegie Corporation Cross-Cultural Education Project of the Univ. of Chicago and with the Center for the Study of Man at the Smithsonian Institution. Results of this fieldwork are reported at greater length in Albert L. Wahrhaftig, "In the Aftermath of Civilization: The Persistence of Cherokee Indians in Oklahoma." Ph.D. diss., Univ. of Chicago, 1975, and "Making do with the Dark Meat: Cherokee Indians in Oklahoma," in *American Indian Economic Development,* ed. Sam Stanley (The Hague: Mouton, in press).

2. Robert W. Buchanan did in fact write a history of this organization ("Patterns of Organization and Leadership among Contemporary Oklahoma Cherokees," Ph.D. diss., Univ. of Kansas, 1972) based largely on fieldwork in the Cherokee Nation and extended interviews with as many of the major participants as chose to make themselves accessible to him. For convenience, we shall abbreviate the full name of the organization to "Five County Cherokee" and shall continue to use that name in recounting events which took place after the organization had decided to change the English version of its name.

3. Stan Steiner, *The New Indians* (New York: Harper, 1968).

4. Wahrhaftig, "The Tribal Cherokee Population of Eastern Oklahoma," *Current Anthropology* 9 (1968), 510-18.

5. Wahrhaftig, "Community and the Caretaker," *New University Thought* 4 (Fall 1966), 54-76.

6. Mooney, "Myths," 16.

7. Janet E. Jordan, "Politics and Religion in a Western Cherokee Community: A Corporate Struggle for Survival in a White Man's World," Ph.D. diss., Univ. of Connecticut, 1974.

8. Wahrhaftig, *Social and Economic Characteristics of the Cherokee Population of Eastern Oklahoma,* Anthropological Studies no. 5 (Washington, D.C.: Am. Anthropological Assoc., 1970); Murray Wax, *Indians and Other Americans* (New York: Prentice-Hall, 1971), 100-3.

9. Wax, *Indians,* 103-4.

10. Mildred Dickeman, "The Integrity of the Cherokee Student," in *The Culture of Poverty: A Critique,* ed. Eleanor Leacock (New York: Simon, 1971), 177.

11. Keetoowah Society, "Four Talks about the Indians from the Keetoowah Society of the Cherokee Indians in Oklahoma," mimeo., 1972, 176.

12. An analysis of the development of this tribal government is presented in Wahrhaftig, "Aftermath of Civilization," ch. 4.

13. In 1907, all living citizens of the Cherokee Nation were enrolled. The roll has never since been reopened. All persons who can trace descent from an ancestor named on the 1907 roll are legally Cherokees and enfranchised members of the Cherokee tribe. There is no residency requirement and no minimum blood quantum. The 1907 roll lists 41,824 persons: 8,703 full-blood Indians, 27,916 mixed-blood Indians (some with as little as 1/256 percent Indian blood), 286 whites, and 4,919 freedmen (Negro exslaves).

14. Murray Wax, Rosalie H. Wax, Robert V. Dumont, Jr., "Formal Education in an American Indian Community," suppl., *Social Problems* 11(4), 1964.

15. Lloyd Fallers, "The Role of Factionalism in Fox Acculturation," in Fred Gearing, Robert M.C. Netting, and Lisa Peatie, *Documentary History of the*

Fox Project: 1948-1959 (Chicago: Univ. of Chicago, Dept. of Anthrop., 1960).

16. Edward P. Dozier, "Rio Grande Pueblos," in *Perspectives in American Indian Culture Change,* ed. Edward H. Spicer (Chicago: Univ. of Chicago Press, 1961), 174.

17. Our use of "assimilation" and "acculturation" here follows Tax; Spicer (1961, p. 497) believes that regarding Pueblo factionalism as schisms between "progressives" and "conservatives" is "entirely too simplified."

18. Leo Kuper, "Some Aspects of Violent and Nonviolent Change in Plural Societies," in *Pluralism in Africa,* Leo Kuper and M.G. Smith, eds. (Berkeley: Univ. of California Press, 1969), 153-54.

19. Robert K. Thomas, "The Origin and Development of the Redbird Smith Movement," Master's thesis, Univ. of Arizona, 1953, p. 73. Morris L. Wardell, *A Political History of the Cherokee Nation, 1838-1907* (Univ. of Oklahoma Press: Norman, 1938), 177-207.

20. This pattern of assimilation is evident in the genealogies and family histories collected by Emmet Starr, *History of the Cherokee Indians and Their Legends and Folklore* (Oklahoma City: Warden, 1921).

21. Angie Debo, *And Still the Waters Run* (Princeton: Princeton Univ. Press, 1940), 379-89.

22. Wahrhaftig, 1975, "In the Aftermath of Civilization: The Persistence of Cherokee Indians in Oklahoma," Ph.D. diss., Univ. of Chicago.

23. Keetoowah Society, "Four Talks," 2, 165.

24. Charles Hudson, "Cherokee Concept of Natural Balance," *Indian Historian* 3(4):51-54, 1970.

25. Clifford Geertz, "The Integrative Revolution: Primordial Sentiments and Civil Politics in the New States," in *Old Societies and New States: The Quest for Modernity in Asia and Africa* (New York: Free Press, 1963), 105-57.

26. Keetoowah Society, "Four Talks," 167.

27. Daniel F. Littlefield, Jr., "Utopian Dreams of the Cherokee Fullbloods: 1890-1930," *Journal of the West* 10:404-27, 1971; Thomas, "The Redbird Smith Movement," in "Symposium on Cherokee and Iroquois Culture," William N. Fenton and John Gulick, eds. Bureau of American Ethnology *Bulletin 180* (Washington, D.C.: GPO, 1961), 159-66.

28. The text of this declaration may be found in Minutes of the Northeastern Oklahoma Cherokees, June 2, 1966. Copy in possession of authors.

29. John Gulick, "Language and Passive Resistance among the Eastern Cherokees," *Ethnohistory* 5:60-91, 1958.

30. Minutes of the Five County Northeastern Oklahoma Cherokees, June 3, 1966. Copy in possession of authors.

31. *Ibid.*

32. *Ibid.*

33. The Mississippi Choctaw requested the services of an anthropologist as a consultant when faced with similar difficulties in integrating whites within the Choctaw tribal bureaucracy (John Peterson; personal communication, 1974).

34. Fred O. Gearing, *Priests and Warriors: Social Structure for Cherokee Politics in the 18th Century,* Am. Anthrop. *Memoir* no. 93, *American Anthropologist* 64 (5, pt. 2), 1962.

35. Fred O. Gearing, "The Rise of the Cherokee State as an Instance in a

Class the Mesopotamian Career to Statehood," in "Symposium on Cherokee and Iroquois Culture," 125-34.

36. Evon Z. Vogt, *The Zinacantecos of Mexico: A Modern Maya Way of Life* (New York: Holt, 1970), 100.

37. Thomas, "The Origin and Development of the Redbird Smith Movement."

Contributors

DUANE H. KING received his Ph.D. from the University of Georgia. He is director of the tribally owned Museum of the Cherokee Indian and holds academic appointments at the University of Tennessee, Knoxville, and Western Carolina University. He is the editor of the *Journal of Cherokee Studies* and has authored more than two dozen publications on Cherokee history, culture, and language.

ROY S. DICKENS, JR., received his Ph.D. from the University of North Carolina at Chapel Hill. He is the author of *Cherokee Prehistory* (University of Tennessee Press, 1976). Mr. Dickens is an associate professor of anthropology at Georgia State University in Atlanta. He specializes in the archaeology and ethnohistory of the southeastern United States.

JOHN PHILLIP REID is a professor of law at the New York University School of Law and a member of the New Hampshire bar. He is the author of *A Law of Blood: The Primitive Law of the Cherokee Nation* (1970) and *A Better Kind of Hatchet: Law, Trade, and Diplomacy in the Cherokee Nation During the Early Years of European Trade* (1976).

BETTY ANDERSON SMITH received her Ph.D. in anthropology from the University of Georgia. Her research interests include prehistory and ethnohistory of Southeastern Indians. She is currently assistant professor of anthropology at Kennesaw Mountain Junior College.

247

WILLIAM C. STURTEVANT received his Ph.D. in anthropology from Yale in 1955 and soon after joined the staff of the Smithsonian Institution, where he is now curator of North American Ethnology and general editor of the forthcoming encyclopedic *Handbook of North American Indians*. He is also adjunct professor of anthropology at Johns Hopkins University. Mr. Sturtevant has conducted ethnographic field work among such tribes as the Florida Seminoles and the Iroquois, and in recent years he has devoted much attention to historical sources relating to Eastern Indians, including manuscripts, paintings, and museum collections.

V. RICHARD PERSICO, JR., holds a Ph.D. in anthropology from the University of Georgia. He has done field research among multiethnic groups in the Southwest. His particular interests include North American ethnology and ethnohistory.

THEDA PERDUE, who received her Ph.D. in history from the University of Georgia, is assistant professor of history at Western Carolina University and is currently doing research work at the Newberry Library. She has published several articles on nineteenth-century Cherokee history and has just completed a book on Cherokee slavery, which will be published by the University of Tennessee Press.

KENNETH PENN DAVIS received his B.A. degree from Oglethorpe University and an M.A. from Georgia State University. He completed his Ph.D. in American history at the University of Virginia in 1975. Mr. Davis served in Vietnam in the Army Signal Corps and currently serves as a captain in the Army Reserve. He is presently employed as a program analyst at the National Archives in Washington, D.C.

GERARD REED received his Ph.D. from the University of Oklahoma in 1967. He taught two years at Bethany Nazarene College in Bethany, Oklahoma, and is currently teaching at Mid-America Nazarene College. Mr. Reed has published an article in the *Chronicles of Oklahoma,* book reviews in several journals, and has read papers at two conventions.

248

RICHARD W. IOBST received his Ph.D. from the University of North Carolina at Chapel Hill. He has done considerable research on the Eastern Band of Cherokee Indians in the nineteenth century. He is archivist at the Hunter Library and director of the Mountain Heritage Center at Western Carolina University.

JOHN WITTHOFT is associate professor of anthropology at the University of Pennsylvania. He began his field work among the Eastern Cherokees in 1946. His special interests lie in ethnobotany and archaeology, and he has published on such diverse topics as Cherokee bird lore, the Green Corn Ceremony, Cherokee steatite pipes, and Cherokee potherbs.

ALBERT L. WAHRHAFTIG received his Ph.D. from the University of Chicago. He and his wife have done field research among Cherokees in Northeastern Oklahoma and have authored a number of publications on contemporary Cherokee life. He is currently teaching at California State College, Rohnert Park.

JANE LUKENS-WAHRHAFTIG studied anthropology at Wake Forest College and was a fellow at the Taylor Museum of Anthropology at the Colorado Springs Fine Arts Center. She has done field work among the Cherokees in Oklahoma with her husband, and, together, they have published articles on contemporary Cherokee life.

Index

Act of Union, post-removal Cherokee
factions, 153, 155
Adair, Edward, 118
Adair, James, 103, 112, 115
Adair County, Okla., 234
African Benevolent Society, 121, 122
Africans, 121, 123, 130
Alabama (as part of Cherokee Nation), 164, 182
Alcohol (use on Qualla Boundary), 214
Allatoona Basin archaeological project, 9
American Board of Commissioners for Foreign Missions, 122, 123
America's Civil War, 160
Amis des Noirs (Haitian antislavery party), 62
Anglo-American political ideals, 92
Apalachee Bay, Fla., 85, 87
Arbuckle, General Matthew, 153, 155
Arkansas, 149, 174, 182
Arkansas River, 136
Armand-Marc, comte de Montmorin-Saint-Hérem (French minister of foreign affairs), 61, 62
Armistead, General, 139
Arthur, Gabriel, 34, 36, 37, 40, 41, 42, 43
Ashmum, Mr. (agent of the African Benevolent Society), obituary of, 121
Augusta (Ga.), 72, 173
Augusta Courier, 140
Axley, Felix, 184, 188

Baldridge, Green Fox, 119
Banks, Sir Joseph, 69, 79
Barnwell map of 1722, 47

Barringer, David, 198
Bartram, William, 4, 7, 24, 46, 50-53
Battle of Horseshoe Bend, 149
Battle of Pea Ridge, 161
Baynton, Captain Benjamin, 79
Beamer, John, 47
Beanstick, Joseph, 132
Beanstick, Moses, 132
Beckwith, George, 85
Bell Field mounds (collapsed earth lodges), 15
Bibb, Henry, 25, 125
Big Cove, N.C., 214
Big Island, 46-47; *see also* Nialque; Cherokee Overhill Towns
Birdtown mounds (N.C.), 22, 24, 26
Black Fox, 98, 105, 117
Blackgum Mountain (location of Keetoowah Society Stompground), 232
Blue Ridge province, 26, 28
Boudinot, Elias C., 99, 114, 132, 139, 149, 153, 187
Bowles, William A. (chief of Texas Cherokees), 65-87
  death, 72
  wife, 85
Bowman (white family in Cherokee Nation), 140
Boyd series (Cherokee ceramics in north Ga.), 29
Brazil, 119
Brewster Period, as Muskogean, 9
British, 34, 35, 39-43, 48, 49, 61-64, 72-76, 84, 86
Brown, Bedford (N.C. senator), 169
Brown, John (Cherokee Old Settler chief), 150
Brown, William (Tenn. judge), 120

Bureau of Indian Affairs, 184, 185, 209, 219, 228, 235, 239, 240
Buren, Martin Van
  President, 185
  administration, 186, 187
Busheyhead, Jesse, 151
Byrd, William (trader), 43

Caldwell, Joseph R., 9, 24
Calhoun, Ga., 133
  Cherokee agency, 171, 178
Cap François, Haiti, 62, 63
Carroll County (Ga.), 135
Carters Reservoir (on Coosawattee River), 20
Cass, Lewis (secretary of war), 134, 141, 142, 143
Catawba Indians, 37, 38, 43
  alcohol abuse, 167
Census of 1835 (Cherokees), 121
Ceramic styles (Cherokee)
  Early and Late Dallas, 20, 26
  Early Lamar, 24
  Early Qualla, 22, 26
Ceramics of northern Georgia, 12–13
Chandler, George W. (lawyer), 188
Charles X (ex-King of France), 144
Chattanooga, Tenn., 50, 73
Chatuga, town of, 93
Chauga site, 11, 24, 52, 53
Cherokee Archaeological Project, 29
Cherokee Constitution, 101, 102, 105, 108, 115
Cherokee County, 184, 193, 213
  (Okla.), 232
Cherokee Indian Advocate, 119, 159
Cherokee Indians
  agriculture, 202
  alcohol, use of, 213–15
  appeal to Washington, 158, 167, 183, 193, 239
  avoid war, 158
  business relations, 220, 229, 241
  clans, 33, 34; relations, 39, 42, 43
  council, 98–99, 108, 111, 125, 131, 138, 139, 141
  Eastern Band, 178, 184, 187, 188, 190, 191, 192, 193, 196, 211, 221
  economy, 203–204, 206, 208, 213, 217, 220, 221
  exports, 203
  factionalism, 142

Cherokee Indians (*cont.*)
  generalissimo, in, 81, 82
  headmen relations, 40–41, 65
  housing, 209
  integration into society, 220, 221
  interpretation of law, 39–40
  lands, 233, 250
  law, 33, 34, 39
  leaders, 75
  lumbering during Civil War, 203
  major goals (present government), 217
  material traits, 34
  national fund, 185
  Overhill, 24, 26, 49
  politics, 92–96
  population, 47, 202
  pottery, 22, 25, 26
  religion, 224, 230–33
  removal to west, 125, 129, 130, 133, 164, 181, 182, 189; see also Trail of Tears below
  replacement of Creeks, 20
  rolls, 209
  settlements, 26, 177, 224, 243
  sequence of historic Cherokee occupation, 9–11
  slaveholders, 120
  social change, 215
  Tomahitans, 36, 39
  Trail of Tears, 183
  tribal council, 97, 209, 229
  tourism, 216, 220
  towns, 46–57, 66
  Western Band, 182, 185
Cherokee Lower Towns, 47–53
Cherokee Middle Towns, 53, 54
Cherokee Mountain, 34
Cherokee Overhill Towns, 56, 57
Cherokee Phoenix, 119, 120, 121, 124, 129, 130, 132, 135, 137, 139, 140, 144, 149
Cherokee Seven Clans Society, 233
Cherokee Valley Towns, 33, 55, 168, 169, 184, 193
Chester, Elisha (U.S. representative), 137, 138, 139
Chickamauga Cherokees, 72, 98
Chickasaw Indians, 38, 81
Chicken, Colonel George, 56, 94, 95
Chilhoe; see Cherokee Overhill Towns
Choctaw Indians, 38, 81

Chota, 24
Churchwell, George W. (lawyer), 188, 191
Civil War, 226
Clark, Governor Henry (Ga.), 199
Clay, Henry, 138, 148
Coe, Joffre L., 11, 15, 29
Colonial Assembly, appeal for assistance, 63
Committeemen, The, 237; see also Five County Cherokees
Community Relation Service, Department of, 232
Confederacy, 160
Confederate States, 160, 161
Congress, activities, 120, 164, 191, 198
Connasitichi; see Sugar Town
Coodey, William Shorey, 154
Cook, Captain James, 64
Cooper, James Fenimore (19th-century writer), 181
Coosawattee River, 20
Cowe mound in Middle Towns, 24, 53
Coweeta Creek (N.C.), 22, 24, 26
Crawford, T. Hartley, 184, 186, 187, 189
  Bureau of Indian Affairs, 190, 191, 192, 193
Creek Indians, 38, 43, 47, 48, 65, 66, 69, 71, 73, 74, 75, 77, 80, 81, 82, 83, 84, 85, 87, 192
Cuming, Sir Alexander, 115
Curry, Ben (superintendent of Cherokee removal), 134, 136, 137, 138, 140, 141, 143, 168

Dahlongea, Ga.; see Georgia
Dancy, Lieutenant F.L. (disbursing agent), 139
Davis, William (property appraiser), 142
Day, Lieutenant William (disbursing agent, 1833), 140
Declaration of Rights of Man and Citizen, 62
Decree of May 1791, 63
Department of Housing and Urban Development, 218
Development of subregion, 28
Dillard, John L. (attorney), 166
Dillsboro, N.C., 183

District of Columbia, 120
Domestic law involving clans of Cherokees, 33, 34
Dorchester, Lord, 76, 77
Doublehead Springs, Okla., 151
Dragging Canoe, death of, 99
Dreadfulwater, Andrew (chairman, Five County Cherokees), 237, 238
Drowning Bear; see Yonaguska
Dudley, Governor Edward B. (N.C.), 189
Dunlap, Brig. General R.G. (Tenn. militia commander), 169

Eaton, John (secretary of war, 1830), 132
Echoe; see Cherokee Middle Towns
Elijay, Sticoe (Cherokee Middle Towns), 53, 95
English, 38, 39, 40, 63
  flag, 64
Estates-General, 62
Estatoe mounds, 24, 48, 50, 52
Etowah site, 22, 24, 114
Etowah Wilbanks-Lamar, 28
European contact, 11, 20, 26, 34, 35, 36, 37, 41, 43, 62, 93, 95, 96, 108-13
Eustis, General (under General Scott), 170
Everts, Jeremiah (Sabbath school teacher), 123

Five County Cherokees of Northeastern Oklahoma, 223, 231-34
  meetings, 235-41
  movement, 243
  purpose, 234
  religion, 242
Fort Cass (Tenn.), 171, 172, 175, 178
Fort Henry (Petersburg, Va.), 35, 36, 43
Fort Lindsay (N.C.), 170
Fort Montgomery (N.C.), 177
Fort Prince George (S.C.), 50, 51, 53
Foster, William S. (colonel during Cherokee removal), 173, 175-77
  prisoners, of, 174-75
Franklin, N.C., 33
French National Assembly, 63
French Revolution, 64

Gabriel (slave), sale of, 124
Garden Creek mound, 24
Gearing, Fred O., 95, 240, 242
General Assembly, 170, 195
General Council, 100, 101, 102, 103, 104, 105, 107, 130
George III, 73
Georgia
  Dahlonega, 129-30
  laws, 123, 170
  New Echota, 24, 50, 74, 82
  officials, 135-41
  property taken by, 144, 148-49, 169
Georgia Cherokees; see Cherokee Nation
Gilmer, Governor (Ga.), 130-31
Golden Ghetto, 208
Gorgets
  Citico style, 19, 22, 26
  face motifs, 22
  Lick Creek style, 22, 26
  mask types, 22
Graham, James (N.C. congressman from Haywood County), 170
Grant, Colonel James, 49
Great Depression, 204, 209
Great removal; see Cherokee Indian removal
Great Terriguo (Tellico), 56
Great White Plague, 209
Green, General Duff, 194, 198
Grenville, Lord, 80, 83, 84, 85

Haiti, as asset to France, 62, 87
Halifax, Nova Scotia (visited by W.A. Bowles), 74-75
Harrington, M.R., of Heye Foundation, 4
Harris, C.A. (Indian Affairs commissioner), 169
Harris, Lieutenant J.W. (removal disbursing agent), 143
Hawkins, Benjamin (American agent), 87, 113, 114
Haywood County (N.C.), 170, 173, 174
Hendrex, William, evaluation of, 142
Herring, Elbert (Indian commissioner), 142
Heye Foundation, sites excavated by, 4, 7

Hicks, Elijah (Ross' brother in-law), 139
Hightower
  river, 131
  town of, 106
Hinton, Mayor (N.C. public treasurer), 189
Hiwassee Island
  culture, 7
  pottery, 22, 24, 26, 28, 55, 168
Holmes, William H., analysis of pottery, 3, 4
Howe, William, 71

Illinois Camp Ground, 153
  location of second convention, 18, 39
Indian John (Occaneechi Indian), 35-40
Indians
  Cherokees; see Cherokee Nation
  Tomahitans, 36, 37
Iron Mountains, 199

Jackson, Andrew, 129, 130, 131, 132, 133, 138, 141, 148, 164, 224
Jamestown, Va., 39
Johnson, Sir John (of Indian Department), 76
Jones, Reverend Evan, 167

Keetoowah Society, 232
Kelly, A.R., site observations (with Heitzel), 11, 53
Kentucky Assembly, favor colonization, 99, 121
Keowe, 48, 50-53
Kitchen map, 52-53
Kittowah, 53
Kneberg, Madeline, 4, 7, 15
Kunnataclagee; see Ridge

Lewis, Tom (member of Bowles party), 71, 80
Light Horse party, 103, 104
Little Egypt, excavation of, 22
Little Keowe, 52
Little Tellico, 55
Little Tennessee River, 69, 174
Little Turkey, 74, 105, 120
London Times, 64, 78, 87
Long, Will West, 210

Long Blanket, 166
Long Hair clan, 33
Lookout Mountain (Tenn.), 66
Loose "tribal state," 28
Lower sites (Cherokee), 24, 36, 48
  maps, 51, 53, 95
Lower towns; see Cherokee Lower
  Towns
Loyalists, 79
Lumbering; see Cherokee Indians
Lumpkin, Governor Wilson (Ga.),
  182

McClintock, Captain William L.
  (first Cherokee removal disburs-
  ing agent), 133-34
McGillivray, Alexander (visitor to
  Cherokees), 66, 72, 73, 77, 78,
  80, 85
McKenny, Thomas (of Bureau of
  Indian Affairs, 1830), 131
Mad Dog's Creek, 80
Maltreatment of Indians in Indian
  hospitals, 235
Mangum, W.P. (N.C. senator), 169,
  194, 198
Marcy, William L. (secretary of
  war), 195
Martin, John (1830 treasurer, Chero-
  kee Nation), 133, 174
Mason, General (Western Cherokee
  commissioner), 196
Mason, John Y. (U.S. attorney gen-
  eral), 196, 197
Medill, William (Indian commis-
  sioner), 158, 159
Meigs, Return J. (Cherokee superin-
  tendent), 114
Methodist Church, separation of, 199
Middle Towns; see Cherokee Middle
  Towns
Miller, John (Loyalist merchant), 72,
  80, 85
Missionaries in Cherokee Nation,
  122, 168
Mississippi River, 136, 144, 165
Mississippian traits of Cherokees, 8
Montgomery, Colonel Archibald, 49
Montgomery, Hugh (Indian agent),
  131, 132, 139, 141
Montgomery, J.M.C. (appraiser),
  134, 142

Mooney, James, 66, 72, 224
Moravians, The, 122
Mounds
  architecture similarities of, 15-16
  Bell Field, 15
  Cherokee, 15
  Wilbanks, 15
Moytoy (chief and commander,
  Cherokee Nation), 115
Muller, Jon D., gorget classification
  of, 22
Murphy (Cherokee County, N.C.),
  183
Murray, John, 72
Muscogee Nation, 87
  see also Bowles, William A.

Nacoochee Mound on Chattahoochee
  River, 4
  excavation of, 4
National Assembly, royal authority
  of, 62-64
National Council (Cherokee), powers
  of, 99, 101, 102, 105, 116, 130
National Guard, of the lower middle
  class, 63
Needham, James, adventures of,
  34-42
"Negro cabins," 118
Negro slaves, 136
  owners of, 118
  payment for, 136
Nelson, Colonel (of Ga. State
  Guard), 132
New Constitution of Fort Gibson,
  formulation, 155
New Echota, Ga., 130, 164, 168,
  170, 177, 178, 181, 189
  Treaty of, 149
New Method (training of soldiers), 83
New York Star, 144
Newnan, General Daniel (Ga. con-
  gressman), 137, 138
Nialque town, 47; see also Big Island
Nikwasi; see Cherokee Valley Towns
Niles' Register, 131
Nootka convention, 78
Nootka Sound, 62, 64, 65, 76
North American explorers, 35, 63
North Carolina Cherokees; see Cher-
  okee Indians
Noyowee; see Cherokee Valley Towns

Occaneechi Indians, 35–39
Ochlochonee River (location of Panton, Leslie & Co.), 85
Oconaluftee Cherokees, as Citizen Indians, 171, 173, 174, 176–78
Oconaluftee River, 165
Oconne; see Cherokee Lower Towns
Oklahoma
  conflict of Cherokees, 225–26
  economy of, 229
  state established, 161
Oklahoma Ozarks
  activities in, 224
  culture, 232
Old Settler (anti-Ross), 154, 155, 158
Omai (Tahitian with Bowles), 79
Original Cherokee community organization; see Five County Cherokees
Otter Lifter, claim of (against federal government), 102
Overhill Towns; see Cherokee Overhill Towns
Owen-Pughe, William (Welsh-speaking enthusiast of Cherokees), 79

Pacific coast, U.S. claim to, 137
Padoucas, "White Indians," 79
Panton, Leslie & Co., 73, 74, 83, 85
Parr, Governor-General (of Quebec), 76
Peachtree Mound (Ga.), 24
Peck, Nicholas (lawyer), 188
Perryman, Tom (Creek chief), 71, 72
Petit, James, judgment of, 124
Philip (King of France), 181
Piedmont province, evolution of, 24, 28
Pitt, William (the younger), 63, 64
Poinsett, Joel R. (secretary of war), 186–92
Polk, James K., 159, 160, 195–98
Porter, James P.H. (friend of W.H. Thomas), 190
Pottery
  Cherokee, 9
  Hiwassee Island, 7
  "lamar tradition," 9, 20, 24
  Norris Basin, 7
Price, Moses, 66, 69, 71, 75, 79, 86
Prince of Wales, 79

Quai d'Orsay, Paris (letter in archives), 61
Quaker work camp, 218
Qualla Boundary, 209, 210, 214; see also Cherokee Indians, Eastern Band
Qualla early burials, 22, 84, 85
Qualla Housing Authority, 218
Quebec, Canada, 76

Railroad Bank of Georgia, 189
Raleigh, N.C., 167, 189
Red Clay, Ga., 141, 143, 144, 182
"Red organization" of Cherokees, 241
Red Power, significance to Cherokees, 223
Redbird Smith, 232, 243
Reid, Governor David S., 194
Revolutionary Tribunal, 62, 65
Ridge, John, 118, 130, 149, 182, 187
Ridge, The, 99, 123
  as Major Ridge, 153
Roan, William (lawyer), 188
Robb, John (acting secretary of war), 138
Robbinsville, N.C., 177, 195
Rocky Mountains, 137
Rogers, J.K. (attorney), 193
Roman Nose, Chief, 169
Ross, John, 118, 130, 132, 139, 140, 141, 143, 149, 150, 157, 159, 160–61, 167, 168, 182, 186
  issue against, 156

"Sabbath schools," 122–23
Saint Augustine, Fla., 38
Santo Domingo, 61, 62, 85
Schermerhorn, John F., 168, 182, 195
Scott, General Winfield, 150, 165, 170, 171, 173, 174, 175, 177, 178, 182, 183
Scudder, Jacob (appraiser), 134
Seminole Indians, 173, 192
Seneca Indians, 53
Sequoyah, invention of alphabet, 151
Settico, 56
Shawnee Indians, 35, 36
Sheffield Register, 78
Shell gorgets, styles, 26
Simson, John (Cherokee chief), 193
Smith, Fines (head, Keetoowah society), 232, 236

Smith, Second Lieutentant A.J., 171, 172, 173, 174, 175
Smithsonian researchers, 4, 29
South Carolina Gazette, 47, 57, 63
Southern Cult, Southeastern Ceremonial Complex, 15, 17
Spain
  against Tomahitans, 38
  visit of Bowles, 78, 86
Spaniards, 37, 38, 63, 65, 72, 84
Springplace, Ga., 122
Sugar Town, 52
Sycamore Shoals, signing of treaty, 164

Tecumseh, 66, 84
Tellico Blockhouse, 69, 93
Terrapin, The, 113
Thomas, William H.
  adoption by Cherokee, 183
  ancestors, 183
  birthplace, 183
  services as attorney of Cherokees, 183–98
  senator (N.C.), 198–99
  wife, 183
Thomas Legion, 199
Tomahitans, 36–43
Trail of Tears; *see* Cherokee Indians
Treaty
  of 1819, 135
  of 1828, 129, 158
  of Hopewell, 181
  of New Echota, 144, 149, 150, 164, 166, 168, 195, 198
Tsali, 165, 170, 171, 172, 174, 175, 177
Tugalo mound, 20, 48, 50, 52
Tugalo River, 53
Tuscarora War, 181
Tuscaroras, international law of, 43
Tyler, President John, 156, 194

United Nations, 82, 84
United States, 62, 65, 86, 113, 116,

United States (*cont.*)
  129, 135, 137, 139, 141
  army, 169, 178
  government, 148–49, 182, 196
  House of Representatives, 232
  law, 225
  loss of thirteen colonies, 62
  War Department, 131, 136, 185, 187, 190, 197
Ustanali, meeting at, 98

Valley Towns; *see* Cherokee Valley Towns
Vann, David, appraisal of, 118
Vann, James, as largest slave holder, 122, 124
Vann, Joseph, appraisal of, 118
Vashon, George (Cherokee western removal agent), 136
Virginia, 35, 37, 39, 42, 43
  frontier, 121, 181

Walker, Felix (N.C. congressman), 183
Walker, John, Jr., 142
Washburn, Cephus (missionary), 150
Wasitani (son of Tsali), 172
Waters, George (slave owner), 118
Watie, Stand, 119, 160, 161
Waxhaw (small Carolina tribe), 37, 38, 41, 42
Western Herald, 140
White Cherokees, 209, 210, 220
White organization as opposed to Red organization, 241
Wilnota (Citizen Indian), 166
Woodfin, Nicholas (attorney), 188
Wool, General John Ellis, 169, 182, 193
Worcester, Samuel Austin
  v. State of Georgia, 148
  U.S. Supreme Court, 138

Yonaguska, 166, 167, 168, 183